Banking Online Fo...

MW00366496

Online resources for businesses

To find out more about banking online and related issues for businesses, go to the following handy Web sites:

U.S. Small Business Administration

www.sba.gov/

Check out this great resource for starting, expanding, and financing a small business (not as small a business as you might think!), plus get information on government relations.

Microsoft Small Business

business.msn.com/

The Microsoft Small Business Web site provides several links to useful resources for business, and it enables you to customize the page for your business needs.

Quicken.com

www.quicken.com

Quicken.com is the online home for all the Quicken products and for a great deal of financial information. Think of it as the online daily newspaper for the Quicken software.

Just as Quicken is focused on financial matters, so is Quicken.com. While the stock market is open, you can view the current averages of the Dow Jones and other popular market indexes. You can also request stock quotes, news, and financial-planning advice.

QuickBooks

www.intuit.com/products_services/
small_business.shtml

The QuickBooks Web site offers software, tools, and more for the small or medium-sized business (from the makers of Quicken).

InsWeb

www.insweb.com/

InsWeb is a leading insurance provider, helping consumers save time and money by providing multiple price comparisons from brand-name insurance companies. From the comfort of your easy chair, you can search and compare rates for auto, home, health, and homeowners insurance. You also find timely information about recent insurance laws, such as California Proposition 103, a new law that entitles some California residents to an insurance rebate.

Quicken Mortgage

mortgage.quicken.com

How much house can you afford? Should you refinance right now? What's the best interest rate that you can get if you apply for a mortgage today? If you're like me, you loathe the process of financing or refinancing your home. As a part of Quicken.com, The Quicken Mortgage Web site is designed to help those of us with serious questions about the mortgage process.

Microsoft HomeAdvisor

homeadvisor.msn.com

The home purchasing and financing business is so complex that every time most people learn something new about it, they immediately are aware of several other things that they don't know. The Microsoft HomeAdvisor is a great online service to help people work through the process of purchasing a home. You find a lot of basic information and terms about the home-buying process to help you build a greater understanding of what you need to do. Current rates for mortgages and a tool to find the best mortgages in your part of the country are also available.

Microsoft Car Finance

carpoint.msn.com

Car shopping with the Microsoft CarPoint online automotive service can help make that next new car purchase much easier. The Web site offers a complete listing and review of all current models, including pricing. When you're ready to buy, you can check out the new car buying service or the used car classifieds.

Corporate Finance Network

www.corpfinet.com

The Corporate Finance Network Web site links you to everything that a financial management person wants to know, including news and information about banks, investment firms, venture capitalists, professional firms, and other companies.

Banking Online For Dummies®

Cheat Sheet

What can you do with online banking?

Try This:	And Get This Benefit:
Check bank balances	Get updated online account information any time of the day or night.
Review your bank statements	You don't have to wait until the end of the month to figure out what cleared the bank.
Transfer funds	Transfer money between any of your accounts any time of the day or night.
Review and download credit card data	Electronically review your credit card balances and statements.
Plan for your financial future	With more of your financial information available to you, you can better understand where your money is going so that you can plan for the future.
Pay bills online	You can pay just about anyone with online banking.
Automatically pay recurring bills each month	With online banking, you set up recurring payments one time and the bank's computers automatically pay the bills each month.

Take the following precautions to ensure a safe online banking experience:

- ✔ Pick passwords that are hard to crack. Take my word for it, FIDO is a pretty easy password to guess. So is PASSWORD. Avoid using the names of pets and family members as passwords.

- ✔ Use a combination of letters *and* numbers in your password, which makes your password much harder to guess.

- ✔ When you select a PIN (personal identification number), don't use birthdays, addresses, phone numbers, social security numbers, or other numbers that anyone can look up and guess.

- ✔ Make your passwords long. If you're allowed to use ten characters, use all ten.

- ✔ Use the password protection that your computer operating system offers. Windows 95 and 98, as well as the Macintosh system 7, have the capability to lock your screen with a password.

- ✔ Don't share your password. Duhhhh!

IDG BOOKS WORLDWIDE

The IDG Books Worldwide logo is a registered trademark under exclusive license to IDG Books Worldwide, Inc., from International Data Group, Inc. The ...For Dummies logo is a trademark, and ———For Dummies and ...For Dummies are registered trademarks of IDG Books Worldwide, Inc. All other trademarks are the property of their respective owners.

...For Dummies: Bestselling Book Series for Beginners

TM

BESTSELLING BOOK SERIES

References for the Rest of Us!®

Are you intimidated and confused by computers? Do you find that traditional manuals are overloaded with technical details you'll never use? Do your friends and family always call you to fix simple problems on their PCs? Then the ...*For Dummies*® computer book series from IDG Books Worldwide is for you.

...*For Dummies* books are written for those frustrated computer users who know they aren't really dumb but find that PC hardware, software, and indeed the unique vocabulary of computing make them feel helpless. ...*For Dummies* books use a lighthearted approach, a down-to-earth style, and even cartoons and humorous icons to dispel computer novices' fears and build their confidence. Lighthearted but not lightweight, these books are a perfect survival guide for anyone forced to use a computer.

"I like my copy so much I told friends; now they bought copies."

— Irene C., Orwell, Ohio

"Quick, concise, nontechnical, and humorous."

— Jay A., Elburn, Illinois

"Thanks, I needed this book. Now I can sleep at night."

— Robin F, British Columbia, Canada

Already, millions of satisfied readers agree. They have made ...*For Dummies* books the #1 introductory level computer book series and have written asking for more. So, if you're looking for the most fun and easy way to learn about computers, look to ...*For Dummies* books to give you a helping hand.

IDG BOOKS WORLDWIDE ®

1/99

BANKING
ONLINE
FOR
DUMMIES®

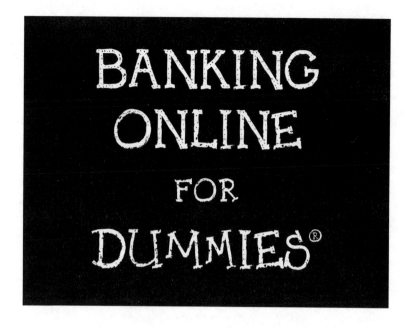

BANKING ONLINE FOR DUMMIES®

by Paul A. Murphy

Michael Meadhra, contributing author

IDG Books Worldwide, Inc.
An International Data Group Company

Foster City, CA ◆ Chicago, IL ◆ Indianapolis, IN ◆ New York, NY

Banking Online For Dummies®

Published by
IDG Books Worldwide, Inc.
An International Data Group Company
919 E. Hillsdale Blvd.
Suite 400
Foster City, CA 94404
www.idgbooks.com (IDG Books Worldwide Web site)
www.dummies.com (Dummies Press Web site)

Library of Congress Catalog Card No.: 99-60535

ISBN: 0-7645-0458-4

Printed in the United States of America

10 9 8 7 6 5 4 3 2 1

1B/RY/QS/ZZ/IN

Distributed in the United States by IDG Books Worldwide, Inc.

Distributed by Macmillan Canada for Canada; by Transworld Publishers Limited in the United Kingdom; by IDG Norge Books for Norway; by IDG Sweden Books for Sweden; by Woodslane Pty. Ltd. for Australia; by Woodslane (NZ) Ltd. for New Zealand; by Addison Wesley Longman Singapore Pte Ltd. for Singapore, Malaysia, Thailand, and Indonesia; by Norma Comunicaciones S.A. for Colombia; by Intersoft for South Africa; by International Thomson Publishing for Germany, Austria and Switzerland; by Distribuidora Cuspide for Argentina; by Livraria Cultura for Brazil; by Ediciencia S.A. for Ecuador; by Ediciones ZETA S.C.R. Ltda. for Peru; by WS Computer Publishing Corporation, Inc., for the Philippines; by Contemporanea de Ediciones for Venezuela; by Express Computer Distributors for the Caribbean and West Indies; by Micronesia Media Distributor, Inc. for Micronesia; by Grupo Editorial Norma S.A. for Guatemala; by Chips Computadoras S.A. de C.V. for Mexico; by Editorial Norma de Panama S.A. for Panama; by Wouters Import for Belgium; by American Bookshops for Finland. Authorized Sales Agent: Anthony Rudkin Associates for the Middle East and North Africa.

For general information on IDG Books Worldwide's books in the U.S., please call our Consumer Customer Service department at 800-762-2974. For reseller information, including discounts and premium sales, please call our Reseller Customer Service department at 800-434-3422.

For information on where to purchase IDG Books Worldwide's books outside the U.S., please contact our International Sales department at 317-596-5530 or fax 317-596-5692.

For information on foreign language translations, please contact our Foreign & Subsidiary Rights department at 650-655-3021 or fax 650-655-3281.

For sales inquiries and special prices for bulk quantities, please contact our Sales department at 650-655-3200 or write to the address above.

For information on using IDG Books Worldwide's books in the classroom or for ordering examination copies, please contact our Educational Sales department at 800-434-2086 or fax 317-596-5499.

For press review copies, author interviews, or other publicity information, please contact our Public Relations department at 650-655-3000 or fax 650-655-3299.

For authorization to photocopy items for corporate, personal, or educational use, please contact Copyright Clearance Center, 222 Rosewood Drive, Danvers, MA 01923, or fax 978-750-4470.

Trademarks: All brand names and product names used in this book are trade names, service marks, trademarks, or registered trademarks of their respective owners. IDG Books Worldwide is not associated with any product or vendor mentioned in this book.

 is a registered trademark under exclusive license to IDG Books Worldwide, Inc., from International Data Group, Inc.

About the Authors

Paul A. Murphy has more than ten years of experience with online services and more than six years of experience with online financial services. He participated in one of the first online banking product launches in the country, and he owns and operates a St. Louis-based online banking and electronic commerce consulting firm, called Murphy & Company. He is the co-author of a book about electronic commerce, and he is the author of several articles about online banking and personal finance that have appeared in *Smart Computing* and *PC Novice* magazines. He is also a frequent speaker at banking and technology conferences. Paul lives in St. Louis with his wife and son. He welcomes your comments about this book, which you can forward to his e-mail address: paul@mcompany.com.

Michael Meadhra is an author and consultant who has written or contributed to more than 30 computer book titles. His credits include several books on the Windows operating system and various Internet-related topics, plus three previous books on online banking and personal finance manager software. His other titles from IDG Books Worldwide include *SmartSuite 97 For Windows For Dummies,* and *Lotus SmartSuite Millennium Edition For Dummies.* In addition to books, he has written innumerable articles for monthly software journals that help readers understand the workings of various software programs. If you have comments about this book, you can reach Michael at meadhra@usa.net.

ABOUT IDG BOOKS WORLDWIDE

Welcome to the world of IDG Books Worldwide.

IDG Books Worldwide, Inc., is a subsidiary of International Data Group, the world's largest publisher of computer-related information and the leading global provider of information services on information technology. IDG was founded more than 30 years ago by Patrick J. McGovern and now employs more than 9,000 people worldwide. IDG publishes more than 290 computer publications in over 75 countries. More than 90 million people read one or more IDG publications each month.

Launched in 1990, IDG Books Worldwide is today the #1 publisher of best-selling computer books in the United States. We are proud to have received eight awards from the Computer Press Association in recognition of editorial excellence and three from Computer Currents' First Annual Readers' Choice Awards. Our best-selling ...For Dummies® series has more than 50 million copies in print with translations in 31 languages. IDG Books Worldwide, through a joint venture with IDG's Hi-Tech Beijing, became the first U.S. publisher to publish a computer book in the People's Republic of China. In record time, IDG Books Worldwide has become the first choice for millions of readers around the world who want to learn how to better manage their businesses.

Our mission is simple: Every one of our books is designed to bring extra value and skill-building instructions to the reader. Our books are written by experts who understand and care about our readers. The knowledge base of our editorial staff comes from years of experience in publishing, education, and journalism — experience we use to produce books to carry us into the new millennium. In short, we care about books, so we attract the best people. We devote special attention to details such as audience, interior design, use of icons, and illustrations. And because we use an efficient process of authoring, editing, and desktop publishing our books electronically, we can spend more time ensuring superior content and less time on the technicalities of making books.

You can count on our commitment to deliver high-quality books at competitive prices on topics you want to read about. At IDG Books Worldwide, we continue in the IDG tradition of delivering quality for more than 30 years. You'll find no better book on a subject than one from IDG Books Worldwide.

John Kilcullen
Chairman and CEO
IDG Books Worldwide, Inc.

Steven Berkowitz
President and Publisher
IDG Books Worldwide, Inc.

VIII WINNER

*Eighth Annual
Computer Press
Awards ≥1992*

IX WINNER

*Ninth Annual
Computer Press
Awards ≥1993*

*Tenth Annual
Computer Press
Awards ≥1994*

WINNER

XI WINNER

*Eleventh Annual
Computer Press
Awards ≥1995*

Dedication

To my wife, Ann: ILYFEAE. — *Paul*

Author's Acknowledgments

My thanks to my literary agent, Chris VanBuren with WaterSide Productions, who took a leap of faith in sharing the vision for this book and sticking with me for more than two years. Thanks also to Ellen Camm, Jill Pisoni, and Sherri Morningstar, the IDG Books acquisitions editors who helped make this book a reality. Thanks to Ryan Rader, the project editor, for his guidance.

A million thanks to Michael Meadhra for stepping in with world-class writing expertise and bringing this project home. Thank you to Peter Weverka for the Microsoft Money chapter. Also, special kudos to Bill Karow, who contributed to this book project.

This book would not have been possible without the help of the folks who work with me at Murphy & Company. Rita Zeitz was a tremendous help with the administrative needs, including permissions and accounting issues, as well as screening my calls while I was writing. Thanks to Lisa Courtney for expertise and willingness to track down facts and review material as I worked through the text.

My thanks to the directory team of Amy Carpenter, Eric Howard, and Rebecca Tapley, as they took on a very important part of the book.

And finally, thanks to several key individuals who have guided, supported, and inspired me: Jeanne Howard, a constant source of help and encouragement since my very first days in this business; Michael Jennings, who provided my first online banking consulting opportunity at Boatmen's Bank in St. Louis; Dennis Laufenburger, the best manager a person could ever hope to have; Tom Ponosuk and Suzanne Milton, for their endless moral support and encouragement; and Doug Braun, a great friend and the developer of the roots of the online banking technology that we see today.

— *Paul A. Murphy*

Publisher's Acknowledgments

We're proud of this book; please register your comments through our IDG Books Worldwide Online Registration Form located at http://my2cents.dummies.com.

Some of the people who helped bring this book to market include the following:

Acquisitions, Editorial, and Media Development

Project Editor: Ryan Rader

Acquisitions Editors: Sherri Morningstar; Jill Pisoni

Copy Editors: Christine Meloy Beck; Elizabeth Netedu Kuball; Stacey Mickelbart; Rowena Rappaport; Tina Sims; Susan Diane Smith

Technical Editors: Jeanne D. Howard; Jack Dewitt

Media Development Editor: Marita Ellixson

Associate Permissions Editor: Carmen Krikorian

Media Development Coordinator: Megan Roney

Editorial Manager: Kelly Ewing

Media Development Manager: Heather Heath Dismore

Editorial Assistant: Paul E. Kuzmic

Production

Project Coordinator: Regina Snyder

Layout and Graphics: J. Tyler Connor, Angela F. Hunckler, Brent Savage, Michael A. Sullivan

Proofreaders: Christine Berman, Rebecca Senninger, Sandra Wilson, Janet M. Withers

Indexer: Liz Cunningham

General and Administrative

IDG Books Worldwide, Inc.: John Kilcullen, CEO; Steven Berkowitz, President and Publisher

IDG Books Technology Publishing: Brenda McLaughlin, Senior Vice President and Group Publisher

Dummies Technology Press and Dummies Editorial: Diane Graves Steele, Vice President and Associate Publisher; Mary Bednarek, Director of Acquisitions and Product Development; Kristin A. Cocks, Editorial Director

Dummies Trade Press: Kathleen A. Welton, Vice President and Publisher; Kevin Thornton, Acquisitions Manager

IDG Books Production for Dummies Press: Michael R. Britton, Vice President of Production and Creative Services; Cindy L. Phipps, Manager of Project Coordination, Production Proofreading, and Indexing; Kathie S. Schutte, Supervisor of Page Layout; Shelley Lea, Supervisor of Graphics and Design; Debbie J. Gates, Production Systems Specialist; Robert Springer, Supervisor of Proofreading; Debbie Stailey, Special Projects Coordinator; Tony Augsburger, Supervisor of Reprints and Bluelines

Dummies Packaging and Book Design: Patty Page, Manager, Promotions Marketing

♦

The publisher would like to give special thanks to Patrick J. McGovern, without whom this book would not have been possible.

♦

Contents at a Glance

Cartoons at a Glance

By Rich Tennant

page 263

page D-1

page 235

page 117

page 7

Fax: 978-546-7747 • E-mail: the5wave@tiac.net

Table of Contents

Introduction

● ●

*W*elcome to *Banking Online For Dummies*. The world of the Internet and the world of banking are both undergoing major changes right before our eyes. I wouldn't say that these two mammoth industries are on a collision course, because both worlds have a lot to share with each other, and online banking, investing, and shopping are just the tip of the iceberg. The online revolution in banking is all very exciting and, because it involves your money, possibly a bit scary.

Be aware that when you start banking online, you will be hooked! You won't want to give up the undeniable measure of convenience when you no longer have to fill out and mail checks by hand. And you'll love the effortless way that you can download your bank statement information into your computer to peruse it at your convenience.

Is This Book for You?

As I wrote this book, I took the liberty of making a few assumptions about you, the reader. You should find this book very useful if you fit the following very inclusive criteria:

- ✔ You have some basic experience with operating a personal computer, so that you know how to turn on the computer, find and run programs, and use a Web browser to view Web sites on the World Wide Web.

- ✔ You have access to a computer at work, home, or school, so that you can follow the many simple steps outlined in the book and take online banking for a test-drive.

- ✔ You have at least a checking account with a bank, so that you can pay bills online. If you have a savings account and credit card accounts, you'll find lots of useful online banking advice for those accounts, also.

- ✔ Your computer meets the basic requirements for Internet access and running the software that you select for online banking. See Chapter 3 for the specifics of exactly what you need.

About This Book

Unless my Internet search engine has blown a gasket, *Banking Online For Dummies* is the first book available that explains the fundamentals of online banking in all its many forms. Most likely, you've heard that your bank offers online banking or is planning to offer it soon. Although you'll see and hear a great deal of fanfare about which online banking options your bank offers, finding out *how* those options work may be a bit of a challenge. This book helps you conquer that challenge.

Banking Online For Dummies was written with every type of computer in mind, instead of being specific to certain computer makes or models. If you log on to a Cray supercomputer every morning at the lab or you just brought home your family's first personal computer, this book explains the process of conducting routine banking transactions with your computer.

The *online banking* that's so frequently mentioned in this book is essentially just the capability to use your computer to complete routine banking tasks (such as transfers, bill payments, statement updates, and so on). Different banks may present online banking using other terms, such as Home Banking, PC Banking, Computer Banking, Bank At Home, Cyber Banking, and other imaginative titles. All these terms share three common elements: a computer, a modem connection, and secure access to your bank accounts.

Another term used throughout this book is *bank* (which shouldn't come as much surprise). I use *bank* as a generic term to include banks and other financial institutions — such as credit unions, savings and loans, and even brokerage houses — where you may do online banking. As you know, these financial institutions differ significantly in the financial services that they offer, but I use the umbrella term *bank* just for the sake of brevity. Your financial institution need not have the word *bank* in its name in order for it to offer online banking.

The examples and figures in this book use as many real banks as I felt would be practical and logical for your understanding as you read the book. Despite my best efforts at diversity in the examples, bank logos and other identification from a few banks appear repeatedly throughout the book. This is an unavoidable side effect of showing realistic examples of online banking in action, so that you are better able to picture the processes that I describe. In many cases, using fictitious sample data to illustrate the processes was impractical or impossible, so I used examples from real banking accounts (of my own and of other agreeable contributors) from real banks. When you see the names of specific banks in the examples, keep in mind that I'm not endorsing or advertising those banks. I'm merely using them as examples.

How This Book Is Organized

This book is organized as a reference, in which you can jump around from section to section or chapter to chapter in order to find exactly the information that you need at any given time. Cross-references refer you to other sections and chapters where you can find information pertinent to the topic that you're reading about. Of course, you can also read the book from beginning to end if you like (but that certainly isn't necessary). The book's chapters are organized into five parts (and an Internet Directory), which I describe in the following sections.

Part I: Understanding Online Banking

The chapters in this part lay the foundation for the discussions to come in the rest of the book. Chapter 1 is a brief introduction to online banking and what it can do for you. Chapter 2 answers questions about which software or Internet options you can use to conduct your online banking transactions. I cover the computer requirements for using online banking in Chapter 3. If you're already hooked to the Internet or have Windows 95 or Windows 98 and a modem, you probably already meet most of the setup requirements discussed in this chapter.

Part II: An Overview of Online Banking

Now that you're connected to your bank, what can you do? Chapter 4 covers accessing your accounts to complete simple tasks like checking balances, reviewing statements, and transferring funds. The magically convenient world of online bill payment is outlined in Chapter 5. If you read only one chapter in this book, read Chapter 5.

Part III: Using Online Banking Tools

Chapters 6 through 10 get down to the specifics of how to use the leading software tools to access online banking and online bill-payment services. Chapter 6 covers Web-based banking at your bank's Web site and some alternatives such as CheckFree and AOL's BankNOW services. Chapters 7, 8, and 9 cover the popular personal finance manager software packages: Quicken, Microsoft Money, and Managing Your Money. Chapter 10 takes a look at online banking for small businesses, primarily through QuickBooks, the leading accounting package for small and mid-sized businesses.

Part IV: Addressing Security Issues

Okay, let's face it. Online banking security is a serious topic — and it should be. You clearly need to know what's happening to protect your financial information, and you need to take the necessary steps to safely participate in online banking. Chapters 11 and 12 explain the security measures that you can use to protect your online banking transactions. I give considerable evidence for the reliability and safety of online banking, in hopes of allaying any fears that you may have about Internet hacking or other threats to your money.

Part V: The Part of Tens

The day after Christmas means that you can find great deals in the stores, the end of college finals means that you get a vacation from school, and the end of a ...*For Dummies* book means The Part of Tens. It's another tradition that nobody really understands, but it works, so I'm not going to mess with it. Because bill payment is one of the most complex online banking topics, Chapter 13 uses the time-honored Part of Tens format to show you ten tips to help you with online bill payments.

The Banking Online For Dummies Internet Directory

The yellow-tinted pages near the back of this book are the *Banking Online For Dummies Internet Directory*, which will be your best friend if you need a new bank for online banking or if you're looking for World Wide Web locations for various other financial services. Just flip through this alphabetized listing to see descriptions for hundreds of financial institutions that you can choose from. (This directory was prepared at great cost to human lives, and it's as accurate as possible, considering the nearly constant changes that occur on the World Wide Web and the less-frequent upheavals among banks. Unfortunately, after printing this book, a few of the listed addresses or services may change, so please don't hold that against me.) Also, for your convenience, a copy of the directory is included on the CD that comes with this book, which should make surfing the banks even easier.

Icons Used in This Book

In keeping with the tradition set by the ...*For Dummies* forefathers, *Banking Online For Dummies* includes several icons in the margins to highlight important points in the text. Look for the following icons in a paragraph near you:

This icon highlights information that you don't want to forget because it will prove useful at some time. Trust me.

This icon points out the really technical information. If you're interested in only the basics, you can skip the paragraphs marked with this icon. But if you get a kick out of knowing a little about what's happening behind the scenes, read these paragraphs to expand your mind.

The real jazzy tricks and great suggestions are located next to this icon.

This book wasn't written by your parents, so when you see this icon, don't ignore it.

This wouldn't be an online banking book without the Internet and the World Wide Web. References to important stuff on the Web are found next to this icon.

Feedback, Please

If you have any comments, suggestions, or questions about this book, I'd love to hear from you. Please feel free to contact me in care of IDG Books Worldwide, Inc.; 7260 Shadeland Station, Suite 100; Indianapolis, IN 46256. Better yet, you can send me an e-mail message at paul@mcompany.com and I'll be happy to answer your questions.

Part I
Understanding
Online Banking

The 5th Wave   By Rich Tennant

"When Roger told me that he wanted to stay in touch with his assets, I didn't expect it to go this far."

In this part . . .

When you plan a tailgate party before a football game, you have to put in a little preparation in order to guarantee your relaxation and enjoyment before game time. The same is true with online banking. Before you can enjoy the benefits of online banking, you need to understand what's involved, make sure that you have all the necessary ingredients (in this case, hardware and software), and notify all the right people (especially your bank).

Okay, online banking isn't quite a party, but it has its rewards and they require preparation. This part helps you get through all the preliminaries.

Chapter 1

An Online Banking Primer

So you're interested in online banking, huh? And why not? Online banking is a hot topic — one whose time has come.

The term *online banking* sounds intriguing, but what exactly does it involve — and how can you benefit from it? Can online banking make your life simpler, help you get your financial chores done faster, or give you more control over your finances? If you ask yourself any of these questions, stay tuned. Answering these questions is what this chapter (and the rest of this book) is all about.

What Is Online Banking?

Online banking isn't some flash-in-the-pan fad that popped up overnight and is likely to disappear just as quickly. It isn't an old idea that's been given a new spin by some marketing genius. Online banking is an enabling technology that's developed and evolved over time and is now entering mainstream use.

A tale of converging technologies

The way that we deal with banks has changed dramatically in a relatively short time. It wasn't so long ago that conducting almost any business with your bank meant going to a bank branch during business hours and transacting your business face-to-face with a human teller. These days you're more likely to interact with your bank by inserting a plastic card into a slot on an *ATM* (automated teller machine) and pressing a few keys. Not only has your point of contact with banks changed from a person to a machine, but you probably also expect to find those machines available 24 hours a day in convenience stores, malls, and parking lot kiosks, as well as at most bank branches.

At the same time, personal computer technology has been spreading. Personal computers (PCs) are now nearly ubiquitous; almost everyone has access to a PC at work, at school, or at home. And PCs are not just stand-alone word processors either. The typical personal computer today is equipped with a modem or network interface that enables you to connect the PC to a network of other computers. Everywhere you turn, you hear about the *Internet* (the worldwide network of computers and computer networks) and about doing all sorts of things *online* (using personal computers connected to other computers through the Internet). Those online activities range from simple e-mail and chats to research, shopping, and now, banking.

Banking customers have grown to accept (and even expect) the convenience of anytime access to their bank accounts through a computer terminal. (After all, an ATM is really just a specialized computer terminal that you can use to access your accounts at the bank.) So, as a banking customer, you can see the logic in substituting your PC for the ATM. Then — presto — you can access your bank accounts from your home, office, or wherever you have a PC with a modem or network connection.

As with many seemingly simple concepts, a lot of complicated stuff goes on behind the scenes to make it all happen. Fortunately, you don't have to get involved with those details in order to use online banking.

Breaking down the elements of online banking

Simply stated, the term *online banking* describes the technology, tools, and processes that give you access to your bank accounts and banking transactions from your personal computer. The specific capabilities of an online banking system depend on the features of the computer software that you use to access the system and on the services that your bank chooses to provide, but typically you can do things like check account balances, get a list of transactions affecting your account, and perhaps transfer funds from one online account to another.

In order for online banking to work, your personal computer must be able to communicate (at least indirectly) with the computer system at your bank. This communication might take place in one of the following ways:

- ✔ Over a modem and phone line connection directly between the two computers
- ✔ Over a closed or private data network
- ✔ Over the public Internet network

Connecting to your bank over the Internet is probably the most common method, but regardless of the details of the connection between computers, the basic principle is the same: Your computer is able to exchange messages with the bank's computer, which means that you can look up information about your accounts at the bank as well as send instructions for conducting various banking transactions.

Your bank's computers run special software programs that provide you with access to information about your bank accounts — and make sure that you're the only one who can see the information. (After all, do you want anyone else to know that you blew your year-end bonus on a new stereo or tickets to the theater?) You need computer software that can communicate with the bank's software, but such software is inexpensive and readily available. You may even already own the software if you use a *personal finance manager* software package (*PFM* for short) to keep track of your budget on your home PC.

Most of the popular PFM programs, such as Intuit Quicken and Microsoft Money, include online banking features in addition to their extensive budgeting, reporting, and other money management capabilities. But you don't have to use PFM software in order to take advantage of online banking. You can access some online banking systems using nothing more than a standard Web browser. The specific online banking features available to you depend on the software you use and on the features that your bank offers. (Chapters 6 through 10 cover the details of Web-based banking and the online banking features of some popular PFM software programs.)

Online banking enthusiasts often bandy about the following terms that you may want to be familiar with:

- ✔ **Electronic banking:** Electronic banking is any system that offers automated access to your bank accounts using electronic media (that is, information conveyed by wires instead of by paper); it includes *ATMs* (automated teller machines) and those automated *telephone banking* systems that allow you to make selections by pressing numbers on the telephone keypad in response to recorded prompts.

ATMs have been around for about 20 years now. Telephone banking is even older — at least in the sense that you could call someone at your bank and conduct some of your banking over the phone. Over the years, telephone banking evolved into a separate service and became almost totally automated, which means that telephone banking can be available 24 hours a day. Online banking is a relative newcomer by comparison, although online banking has existed in various forms for more than ten years.

✔ **Online personal finance:** Online personal finance goes beyond simple banking to encompass other finance activities that you can perform online. Examples include researching investments, buying and selling stocks, applying for mortgages, and shopping for life insurance.

✔ **Online bill payment:** Online bill payment enables you to send online instructions to your bank so that the bank can make payments on your behalf. Basically, this means that you can write electronic checks by simply filling in an on-screen form. Although bill payment is a banking-related activity that you can do online (and, therefore, falls under the umbrella of the *online banking* moniker), most banks consider online bill payment (issuing checks) a separate service from online banking (the capability to view balances and lists of transactions). You can have online banking access to an account without necessarily being able to write online checks on that account, and vice versa.

This book focuses on online banking and online bill payment, but I occasionally refer to other forms of electronic banking and online personal finance where appropriate.

Online banking gives your personal computer most of the capabilities of an ATM or a telephone banking system. But online banking can enable you to do things that you can't do at an ATM. The availability of a full keyboard, a mouse, and a large on-screen display means that banks can display more information and achieve a richer interaction with the user through online banking. As a result, online banking is easier than using an ATM or telephone banking system and can furnish you with more detailed information about your accounts.

Online banking sounds like everything you need, doesn't it? But don't toss your ATM card yet. You still need the ATM (or a human teller) when you want to get cash and make deposits. Online banking systems can't handle transactions that require dispensing currency or collecting printed checks and cash that you want to deposit to your account. (You can't use your computer to print out your own currency — at least not legally — and stuffing a deposit envelope into the floppy disk drive slot on your computer can't magically transport the deposit to the bank, no matter how much you wish that it could.) See Chapter 4 for information about Smart Cards, a new technology that may become the electronic cash of the future.

How Can Online Banking Help Me?

Suppose that you arrive home late one night. As you prepare to leave on a trip early the next morning, you notice a stack of mail that includes some bills that must be paid before you return. Fortunately, online banking enables you to make quick work of that chore. You turn on your computer, and in just a few moments you log on and check the balances on your bank accounts. The balance in your joint checking account is lower than you expected, so you check the detailed list of transactions and discover that you forgot to record a cash withdrawal from the ATM and that your significant other neglected to tell you about a couple of purchases. You need to transfer funds from another account if you're going to have enough money to cover those bills you need to pay. But a transfer is no problem. With online banking, you can transfer funds with a just few clicks of your mouse. After you deal with the transfer, you're ready to tackle those bills. You type a name, type an amount, and click the mouse a few times to enter each bill payment. The bank takes care of getting the payments to your creditors according to your instructions. There — you're done.

From start to finish, the whole online banking session takes just a few minutes. You don't need to make a trip to the ATM to check your account balance or frantically search for receipts to figure out why the bank's balance doesn't match what you expect. Transferring funds and paying bills take just a few keystrokes and mouse clicks, and you don't have to tear off bill stubs, stuff envelopes, or lick stamps. Your financial chores are complete and you can concentrate on preparing for your trip without worrying about mailing those bills or stopping at the bank or ATM on your way out of town.

The scenario above illustrates some of the capabilities and advantages of online banking, and probably every online banking user can think of a different version of this scenario. You need only a little imagination to think of many more ways that you can use online banking capabilities, such as:

- ✔ Getting an up-to-date balance for your bank account
- ✔ Identifying which checks have cleared the bank by reviewing a list of recent transactions that affect your account
- ✔ Checking the transaction details for ATM cash withdrawals, debit card purchases, and other transactions that you may have forgotten to record
- ✔ Confirming the date and amount of direct deposits (paychecks, tax returns, government checks, and so on) into your account
- ✔ Transferring funds from one account to another
- ✔ Making a payment on an installment loan or credit card account at your bank
- ✔ Sending a check to a creditor to pay a bill

✔ Downloading transaction information and automatically inserting it into personal finance manager software

✔ Simplifying the process of reconciling your records to your bank statement by automatically comparing information in your personal finance manager software to online data from the bank

✔ Doing all this and more, and doing it any time of the day or night, including evenings and weekends

All the capabilities in this list may not be available from your bank, and some of them require personal finance manager software such as Quicken or Money.

Actually, the advantages of online banking can be summed up in one word — *convenience*.

Online banking gives you a way to access your bank accounts 24 hours a day, 7 days a week, so that you can do your banking when and where it's convenient for you. If you want to check account balances and pay bills in your underwear at 2:00 a.m., you can. Compare the convenience of online banking to attempting to do the same thing with traditional banking at a branch or an ATM. You can forget about trying to find a bank branch open at that time of night. Although an ATM is probably available, you need to put some clothes on before trekking out to the machine location. And when you finally reach the ATM, you still can't do many of the things that you can do with online banking.

Information about your bank accounts is always available — as close as your computer. In a busy world, that convenience is a powerful incentive to use a new technology such as online banking. But convenience isn't the only advantage; online banking can actually help you make better financial decisions.

With online banking, you get better information about the status of your accounts — more information available in a more timely manner — and better information enables you to make better decisions.

For example, you can check your account balance at an ATM, but that balance is almost meaningless if you have a number of outstanding checks that may, or may not, have cleared the bank yet. You can't be sure where you really stand unless you can see a list of the transactions in the account, but you get such a list only once a month when your statement arrives in the mail — and it's several days out-of-date by the time it arrives. Bummer!

Online banking, on the other hand, gives you access to an up-to-date statement, complete with transaction details, anytime you want one. You can monitor all your accounts closely and manage your funds to maximize interest income or minimize service charges and overdraft fees.

As an added bonus, being able to do things faster and easier means that you're more likely to do them when you need to. So, instead of making a mental note to stop at the bank tomorrow to see whether that missing check has cleared (which you may forget to do), you can do it online right now — while you're thinking about it. You have no need (or excuse) to procrastinate when you can complete the task in moments.

What Do the Banks Get Out of It?

Online banking isn't just a convenience for customers; it's also a good deal for banks. Online banking lets banks offer more services and serve more customers at a lower cost. The computer facilities needed to support online banking aren't exactly cheap, but they're much less expensive for banks to build and maintain than brick-and-mortar branches with human tellers. Online banking is even less expensive for banks than serving customers with ATMs.

The cost savings associated with online banking have the potential to help banks be more competitive by improving services while charging lower fees than are otherwise necessary. Online banking also affords banks the opportunity to expand their customer base by extending services to customers in outlying areas where it's impractical to build branch buildings.

Why should you care?

Well, if online banking is good for banks and is convenient for customers, you can expect the technology to be developed, expanded, and enhanced all the time. Online banking isn't some test program that will receive a short trial and then be discontinued when it proves to be unprofitable for the bank. On the contrary, online banking is a proven concept that furthers the bank's strategic mission of providing more services at lower costs. Many online banking programs around the country are being phased in, and though some services are still in a trial stage, only the details of implementation are being tested in the trial programs. The concept of online banking is here to stay.

What's the Catch?

If all this online banking stuff sounds almost too good to be true, you may start to look for a catch. And your well-founded suspicion may be justified — somewhat. But I think you'll find that the catches explained in the following sections are mild and easy to accept.

Catch number one: Availability

The biggest catch is that online banking may not be available to you — at least not from your current bank. Your bank has to do a lot of work to make your accounts available to you online, and even more work to ensure that you're the only one who can access your accounts. Setting up an online banking system takes a lot of time and expense. As a result, not all banks offer all the online banking features that you may want — at least not yet.

That leaves you with a dilemma. You may have to choose between getting by with what your bank offers or changing banks to get the online banking features that you desire.

You don't want to move your accounts and your banking relationship to another institution without really good reasons, and the availability of a particular online banking feature alone probably isn't sufficient justification to change banks. Don't worry, though, because online banking is very popular with banks, so most of them will offer it sooner or later. If your bank doesn't offer online banking now, your best strategy may be to have patience and wait for your bank to come around. However, if you're relocating to a new city or moving your bank accounts for some other reason, you may want to make the availability of online banking a factor in choosing your new bank.

Catch number two: Security concerns

Another potential catch is concerns about security.

Online banking requires your personal financial information to bounce around over the Internet and various computer networks as it travels between your personal computer and the bank's computers. Consequently, you may be worried about the danger of some computer hacker getting into your accounts or learning the details of your personal finances.

You can put your mind at ease. Online banking enjoys a level of safety that is comparable to conventional banking activities (such as visiting a teller and performing transactions via an ATM).

The security of all banking transactions — including online banking transactions — is a major concern of banks and of the regulatory agencies that oversee them. Consequently, banks and other organizations that offer these services go to great lengths to ensure that your online banking transactions are secure. The following list describes some of these security measures:

✔ Financial institutions employ elaborate measures to protect their computer systems and the data that they contain from *any* unauthorized access.

✔ Access to your particular accounts is protected by secret passwords known only to you and the bank. The system of user identification and passwords ensures that only you can see your account information and that the account you see is not your neighbor's.

✔ Data transmissions between your computer and the bank are encrypted to make them unintelligible to unauthorized parties who may intercept the data.

✔ In the extremely unlikely event that something goes wrong and an unauthorized person does manage to gain access to your account, you are protected by the same regulations that limit your liability to only $50 if your credit card is lost or stolen and used fraudulently (provided you meet certain requirements, such as reporting the loss in a timely manner).

Online banking security encompasses a lot more than I hint at in this brief overview. In fact, security is such an important topic that I devote two chapters to it later in this book. Check out Chapters 11 and 12 if you're interested in more information about some of your bank's security measures and what you can do to enhance your own online security.

Chapter 2

Investigating Your Online Banking Options

So you decided to take the plunge into online banking, eh? Good for you! Online banking can provide lots of options that help you organize your finances while saving you time and effort.

More banks, credit unions, and savings and loan associations offer online banking every day. Facing the ever-growing morass of possibilities, however, you may wonder how in the world you're going to decide which online banking products and services are right for you. That's where your friendly *Banking Online For Dummies* author — here I am! — comes swooping in to help. In this chapter, I outline your options as you enter the world of online banking.

Before you jump in with both feet, you need to make some decisions. These include reviewing your bank's online offerings and the types of financial details you want to keep track of. I cover all of this in this chapter.

The Current State of Online Banking

Most bank checking accounts share certain basic similarities, but the details (such as the fee structure and other services and features that are bundled with the account) vary significantly from bank to bank. Typically, each bank offers an assortment of accounts with different features to appeal to customers with different needs. So, too, do online banking offerings differ.

You may be able to use the online banking features built into a personal finance manager (PFM) software program such as Quicken or Microsoft Money. Or you may have access to online banking at your bank's Web site. Or you may use software supplied by Your bank to do online banking. (See the sections "Choosing among Your Online Banking Options" and "Personal finance manager software" later in this chapter for details.)

Ideally, you could choose how to access online banking and the specific features you use based solely on your needs and preferences. The truth, however, is that your options may be limited by what your bank offers.

Although many banks offer multiple online banking options, a large number of banks offer only a single online banking solution at this time, such as Web-based banking. You can't use the online banking features of a PFM unless the bank supports connections to that brand of software. Work aplenty is going on behind the scenes between banks, online banking vendors, and bank networks to give consumers more flexibility in their online banking. For the short term though, what your bank offers is pretty much what you get — unless, of course, you're willing to change banks.

Choosing among Your Online Banking Options

Just as with the rest of your computer choices, you have options, options, and more options in today's online banking market. Understanding your various options is easier if you group them into categories based on the way you access the features that your bank offers. You can access online banking features in three main ways:

> ✔ **Via the Web:** You can use a standard Web browser (such as Netscape Navigator or Internet Explorer) to access account information via your bank's World Wide Web site on the Internet. (More details to come in the section "Web-based online banking.")

✔ **Via a commercially available personal finance manager software package:** Personal finance manager software packages are stand-alone programs that enable you to track and manage all your financial information (multiple bank accounts, investments, and more). They also have the capability to exchange information with your bank online — provided your bank supports such a connection. The most popular packages, covered in separate chapters later in this book, include Quicken, Microsoft Money, and Managing Your Money.

✔ **Via a proprietary software package that your bank offers:** (Proprietary software is also commonly referred to as *bank-branded* or *private-label* software.) Bank-branded software packages share much in common with personal finance manager software because bank-branded programs are usually stand-alone programs that run on your computer and enable you to connect to the bank for online banking. Bank-branded software runs the gamut from full-blown PFM packages to more limited packages that only let you review account information and complete simple tasks like paying bills. Typically, bank-branded software offers fewer features than commercial PFMs, but the features are often simpler and easier to figure out.

Several factors influence your choice of online banking options, but your choice usually comes down to a combination of what your bank actually offers and which of these options best fits your computing needs.

Web-based online banking

Perhaps the most common online banking option offered by banks today is Web-based banking — providing access to information about your accounts via the bank's Web site on the Internet.

The *Web* (short for the *World Wide Web*) is an exciting, often convenient tool for accessing practically unlimited amounts of information on the Internet. Considering all the attention heaped on the Internet and the Web, the fact that people often confuse the terms isn't all that surprising.

The *Internet* is a global network of computers that have all adopted the same method for exchanging data. If you want to use the Internet, it doesn't matter what type of computer you have. If you can load the necessary tools on the computer to access the Internet, your computer can exchange data and information with all the other computers on the Internet.

On the other hand, the Web refers to that portion of the information available on the Internet that is formatted in *HTML (HyperText Markup Language)* for easy access and viewing via common Web browsers such as Netscape

Navigator and Microsoft Internet Explorer. Viewing Web pages with a browser creates a graphically rich environment where you can click a *link* — a highlighted word, phrase, or graphic — to view another Web page, visit another site, or send information to another computer.

Actually, Web pages and Web sites (collections of related Web pages) can exist on private, local networks called *intranets,* and on individual computers, as well as on the global Internet. However, the vast majority of Web sites are on the Internet and are accessible by any other computer connected to the Internet.

The Web is the only portion of the Internet that most people use, so it's not surprising that so many people incorrectly say "the Web" to describe the Internet, much as they use the word "Xerox" to refer to photocopying. Other tools for accessing information on the Internet are available, but you don't *need* tools such as FTP (File Transfer Protocol) utilities and chat programs to do your banking online. Need more information about the Internet? Grab a copy of *The Internet For Dummies,* 6th Edition, by John Levine, et al. (IDG Books Worldwide, Inc.).

So what *does* it take to do online banking on the Web? I discuss hardware and software requirements for online banking in more detail in Chapter 3, but the basic requirements for Web-based online banking are the same requirements for other Internet access and Web browsing. Everything you need is typically included as part of the package when you buy a new computer, so you probably already have all the following:

- ✔ **An account with an Internet service provider:** An Internet service provider (ISP) is a company that helps individual users (like you) connect to the Internet by providing groups of modems and other hardware and taking care of all the technical details of maintaining the network. An ISP provides you with a user ID and password to access the network and, from there, the Internet. You can get Internet access from an independent ISP or through an online service such as America Online. You may also have access to a similar service by virtue of being connected to a computer network at work or at school.

- ✔ **A modem or other physical connection to the network:** Your computer needs some kind of physical connection to the worldwide network that is the Internet. Usually, a modem connects your computer to a phone line, which links to computers at your ISP. However, your computer may be part of a local area network (LAN) that is connected to the Internet, or it may be linked to the Internet through some other connection (such as a cable modem).

✔ **A Web browser and other Internet access software:** A Web browser is
a viewer that enables you to see and interact with Web sites. The odds
are that a Web browser (Internet Explorer) and all the other software
needed to access the Internet are part of your computer's operating
system (probably Windows 95 or Windows 98). Don't worry — you
don't need to be a computer geek to get it all configured and operational. Your ISP is glad to help you get everything installed and set up
correctly. In fact, your computer may include a feature that automatically installs the appropriate software and establishes an account with
a leading ISP when you click an on-screen icon.

Web-based online banking uses the Web as a pipeline between you and your
bank. Gaining access to your personal finance information usually entails
just three simple steps:

1. Log on to the Internet with your computer.

2. Display your bank's online banking Web site in your Web browser.

3. Enter your user information (typically your name and password, or
   account number and password).

After you identify yourself, the bank's computer system gives you access to
information about your accounts. You can check transactions, transfer
funds, and perform any online banking transactions that your bank's Web
site permits.

Web-based online banking works with current and recent versions of both
the leading Web browser programs — Netscape Navigator and Microsoft
Internet Explorer. You don't need any additional software and you can
access your bank's site from any computer that provides access to the
Internet.

So why is Web-based online banking (and online banking, in general) growing so fast? Check out the following reasons:

✔ **Offering online banking through the Web is more affordable for
banks than developing private data networks.** Some of the online
banking pioneers like Chase, Citibank, Wells Fargo, and NationsBank,
have spent *millions* of dollars on researching, developing, and implementing online banking services — often using proprietary, private
networks. These funds are money well spent — these banks have
earned top spots with online banking rating services. But if online
banking always required such hefty expenditures, only the industry
heavyweights could afford to do it.

Today, even the smallest community banks and credit unions can offer online banking. The cost is no longer prohibitive for most banks, because banks don't have to develop all the software and services in-house. Now, many community banks and credit unions (instead of just a select few) contract with service bureaus to install and maintain all their other computer systems, so many banks simply retain the same service bureau to facilitate the computer needs necessary for online banking. When a service bureau develops a new application — like online banking — for its customers, it can spread the costs over multiple banks, lowering the actual cost to each bank. Furthermore, by using standard facilities and technologies like the Internet and the Web, development costs are reduced significantly. For the first time ever, the cost for a community bank or credit union to install and maintain online banking during the first year can be as low as $50,000.

✔ **More people own personal computers because the prices continue to drop.** For $1,000 or less, you can get a powerful computer system that's designed for the average family wanting to surf the Internet, let the kids do schoolwork, and play realistic games. As computer prices drop and capabilities climb, the number of households with computers increases. Businesses can afford more computers, too, so computers are finding their way onto almost every desktop.

The availability of personal computers, coupled with their common use as Web-surfing appliances, gives consumers easier access to Web-based activities and a higher comfort level with them (which translates to greater trust). These increases bring on an exponential growth in consumers' ability and willingness to try Web-based online banking. As the number of potential users grows, so does the bank's interest in online banking as a cost-effective way to deliver banking services to its customers.

✔ **Internet access is popping up everywhere.** Airports, hotels, coffee houses, schools, and copy centers all offer Internet access. Because Web-based online banking uses the Internet, more places offering access to the Internet means more places for you to conduct online banking. This growth is similar to the ATM explosion of the 1980s, when ATMs began to pop up at gas stations, grocery stores, malls, and seemingly everywhere else.

✔ **You can use the same software that you use to access the rest of the Web.** As a result, many online banking customers take a look at their bank balances at the same time that they check the weather, their stock portfolio, and the latest sports scores. Also, if you're free from having to load, run, and maintain a separate software package, you can bank online from other places, such as at a hotel when you're on the road, or at a friend's home.

✔ **New security features protect your data.** One of the main reasons that earlier generations of proprietary online banking software were so cumbersome and expensive was the need to protect the privacy and security of your bank account information. That situation has changed because modern Web browsers support Secure Socket Layer (SSL) and 128-bit encryption. This (and other) technology ensures that your private account information remains private by transferring information between your computer and the bank using an effectively unbreakable code. (See Chapters 11 and 12 for more information on security.)

A good example of an institution that utilizes Web-based banking is Security First Network Bank. One of the first Web-only banks, SFNB is a pioneer in the Web-based online banking world. SFNB has only one physical location — in Atlanta (largely because it's required to have a physical location, according to the rules associated with obtaining a bank charter) — but it serves customers all over the country.

From the SFNB lobby, shown in Figure 2-1, you can access online banking at SFNB by entering your customer ID and password; after that, you can select an option from the menu.

Figure 2-1:
The SFNB
online
lobby.

Personal finance manager software

A personal finance manager *(PFM)* is software that you buy and load on your computer to manage all your financial affairs. Quicken, Microsoft Money, and Managing Your Money by MECA are the leading PFM software packages available today. After you load the PFM software onto your computer, you enter your bank transactions into the PFM's account register just as you enter your transactions into the paper check register in your checkbook.

The good news about PFMs is that they enable you to manage your finances more easily than with conventional paper registers by letting you create and maintain an electronic version of your checkbook register. With old-fashioned paper registers, you enter the check number, the date you write the check, whom you write the check to, and the amount of the check. If you're like me, you probably also scribble some note about the reason for the payment in case the payee's name doesn't make the reason obvious. PFMs are designed to let you add considerably more information about each transaction, including categories (and even subcategories) for each entry in your electronic register. After you invest the time and effort entering all that data, you can reap the dividends by generating reports and charts that help you analyze and manage your finances. See the "Other special features of PFMs" section later in this chapter for the full story on how categories work.

The bad news about PFMs is that if you don't keep track of *every* banking transaction (deposits, withdrawals, checks, direct debits, transfers, ATM transactions, ATM transaction fees, and so on), the data in your PFM doesn't reflect the correct amount of money that you have in the bank. PFMs require a lot of manual data entry. As a result, many people find maintaining their PFM account registers to be a *huge* hassle without electronic help from a bank!

Fortunately, there is a solution to this massive data entry challenge. The leading PFMs include integrated online banking features that enable you to connect to the bank, download data about your banking transactions, and then add that data to your PFM's account registers automatically. You never miss recording a transaction, and you practically eliminate the occurrence of typing errors.

Another alternative is to download your account data from your bank's Web site and save it in a separate file on your hard disk (if your bank's Web-based banking service offers this option). You can then import this data into your PFM's account registers. It's a little better than entering all the transaction data by hand, but it's usually no substitute for the convenience of using the PFM's integrated online banking features.

PFMs aren't for everybody. (Not everyone wants or needs to keep track of that much detail about his or her finances, or is willing to spend the time doing it.) If you want to use a PFM, you need to find out whether your bank supports *fully integrated* online banking with one or more of the popular programs, and if so, which ones. Not all banks support online banking with PFMs, and it's rare for a bank to support all three of the popular PFMs. Unless you're willing to switch banks, you probably have to resign yourself to using the PFM that your bank supports instead of choosing the software that appeals to you.

In Part III of this book, I outline the details of banking online with the three leading PFM software packages: Quicken, Microsoft Money, and Managing Your Money. These three packages represent more than 95 percent of the installed PFM software market.

The three packages share the following features:

- ✔ **A Windows version** of the PFM software
- ✔ **Account registers** to track transactions and balances in multiple bank accounts, credit card accounts, investment accounts, and so on
- ✔ **The ability to categorize transactions** in order to facilitate expense tracking and budgeting
- ✔ **Some type of financial planning tools**
- ✔ **Lots of charts, graphs, and reports** to help you look at your financial position
- ✔ **The capability to export data** for analysis to a spreadsheet or other third-party program
- ✔ **Basic online banking functions,** including balance inquiry, statement review, funds transfer, and bill payment

Quicken

Quicken is the most popular PFM on the market today. Independent research suggests that about 60 percent of people who use a PFM use Quicken. Quicken also offers the most financial planning tools and resources of the popular PFMs (but Money is a close second in the feature race). Intuit, the maker of Quicken, also offers TurboTax, the leading computer-based tax preparation software.

If you do decide that Quicken is the right PFM for you, you need to decide which version of Quicken you want to use. In addition to a standard or basic version of the Quicken software, Quicken has several versions with different features and pricing. Quicken's online banking features are covered in Chapter 7.

For Quicken product information, visit www.quicken.com.

If you choose Quicken as your PFM, you may want to make a trip back to the bookseller and pick up a copy of *Quicken 99 For Dummies* by Steve Nelson (IDG Books Worldwide, Inc.). You can get the latest information on Quicken at its home page (shown in Figure 2-2). The *Banking Online For Dummies* CD, at the back of the book, also includes a trial version of Quicken 99.

One important thing to know about Quicken: It's the only major PFM you can get in a Macintosh version.

Managing Your Money by MECA

Managing Your Money (MYM, pronounced "mim") is a full-featured PFM offered by MECA software. The current version of MYM was developed for a group of banks that wanted its own software package to offer to its customers instead of the Money and Quicken products.

Will MYM meet your financial needs better than Quicken? That question, in its proper place, comes second. You must first ask, "Does my bank offer MYM?" If your bank doesn't offer MYM and the ability to update your data electronically, MYM simply isn't an option for you.

If your bank does offer MYM, you can choose from MYM's slew of features — most notably, the SmartDesk screen (shown in Figure 2-3). You can access nearly all MYM features from this screen.

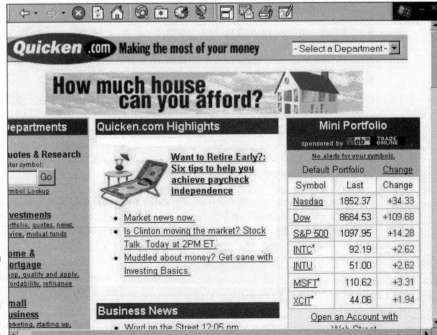

Figure 2-2:
The Quicken home page.

Figure 2-3:
The
Managing
Your
Money,
NationsBank
edition,
SmartDesk
screen.

Microsoft Money

Money is a strong competitor to Quicken and MYM because it has all the functionality that you can expect from a full-featured PFM.

You can find everything that you possibly want to know about Microsoft Money at the Microsoft Money Web site (shown in Figure 2-4) at `www.microsoft.com/money`.

Death, taxes, and . . .

You can count on *three*, rather than two, certainties in life: death, taxes, and the fact that a bank wants its name on anything that it gives to its customers. MECA prepared itself for the last certainty by providing its software as a locally branded product and service to several major banks in North America. In the early- to mid-1990s, banks clearly saw that online banking was an upcoming channel for connecting with customers, but many banks were reluctant to commit resources to developing custom software for such an unknown quantity. The obvious alternative was to purchase a commercially developed product. Quicken was already way out in front of the PFM market and picking up speed. The logical choice for many banks was to sign on with MECA and give customers an alternative to Quicken with a bank-branded version of MYM.

Figure 2-4:
The
Microsoft
Money
home page.

As with Quicken and MYM, if your bank installs the necessary equipment and software functionality to provide account data and handle bill-payment requests for Money users, online banking and bill payment are great add-ons to the traditional PFM features.

The Money software is organized around the graphically oriented welcome screen that you see when you run the software (as shown in Figure 2-5). Information on the first screen includes a list of bill payments that are due, balances with current accounts, and other useful information.

Money, however, includes a cool feature that the other PFMs don't have: its Active Statement technology. *Active Statement* is a tool that Microsoft provides to let you manage the process of importing data into Money from Web-based online banks. If you use Money as your PFM and your bank offers online banking via the Web, you can use Active Statement to update the data in your Money registers.

Thanks to the fact that Microsoft is trying to close the sales gap between Money and Quicken, Money is usually cheaper than the other PFMs to purchase, and it's sometimes available for free or for a nominal charge from your bank. Try out the trial version of Money included on the *Banking Online For Dummies* CD, located at the back of this book.

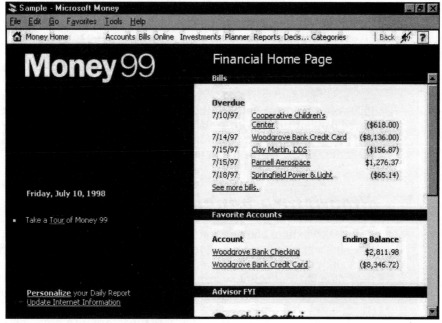

Figure 2-5:
The
Microsoft
Money
welcome
screen.

Other special features of PFMs

One benefit of most PFMs is the ability to categorize transactions. A *category* is another column of information that you can append to an entry in your PFM register. In the category column, you can add information to remind you which type of transaction you performed; for example, you could attach a category like "auto expense" when you make a car payment. Categories enable you to summarize your spending information to easily track where your money is going. The capability to add an almost unlimited amount of extra information, such as categories, is one major advantage that online registers have over traditional paper registers.

Subcategories allow you to detail the categories even more fully. When I fill up my car with gas, for example, I record the transaction with the main category of Auto Expense and the subcategory of Fuel & Oil. If you keep your PFM software and registers up-to-date, you can run informative reports to help you analyze your income and expenses, improve the budgeting of your money, prepare your taxes, or gather information for that next loan.

Because PFMs are designed to help you manage *all* your finances, they enable you to keep track of many different types of accounts (checking accounts, investments, credit cards, loans, and more) and create reports and charts that consolidate information into an overall picture of your financial situation. The leading PFMs all include features that help you create a budget and compare your actual spending to your plan. These programs typically include features that help you play out what-if scenarios to compare things like the cost of loans, the advantages of refinancing a mortgage, and how much retirement income you need.

PFMs offer far more detail at the transaction-by-transaction level than Web-based banking does. With Web-based online banking, on the other hand, you can perform transactions and keep track of balances in a key bank account without taking the time to list and categorize every transaction.

Proprietary banking software

Proprietary online banking software is built from scratch or modified to fit the bank's exact preferences for look, feel, and functionality. Depending on the bank's desires and budgets, proprietary software can be as simple as providing basic account access and bill payment, to a complete software package that has numerous functions like the PFMs mentioned earlier.

Proprietary software almost never uses the Internet to exchange data between the customer and the bank; rather, a private data network typically serves for data exchange. A private data network (also called a closed network) uses its own modems for consumers to call with their modems. You accomplish the goal of connecting your computer with the bank's computer, but your information traverses a private network, controlled by the bank and its contractors, instead of traveling over an open, publicly accessible network like the Internet.

In the early days of the Internet, before Internet security issues were adequately addressed and before Internet access was as ubiquitous as it is today, many banks chose private networks over the Internet for their online banking connections because the private data networks offered better security and control. Given that banks provide local numbers in their areas for their customers to call, private data networks remain a good means of handling online banking access. (However, the Internet is now a viable alternative that is both safe and convenient. As a result, you'll probably see a gradual shift away from the private data networks in the future.) A few years ago, Web-based online banking over the Internet was unheard-of, because the Web browsers, security features, and widely available Internet access that make Web-based banking possible were not yet in place. Online banking required stand-alone programs to communicate with the bank's computers over a direct modem connection or a private data network. A select number of large banks developed proprietary software to provide online banking services.

During this time, PFM software developers added online banking features to their products. PFMs provided more features than the early proprietary software programs, but the added features meant added complexity, and in addition, the PFM software companies charged banks a premium for connecting to the software (which translated to some meaty charges for you and me). Consequently, banks saw continued development of propriety software as an attractive alternative.

Today, online banking is heading toward PFMs and Web-based banking, and away from proprietary software, due to the greater convenience that these solutions afford and the elimination of the substantial software development expenses attributable to proprietary software. As more people use PFMs, the cost per user for that option is coming down. For those users who don't want or need a full-fledged PFM, Web-based banking on the Internet is rapidly becoming the preferred option for banks because they don't have to develop and distribute a separate software program for customers to use, and telecommunications costs are usually lower on the Internet than on a private data network.

Checking Out the Online Features That Your Bank Offers

First and foremost as you enter the world of online banking, you want to figure out whether your bank offers online banking products and services and, if so, which ones. The following list gives you the three main ways to find out:

✔ **Look online.** If your bank has any type of online banking offering, chances are it also has a Web site. Just because your bank has a Web page doesn't mean it offers online banking, but the Web page is a good place to start. If you don't know the address of your bank's Web site, you can start by looking in the directory section of this book. If you don't find your bank listed there, try taking a stab at the site's address — just put the name of the bank between www. and .com. (If your bank is Wachovia, for example, try typing www.wachovia.com in the URL box of your browser.) If the bank name doesn't work, try initials, such as www.anb.com for Amarillo National Bank. When you exhaust the easy guesses, move on to the search engines.

Search engines are electronic card catalogs for finding everything and anything on the Web; a good search engine is the best way to locate what you seek on the Web. To use a search engine, point your Web browser at a search engine (examples: Yahoo!, at www.yahoo.com;

Excite, at `www.excite.com`). Check out `www.search.com` for a great collection of all the major search engines. Just type the name of your bank in the search field and press Return. If your bank is online, it's bound to show up in the search results. Click the name of your bank to go straight to the bank's home page, where you should be able to find details about the online banking products and services that it offers.

- ✔ **Visit the bank and ask.** Next time you go to the bank, ask a teller (or, better yet, the branch manager) if the bank offers online banking. Some banks announce their offerings through messages on ATM receipts, newspaper ads (how retro), advertising placards in the lobby, and inserts in your monthly account statement.

- ✔ **Call your bank's customer service department and ask.** Give your bank a call and ask whether it offers online banking. If so, the customer service person can probably give you the URL for the bank's Web site or send you the information in the mail.

How Much Should You Pay for Online Banking?

Web-based banking, online banking via PFMs, and online banking via proprietary software typically require different usage fees. Here's a rundown of the pricing for the economically minded (and aren't we all economically minded?):

- ✔ **Web-based online banking:** The current trend among Web-based online banks is to charge you no fees to access basic online banking features like checking your balances, reviewing statements, and transferring funds, but to charge somewhere in the neighborhood of $5 to $7 per month for bill payment.

When banks set the price for their bill-pay services, they usually set a limit on the number of online bill payments (typically 10 to 20 payments) you can make for the monthly fee. The bank charges you more whenever you make more payments than the allotted number in a given month. The average online banking household makes about 8 online bill payments a month, however, which motivates some banks to include unlimited bill payments under the monthly fee.

- ✔ **PFM-based online banking:** Most banks charge a fee for access to basic online banking tasks and an additional fee for bill payment. The combined fees can rise above $10 with some banks. (One fee, or both fees, may be included as part of a list of bundled services that you get for a fixed service charge. Also, the fees may be waived if you keep a certain minimum balance in your account.) The higher cost for PFM-based online banking often stems from fees that software vendors like Intuit (Quicken) and Microsoft (Money) may charge the bank for providing a conduit to the customer through the vendor's software. Some banks require you to purchase your own copy of the PFM software, which may entail an up-front expense in the $20 to $90 range.

✔ **Private label software:** No standard pricing applies to private label software. The bank usually provides the software to its customers free of charge. Some banks also give basic account access services away for free and charge only for bill payment; others charge for both. If you're what most banks call a *private banking client* (translation: you have big bucks in the bank), however, you may not have to pay for either. The bank usually waives your fees for all online banking transactions, as well as most other banking services.

Examining Other Electronic Banking Alternatives

If you're not a big fan of Web-based banking or online banking via a PFM or your bank's proprietary software, you still have a few other options to consider. Several banks have teamed up with online services like AOL to offer online banking. Some banks have also installed or upgraded telephone-based banking systems for paying bills and transferring funds.

The BankNOW service

America Online (AOL) is the most popular online service in the world, with more than 12 million customers today (and the number keeps growing). AOL's online banking service is called BankNOW. Perhaps the fastest way to navigate to the BankNOW area on AOL is to use its keyword (typing a word or name at the keyword prompt instead of clicking on-screen buttons). You can enter the keyword BankNOW to jump directly to the welcome screen shown in Figure 2-6.

The AOL finance and investment content areas are some of the most heavily visited computer sites in the world, more popular than anything on the Internet. I cover how to use AOL's BankNOW service in greater detail in Chapter 6, but here I focus on *why* people use the BankNOW service.

Figure 2-6:
The AOL
BankNOW
welcome
screen.

Before you can use the AOL BankNOW service to bank online, you need to subscribe to the AOL service. Also, your bank must have a relationship with AOL that allows AOL to exchange data with your bank's online banking systems. Judging from the list of banks available through BankNOW, this is primarily an offering for the largest banks, including Wells Fargo, Union Bank of California, and others. You can always find the list of participating banks on AOL, via the keyword BANKING CENTRAL.

BankNOW uses a small add-on piece of software that you can download free of charge when you establish your online banking relationship through AOL. The software provides a convenient system for the people who use it, because it integrates online banking with their favorite online service where they check stock quotes, loan information, and other financial content. You can also appreciate the convenience of having all your online transactions in one place, such as AOL.

On the other hand, all the banks that allow access via the BankNOW service also offer other online banking options, including Web-based banking and PFM support. So, you don't have to use AOL and BankNOW to do online banking with any of these banks. Also, anyone who has America Online Version 3.1 or higher can access the Internet and the Web via AOL, and the Web is where the bulk of online banking development efforts are occurring.

The CheckFree alternative

If all you want to do with your computer is pay bills, take a look at CheckFree.

CheckFree (www.checkfree.com) is the largest payment processing company in North America. (See the CheckFree home page in Figure 2-7.) It serves as a transaction broker, keeping track of funds transfers between businesses and consumers, as well as funds transfers between businesses and other businesses.

In addition to offering bulk payment processing services to banks and corporations, CheckFree offers online bill-payment services to individual consumers via the Web. You can't check your account balance using CheckFree, but you can pay your bills without signing checks or licking stamps.

To use the CheckFree Web BillPay service, simply visit the CheckFree Web site and follow the instructions to enroll in the service. After you enroll in the service, CheckFree allows you to create a list of your payees on the CheckFree Web site (protected with all sorts of security and passwords). After your payees are listed, simply tell CheckFree when to pay them and how much. CheckFree takes care of the rest. The bill-payment process is essentially the same as the online bill-payment service from your bank (which is covered in detail in Chapter 5).

Figure 2-7:
The
CheckFree
home page.

The only downside to CheckFree is that it's slightly more expensive than most banks that offer online bill-payment services. That's because CheckFree has no other opportunity to recoup its cost of doing business with you, whereas almost all banks offer online banking services at or below cost with the expectation of getting other business from you down the road.

Figure 2-8 shows the Web BillPay home page on the CheckFree Web site.

Everything you need to know about CheckFree's Web BillPay service, as well as how to enroll in it, is available at this Web site: `www.mybills.com/CheckFree/`.

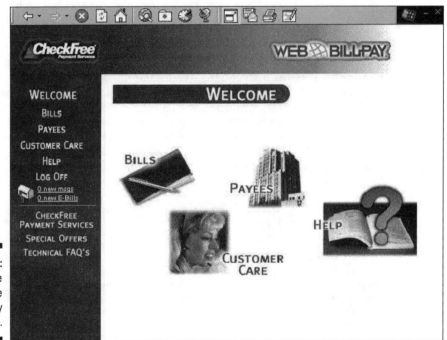

Figure 2-8:
The CheckFree Web BillPay home page.

Chapter 3

Gathering Everything You Need to Bank Online

. . . .

In This Chapter

▶ Getting the right hardware and software

▶ Getting on the Internet

▶ Choosing a Web browser

▶ Accessing your bank with the Internet or a private dial network

▶ Reviewing bank account fundamentals

. . . .

*I*f online banking is the reason you're taking the plunge and getting connected to the Internet or an online service, this chapter is for you. I go over the hardware and software that you need in order to make online banking work.

Oh — you're already connected to the Internet? And you use personal finance manager (PFM) software (say, Quicken)? In that case, you almost certainly have all the basic hardware and software requirements covered. So you may just want to skim this chapter to review your options or even skip ahead to the next chapter and start figuring out the inner workings of online banking.

Is Your Computer Adequate for Online Banking?

You need access to a computer for online banking — but not just any computer; you want one that's up to snuff. Your computer doesn't have to be the latest and greatest hunk of high-tech hardware available, but you don't want to trust your online banking to an antiquated system that's likely to crash right in the middle of a transaction. You also need software. The specific hardware and software that you need depends on the method you use to connect to your institution for online banking.

Figuring out whether your computer (or anybody else's computer, for that matter) is hardy enough to handle online banking is fairly simple. (It may take a little research, but it's still fairly simple.) The first question that you need to ask yourself (and your bank) is which of the three main online banking options you plan to use. You can read Chapter 2 for an overview of the online banking options available in today's market. Then check with your bank to find out which options it supports. After you know which options are available, you can pick the one that best suits your needs; then you can check your computer system against the requirements for that option.

The following list covers the requirements for the three main types of online banking:

✔ **Web-based banking:** If you plan to use Web-based banking, your computer needs are simple. You need the following items:

- **An Internet connection:** You need a direct Internet connection via a local area network (LAN) at your workplace or school, or you can use a modem to connect to an Internet service provider if you're connecting from home. You can use a Windows-based PC, a computer running Linux or another flavor of UNIX, or a Macintosh. Almost any hardware and software combination that allows you to connect to the Internet is fine, as long as the connection isn't exceedingly slow (anything slower than a 14,400 bps modem isn't practical) and you're not otherwise restricted from accessing graphical content on the Web. (See "Accessing the Internet" later in this chapter for more details.)

- **A Web browser:** You need a Web browser to view your bank's Web site and gain access to your accounts. (If you don't have a Web browser, you can easily add one. See the "Choosing a Web Browser" section later in this chapter.) To maintain security, the browser must normally support Secure Socket Layer (SSL) encryption. Supporting SSL is an easy requirement to meet because the leading Web browsers — Microsoft Internet Explorer and Netscape Navigator — both fill the bill. (More on Web browsers in the "Choosing a Web Browser" section later in this chapter.)

That's it. Basically, if you can surf the Web, you can use Web-based online banking. Most new computers come with a Web browser preinstalled, so you're all set for Web-based online banking if you recently bought a new machine. I cover some of the issues involved in establishing an Internet connection and selecting a Web browser later in this chapter. If you're interested in more in-depth coverage of these topics, you can find this information in *The Internet For Dummies,* 6th Edition, by John R. Levine, et al. (IDG Books Worldwide, Inc.).

✔ **Personal finance manager (PFM) software:** If you plan to use a PFM program such as Quicken, Money, or Managing Your Money, the box that the software comes in usually tells what kind of hardware it requires. You need to check the system specifications for your computer against those requirements, but the following list gives you a rough idea of what to expect:

- Most PFM software is designed to run on a Windows-based PC. If your computer runs Windows 95 or Windows 98 and handles other Windows programs, it should be adequate for running PFM software as well. Some PFM packages can run on older Windows 3.1 systems, but the latest versions of the market leaders, Intuit Quicken and Microsoft Money, both require Windows 95 or Windows 98. If you use a Macintosh computer with System 7.0 or higher, you have the computing horsepower to run PFM software as well, but unfortunately, only Quicken offers a version for the Macintosh.

  If you plan to use a PFM program, you need to use the latest version of your selected software — for two very important reasons. First of all, online banking is a relatively new feature that has undergone dramatic changes in the last few years. Therefore, only the latest versions of the PFM software offer the full menu of available features and capabilities. Another important issue is how the software handles dates as the year 2000 approaches — the so-called *millennium bug* or *Y2K* (Year 2000) issue. You can be sure that the latest versions of the software are Y2K-compliant, but older versions of the same programs may not be.

- You need an Internet connection or a modem (or an Internet connection over a modem). This may be listed on the software box as an option rather than a requirement, but it's necessary if you plan to connect to your bank for online banking.

- Many PFM software packages, especially the deluxe versions, require a CD-ROM and audio capability in order to use multimedia features of the software. In some cases, the system requirements may list a certain speed CD-ROM, such as 6X. Some may even require *MMX Technology,* which refers to the newer Pentium processors with MMX capability. (All Pentium II processors are MMX-enabled.) You probably need a CD-ROM in order to load the software. However, you may be able to get by with a CD-ROM that is a little slower than recommended if you're willing to put up with slow, jerky multimedia playback. If you don't know what 4X and 6X mean, or if any of the hardware requirements sound like a foreign language, take information about your computer system to the local software store and ask for assistance.

✔ **Proprietary, bank-branded software:** The software in this category was developed to your bank's individual specifications, and it's likely that it differs from other available online banking software. (That's why it's called "proprietary.") As a result, it's almost impossible to make blanket statements about the system requirements for bank-branded software. The odds are that the bank-branded software will be a Windows program and that it will require a modem for connection to the bank via a private data network instead of the Internet. However, the software from your bank could be different. If you plan to use bank-branded software for online banking, you'll need to contact the bank for information about the specific system requirements for their software.

Almost every Windows-based computer sold today is equipped with enough hardware to offer Web access, so if you bought a new computer recently (or are planning to buy one), you're probably in good shape for online banking. PFM software requirements are also well within the capabilities of all but a few new computers sold today.

Do your banking on the TV — with WebTV

Although computer prices drop regularly, you can still expect to sink $1,000 to $1,500 in any new personal computer system complete with all the required doodads. This cost is quite an investment if you don't have much use for a computer or you just want a low-risk way to try online banking. One low-cost alternative, fairly new in the long line of innovations that computer manufacturers keep bringing us, is WebTV. WebTV, now owned by Microsoft, offers a set-top box with a keyboard and some limited features for just a few hundred dollars. Simply plug the device into the power outlet, plug it into your regular phone line, and then plug it into your TV like a video game or cable TV connection.

Turn on WebTV, and a user-friendly menu greets you and then guides you onto the Internet. WebTV is easy to use; it acts about the same as a Web browser acts on a normal computer. Instead of pointing and clicking with your mouse on-screen, though, the WebTV cursor moves only to the *hyperlinked areas* — that is, the hot spots that you can click to get more information. The keyboard enables you to enter text into on-screen forms

and e-mail. WebTV offers much of the flexibility of a regular Web browser, but at a much lower cost. It's slightly different than browsing the Web on a PC, but similar enough — it's still point and click. You can't run regular PC software on a WebTV and you can't download files, but it sure makes getting onto the Web easy and cheap.

Note: You still have a monthly bill. WebTV service costs about the same per month as an Internet account via an Internet service provider (ISP) for a PC; it's the initial cost of WebTV that's lower.

WebTV enables you to access your bank's Web site, but it may not be the best solution for online banking. Small print and graphic details that are designed for display on high-resolution computer monitors can be hard to read on your lower-resolution TV screen unless the bank prepares a special version of its Web site for WebTV users. Also, as with Web browsers, encryption is a major issue (as described in "Choosing a Web Browser," later in this chapter). Make sure that your bank certifies that its Internet banking services are WebTV-compliant.

Accessing the Internet

Whether you use Web-based online banking or the online banking features of a PFM program, you probably connect to your bank via the Internet. How you configure your computer for Internet access and the procedure you use to establish an Internet connection can vary, depending on the kind of Internet access you have. The following sections cover the types of Internet access that you can choose from and give you some advice on the best ways to get connected.

Using a direct Internet connection

Large companies, government agencies, and universities that have a number of employees or students connected by a local area network (LAN) may opt to provide Internet connectivity through a direct Internet connection. The company can arrange to have a high-capacity telecommunications line installed that creates a full-time link between the LAN and the Internet. With such a system installed, anytime you're logged onto the local network, you're also connected to the Internet. You don't have to deal with a separate dial-up or log-on process required to connect to the Internet — you just pop open your Web browser and poof! — you're up and running.

Naturally, a direct Internet connection requires some security measures, such as firewalls and other precautions, to prevent outsiders from using the connection between the Internet and the LAN to go rummaging through a company's machines. However, these security measures usually work behind the scenes and are invisible to you as you do your banking.

Direct Internet connections can vary in speed and capacity based on the number of employees connected and their individual needs for *bandwidth,* or connection speed, to their desktop PCs. Even slower direct connections are faster than nearly any other method of Internet access.

Because a direct Internet connection is part of the services of a local area network, you don't have to worry about how to set up and configure the connection — the network system administrator or computer support staff takes care of all that. Chances are that the support staff configured your computer for Internet access at the same time that they set up the other network connections. If not, ask someone on the staff to add Internet connectivity to your system.

Keep in mind that companies provide Internet connectivity for business-related activities. Check your employer's Acceptable Use Policy before frolicking happily onto their connection to perform your own personal banking — your employer may frown on employees using company property for personal use.

Using a modem for a dial-up Internet connection

If you don't enjoy the luxury of a direct Internet connection, you probably get Internet access through an Internet service provider (ISP) or online service (such as AOL) and connect to that service via a modem and phone line. This method isn't as fast and convenient as a direct Internet connection, but it works. Dial-up Internet connections are the most common type of Internet connections used today.

A modem (short for Modulator-Demodulator, for the computer trivia buff) lets you use your regular telephone lines to connect your computer to other computers. The modem may be installed inside the computer or in a separate box that's connected to the computer by a cable. After the modem is installed (most new computers come with a modem preinstalled), all you need to do is hook the telephone wire into the jack, and make sure that your computer knows that the modem is there. (In Windows 95 or 98, click Start➪Settings➪Control Panel and then double-click Modems. If your modem isn't listed in the Modems dialog box that appears, contact your PC provider or local guru.) Connection speeds via modem continue to grow — current modems top out at a speed of 56 kilobytes per second.

If your computer didn't come with a modem, make sure that the modem you buy adheres to the new *V.90 standard,* the international standard for 56K connectivity. V.90 compatibility is primo, offering the fastest modem connection speeds you can find. For help and advice on installing your new modem, see *Upgrading and Fixing PCs For Dummies,* 4th Edition, by Andy Rathbone (IDG Books Worldwide, Inc.).

In addition to the modem hardware, you need software installed on your computer to control the modem, dial the ISP's phone number, and handle the details of connecting your computer to the ISP and to the Internet. (In Windows 95 and 98, the Dial-Up Networking feature handles most of these chores.)

You can set up all this stuff manually if you insist (ugh!), but it usually isn't necessary. Most ISPs and online services have software programs available that can automatically install the required software and configure it for you. The set-up program may be preinstalled on a new computer, or it may come on a disk or CD. All you have to do is click the set-up program's icon or insert a disk or CD into the correct drive on your computer; then you follow the instructions that appear on-screen.

Using an alternative type of Internet connection

In addition to direct Internet connections and dial-up connections over a regular phone line, you can use other methods to connect your computer to the Internet. You're not as likely to use the following alternative Internet connections, but I list them here so that you at least know that they exist:

- **ISDN and ADSL:** These special kinds of telephone service can provide high-speed data communications as well as voice communications. A special adapter, similar to a modem, connects your computer to the phone line. ISDN and ADSL are available in limited areas and can be tricky to set up. If you're interested, check with your local phone company and Internet service provider for more information.

- **Cable modems:** The same cable that brings dozens of TV channels into your home can bring an Internet connection, too — if your cable company provides the service, that is. Configurations vary, but typically a cable modem, either a separate unit or a feature built into the TV set-top box, provides a connection point between your computer and the cable. To connect your computer to the cable modem, you usually need a network interface like one you use to connect your computer to a local area network. Cable modems offer faster Internet connections than dial-up connections, but the technology is available only in limited areas. Check with your local cable TV company for information.

- **Satellite dish antenna:** Just as a TV cable can provide a connection to the Internet, a satellite dish antenna can provide a communications pipeline to bring Internet data to your computer. In theory, the system is similar to the cable modem except that the data is broadcast from a satellite and picked up on a dish antenna instead of traveling over wires. Because your home antenna is a receive-only unit, you need a separate Internet connection to send information (such as the address of a Web page that you want to view) out onto the Internet. The cost and complexity of this option makes it suitable for serious computer geeks only.

Choosing an ISP

To access the Internet and the World Wide Web, you need to contact an *Internet service provider* (ISP). (By the way, just about everybody refers to Internet service providers as *ISPs.*) ISPs buy large, high-speed connections to the Internet (similar to *wholesale*) and sell them to consumers (similar to *retail*) who want an online connection through a modem. You sign up with an ISP to furnish your Internet connection, similar to signing up with a phone company to receive your phone connection. You can choose from a number of ISPs, some local and some that serve regional and national areas, and if you find one that's not up to snuff, you can try another.

All ISPs offer the same basic service — access to the Internet. In addition to providing an Internet connection that you can use to access the Web, most ISPs give you an e-mail address and maintain e-mail servers and news servers, and provide Web site hosting and other services. Online services (such as America Online, CompuServe, Prodigy, and Microsoft's MSN) also provide Internet access, but they add a lot of other exclusive services for their members, such as special software, chat rooms, discussion forums, file download areas, news services, and more.

When choosing an Internet service provider, your first choice is between an online service and a regular ISP. If you want the other features of an online service, that's the way to go. But if all you're looking for is Internet access for e-mail and Web surfing (and online banking, of course), then a local or regional ISP may be a better choice. Local ISPs are usually listed in the Yellow Pages telephone directory, and you can find ads for other ISPs in computer stores and magazines (and probably in your post office box as well).

When you start to compare ISPs, you want to look at more than just the prices that they charge for services. Reliability and customer service are the main factors to consider when you choose whether to go with one ISP versus another. Some ISPs do a better job of maintaining their equipment and answering the customer service line than others. A huge part of customer service is the *user-to-modem ratio,* a fancy way of saying, "Can I actually get through to this ISP or do I receive constant busy signals?" Another factor to consider: How easy is it to get your computer set up to access the Internet through a particular ISP? Look for a good set-up program that automates configuring your system and installing software and for technical support service that's available when you need it.

The most helpful resource for advice on picking an ISP is word of mouth. Ask your friends and neighbors which ISP they think is best. Ask how the installation process went and whether the ISP's technical support staff is helpful. Find out how often and what time of day your friends get busy signals. Most ISPs offer a *risk-free trial* where you can try their service for a month and cancel within the first 30 days without charge if you're not satisfied with the service.

Flat-fee service versus limited access

Of course, one of your considerations in selecting an ISP is the cost of Internet access. Although cost can vary by ISP, you can generally sign up for one of two types of rate plans: flat-fee or limited access. Under a flat-fee arrangement, the ISP lets you dial in and surf the Web as long as you want for a flat fee (usually about $20 a month). This option is great if you're like me and use the Internet several times a day to check e-mail, read the news, and, of course, bank online. With unlimited access for a flat fee, you can feel free to explore the resources on the Web whenever you want without worrying about running up a big bill for online time.

Even though you're not being charged extra for the amount of time you spend online, you don't want to keep an Internet connection open when you're not using it just to avoid the inconvenience of having to reestablish a connection later. This practice isn't fair to other ISP subscribers who may be waiting for access to a phone line and modem. Most ISPs have policies that prohibit attempting to maintain a connection when you're not actively using it. The ISP may disconnect you after several minutes of inactivity, and your access account can be canceled for repeated abuse of this policy.

If your Internet access is limited to conducting a few banking tasks and checking e-mail a few days a week, you may want to consider a limited access or metered rate. Instead of paying $20 or so for unlimited access each month, you pay a lower fee for a limited amount of time online and then pay a per-minute rate (like the charges for long-distance telephone calls) for any time you use over and above the monthly allotment.

For example, MindSpring, a nationwide ISP based in Atlanta, offers five hours of Internet access each month for $6.95, with additional hours available for $2 each. Chances are, your local ISP also offers a lower, metered rate. If you don't spend a lot of time online, this option can save you money. Carefully consider this option based on your habits, though — it doesn't take many extra hours of usage to put you past that $20 per month figure.

The *Banking Online For Dummies* CD (see the inside back cover) includes an Internet starter kit from MindSpring.

Gaining Internet access while away from home

When choosing an ISP, you may want to consider not only the service the ISP offers in your local area, but also its ability to offer you reliable Internet access when you're traveling in other cities or places that don't have local access to the Internet.

This access serves two important purposes. First, the cost of connecting to the Internet by making a long-distance call from a hotel room is really expensive (trust me — I travel about 150 nights a year). Second, many people still live or vacation in parts of the country where you can't access the Internet with a local call. Either way, choosing an ISP that provides local access numbers in many of the largest metropolitan cities and a toll-free number for access from all other areas is worth considering. The ISP probably charges an hourly fee for using the toll-free number (so it isn't really toll-free), but it's usually much cheaper than paying hotel phone charges or for options such as calling cards and third-number billing to your home phone.

Choosing a Web Browser

In order to use Web-based online banking, you need an Internet connection and a Web browser. Even if you use a PFM program or bank-branded software for online banking, you probably need a Web browser to view other online financial resources and information.

Web browsers are software packages that allow you to access information on the World Wide Web and display it on your computer. Several different Web browsers are available in versions for just about every computer platform. The leading Web browsers for Windows and Macintosh computers are Microsoft Internet Explorer and Netscape Navigator.

Both of the leading browsers are available for free from a number of sources. If you have Windows 98, or a newer copy of Windows 95, Internet Explorer is automatically installed along with the Windows operating system. It's also included in a package with a number of other Microsoft software programs, and it's available for download from Microsoft's Web site. Netscape Navigator is available to download for free from Netscape's Web site and comes bundled with several third-party computer programs.

You can choose to use Netscape Navigator or Internet Explorer (or another browser). You can even have more than one browser installed on your system and use them interchangeably. However, if you use Windows 98 or Windows 95 with Internet Explorer 4, don't attempt to remove Internet Explorer from your system. Doing so messes up your system. If you prefer Netscape Navigator, just leave Internet Explorer alone and install and use Navigator to view Web pages.

Begging the pardon of both Netscape and Microsoft, in regard to online banking, which Web browser you choose isn't that important. What matters is whether your Web browser is compatible with your bank's requirements. So, the first step in selecting a Web browser is to check with your bank to see which browser, if any, the bank requires. If your bank supports one of the leading browsers, it probably supports the other, but check with the bank to be absolutely sure. A bank, like any Web site owner, wants to make its Web sites and information available to the largest possible audience.

What's more important than the brand of Web browser you choose is to make sure that you're using a fairly recent copy of that Web browser. Browsers have gone through a lot of changes in just a few years, and older versions of the browsers probably don't support all the features you need for successful online banking. If your computer has access to the Internet and a copy of the latest Internet browser, you're all set for Web-based online banking. Why? Because these newer browsers (Version 4 or later of both Internet Explorer and Netscape Navigator) incorporate the latest encryption methods.

Encryption is the process of scrambling data so that no one other than you and your bank can read your data as you send it across the Internet. This technology keeps your personal financial information private and secure despite the fact that it travels over a public network. I cover security in greater detail in Part IV.

If you aren't sure whether you have an appropriate browser, don't worry! Through the magic of compact disc (CD) technology, a copy of both Microsoft Internet Explorer 4.0 and Netscape Communicator (which includes Navigator 4) are loaded on the CD neatly affixed inside the back cover of this book. If online banking is bringing you to the Web for the first time, consider making a return trip to your favorite bookseller to get the latest edition of *The Internet for Dummies,* 6th Edition, by John R. Levine, et al. (IDG Books Worldwide, Inc.).

Considering the technological advancements in Web sites and browsers

In the early days of the World Wide Web, a Web site with a company logo, an address, a phone number, and a few other static pieces of information drew high praise and even some response from people. As the Web development community and its tools mature (and as people tire of looking at Web sites that are essentially electronic business cards), Web developers have been asking, "What can we do to make our Web sites more interesting?"

The answer they found is to incorporate programming features and function-ality into Web pages so that they become online applications. Recent versions of the leading Web browsers include the capability to display these new applications as their programmers intended. (That's another reason you need to make sure you're using an up-to-date Web browser.)

Many banks are implementing Web-based online banking with sophisticated programming code behind the scenes so that you can have the functionality of a traditional software package *without* having to buy and install the software. Some sites track where you've been on the site, so that upon your return you're taken to where you left off, and some sites run stock tickers customized with stocks that you select. In other words, many Web sites now act like full-featured software programs and are much more exciting than early Web sites. Are you wondering how that helps you as an online banking customer? Well, for example, it lets you tailor a bank's Web site to suit your needs — and still access it via a standard Web browser. (So you get some of the benefits of expensive PFM software without having to buy it.) Capabilities that used to require installing separate, stand-alone software on your computer can now be delivered on the Web.

Getting a taste of Java

Java, developed by Sun Microsystems, is a fully functional programming language designed to run from a Web browser and numerous other platforms. Programmers with traditional programming experience can easily apply their programming skills and build highly interactive Web site applications with Java. Recent versions of the popular Web browsers support Java and display Java-enhanced Web sites.

FTB Online from First Tennessee Bank is the first bank in the U.S. to offer an online banking system developed entirely with Java. FTB Online (shown in Figure 3-1) offers account balances, statement review, funds transfer, and bill-payment services using the Java programming language. FTB Online also offers an interactive financial planner, which enables you to input your current financial information and future goals. FTB Online evaluates the data and returns financial planning advice online based on the programming of the financial planner — *without* requiring you to download, install, and run a new piece of software (thanks to Java).

What happens when you visit FTB Online for the first time? Your Web browser downloads the FTB Online Java code to your computer and then runs it for you. The code automatically loads on your computer and runs in the background; you never need to run a separate piece of software while you view your FTB Online banking information.

Java-enhanced applications, referred to as *Java applets,* are designed for execution over a network or the Internet. Extremely small in size, they download each time a computer accesses the site. In this way, users always have the most current version available, eliminating the need for keeping track of versions and doing manual software updates, because Java automates the process. Wider use of Java in Web pages is important for online

Figure 3-1:
The FTB
Online
home page.

banking because it enables you to perform advanced computing functions
without having to buy, install, and update a regular piece of software. And
because the software is Web-based, you have the freedom to use just about
any computer to conduct your online banking transactions; the software
loads each time you visit the Web site.

Java is perhaps the best-known example of a Web programming tool. But
Web developers can use a number of other programming tools (such as CGI,
Perl, JavaScript, ActiveX controls, active server pages, and DHTML, to name
just a few) to add features to their sites. Many of these programming tools
and techniques require complementary support from the Web browser
software in order to function properly. As an end user, you don't need to be
concerned about the programming language or tools used to create the Web
sites you visit. You just need to make sure that you can use and view new
features by using a Web browser that supports current technologies.

Connecting to the Bank

To make online banking work, you need to receive information about your
accounts from your bank's computer system and have it displayed on-screen.
That requires a connection between your computer and the bank's computer system.

Of course, you don't get direct access to the bank's main computer in order to manipulate any data there. That would be a totally unacceptable breach of security! What you can do is send requests for information to the bank's computer facility, where the requests are filtered and processed by several layers of security before access is granted to information about your account (not the account data itself, mind you; just information about your account). A response to your request eventually makes its way to your computer along a similar path.

When I talk about connecting to the bank and to the bank's computer, I'm really talking about communicating with the computer servers that process requests for information, not connecting to the main computers where customer data is stored.

Basically, you connect your computer to a network (often the Internet), which the bank's computers are also connected to. Then you send information back and forth between your computer and the bank using that data communications network. I detail all the methods by which you can connect to the Internet in the "Accessing the Internet" section of this chapter. The following list describes the three most common options for connecting to your bank:

- ✔ **Connect, via modem, to a private data network:** Most proprietary online banking software from banks, as well as some PFMs, uses a private data network to link customers to the bank for online banking. A *private data network* is a simple technology that removes the need to connect to the Web. Private data networks work as follows: Somewhere in the banking software program is a *dialer.* A dialer is a small program (or just a section of computer code in a larger program) that wakes up your modem, dials a predefined phone number, and connects you to the bank. When you dial into a private data network, the dialer limits what you can do on the network (in this case, you can complete your banking transactions, but that's about it), and then the dialer hangs up the connection after you finish your business. You're connected to a bank of modems located at the bank's offices or (more likely) to modems provided by the bank's telecommunications contractor. Many people believe that private data networks are more secure than the Internet because the private data network is a closed, tightly controlled environment. However, the use of encryption can make the public Internet so secure that any difference between a private data network and the Internet becomes a moot point. (See Chapter 12 for details on security and encryption.)

- ✔ **Connect, via modem, to the Internet through an ISP:** Technically speaking, connecting to the Internet through a modem connection with an ISP works exactly the same way as connecting to a private data network. Dialer software controls the modem and places a call to a modem at your ISP and then establishes a communication link between the computers. The differences are that the dialer software may be separate instead of built into the online banking software, and you probably need to enter a user ID and password to log on to the ISP's system. Also, after you connect to the ISP, you are, by extension, connected to a public network that offers access to potentially millions of Internet sites and much more data than any single private data network can offer. The public nature of the Internet carries some security risk for your data, but that risk is more than offset by the use of strong encryption that protects your online banking data.

✔ **Use a high-speed Internet connection at work or school:** If your office or school has a direct connection to the Internet (which I explain in detail in the section "Using a direct Internet connection"), you're in for a pleasant surprise, because a direct Internet connection is fast and responsive compared to a dial-up modem. In a direct connection, your computer is connected to a network of computers at work or at school. That network is wired into the Internet and information can pass from the local network to the Internet and back. You go through a normal log-on procedure to gain access to your local network. After you have access to the local network, you have access to the Internet as well. When you use a direct Internet connection, Web-based online banking and the PFM features supported by Internet access look, feel, and react the same as with a modem connection — only faster.

Figure 3-2 diagrams examples of some of your options for connecting to your bank.

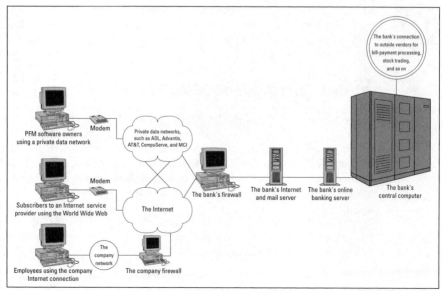

Figure 3-2:
Connecting
to your
bank.

Understanding Bank Requirements

Each bank has different policies regarding their online banking services. Whatever type of service your bank offers, you can expect to have to go through some kind of sign-up procedure before you can capitalize on online banking. After you formally request the service, your bank issues you a user ID or account number and a password or personal identification number (PIN) — like the one you use with your ATM card — that you can use to identify yourself online in order to gain access to your accounts.

Filling out an application

All banks require you to complete and sign a registration application before they allow you to start banking online. The application may require no more than clicking a button or checking a box to indicate that you agree to the terms of the services to be offered — and if you already have an account with that bank, these banking online terms are probably remarkably similar to the terms you agreed to when you first opened your accounts.

Some banks let you sign up directly online, but not all of them do. Some banks require a paper application, which isn't exactly progressive in these high-tech times — but don't get too mad at the bank. The banks are reacting to the requests of their bank examiners and other folks who oversee operational and security issues.

Don't be surprised if the bank insists on sending your user ID and password to you by mail — probably in two separate letters. This is a security measure that helps prevent unauthorized access by sending sensitive information to the same address to which the bank mails your account statements.

Specifying an account

When you apply for online banking, you need to specify at least one account for online banking purposes. In nearly all cases, you want this account to be the one that funds your bill payments. In most cases, if you have more than one account at your bank, you can access your other accounts with the same online banking ID. Many people use their online banking service to manage all their bank accounts. Some of the more progressive banks also include the ability to view loan accounts, credit cards, and lines of credit. Your bank may automatically give you access to all your eligible accounts when you sign up for online banking, or you may need to specifically request online access to each account.

Managing different types of accounts

Managing multiple accounts, such as separate accounts for your spouse or kids, is quite simple after you establish your online banking relationship with the bank. Hooking multiple accounts to your online banking access ID allows you to see all your balances, transfer funds between accounts, and check details, such as the verification of funds transfers.

Part II
An Overview of Online Banking

The 5th Wave — By Rich Tennant

©RICHTENNANT

"I like the convenience of online banking, but the overdraft penalties are more immediate."

In this part . . .

This part shows you how to get started with some of the basic online banking tasks and it introduces you to the array of online banking methods that you can choose from. You also begin to pay your bills online — from the comfort and convenience of your computer keyboard. You'll wonder how you ever survived the drudgery of paying bills before you jumped on the online bill payment bandwagon.

Chapter 4

Getting Started with Online Banking

*O*nline banking is on its way to a computer near you! As a matter of fact, it may already be there. Many banks are currently offering online banking to their customers, and more banks have announced plans to install online banking in one form or another. You, being hip enough to pick up this book, are naturally on the leading edge of this trend. (Take a moment to pat yourself on the back.) Depending on your particular needs — which I explore a little later in the chapter — you have the choice of Web-based banking, using the online banking features of a personal finance manager (PFM) software program, or using proprietary online banking software from your bank. See Chapter 2 for all the details that can help you choose which type of online banking is right for you.

In this chapter, I outline the advantages and disadvantages of the various online banking options. You also get to jump in, do some actual banking online, and get accustomed to the major online banking features.

Choosing Your Path: Web-Based Banking or PFM Software-Based Banking

You can do just about anything with online banking that you can do in a bank branch, although you can't use your computer to deposit or withdraw cash. Well, actually, you may find a few other exceptions: You can't use your online banking connection to store important papers in a safety deposit box and you can't swipe the bank pens, either. Banks already offer many more online services than were offered by the first online banking programs just a few short years ago, and new services are coming online all the time. For example, a whole group of people is already working on ways to allow you to withdraw cash from your computer using the new Smart Card technology. Unfortunately, you're on your own with the pens.

Cash at your desktop with Smart Cards

Several companies have developed a way to dispense money at your desktop. No, I am not talking about printing $20 bills from one of the new color laser printers, but rather a technology called *Smart Cards* that can distribute money over the Internet.

Smart Cards are similar to the credit cards, debit cards, and ATM cards that you use now, except that Smart Cards include an embedded computer chip that can hold far more information than the account number stored on the magnetic strip of a typical credit card. (That's why they call them "smart" cards.) Smart Cards are already popular in Europe and are currently being introduced into the United States.

The computer chip on a Smart Card can keep track of a monetary balance and process additions and subtractions that affect the total. This enables the Smart Card to function like an electronic wallet for people who make small purchases, like buying a cup of coffee in the morning, but don't want to fool with loose change. The strange-but-true part of this technology is that although no coins are minted or paper bills printed in this instance, money is stored in the form of computer memory on the card. And yes, if you lose the card, you lose your money.

To use a Smart Card, you first need to buy one at an ATM or from a merchant. The Smart Card already has a monetary value (say $20) loaded on it. When you buy your double grande latte at a coffee shop that accepts Smart Cards, you can present your Smart Card instead of money. The merchant puts your card in a Smart Card machine and deducts the cost of your cup of Joe. The process is similar to making a purchase with a debit card, except that the merchant doesn't need to have a live connection from the purchase terminal to a bank processing center and you don't need to wait for authorization from the bank in order to complete the transaction. This factor makes Smart Cards potentially more autonomous than debit cards — more like cash.

Just as the merchant can deduct the cost of a purchase from your card, you can add money to your card by transferring funds from your bank account to the card using an ATM or a terminal at your bank. In addition, computer accessories (usually special keyboards) that can read and write to Smart Cards are already available. So, it's only a matter of time before you'll be able to use online banking to transfer money to your Smart Card.

You don't have to wait for some pie-in-the-sky future to get real benefits from online banking. The online banking systems in place today can enable you to do all the following:

- ✔ Review your current bank account balances
- ✔ Review your account statements, complete with transaction entries that were posted as recently as last night
- ✔ See which checks have cleared your bank
- ✔ Confirm that direct deposits and automatic deductions occurred as scheduled
- ✔ Pay bills to just about anyone
- ✔ Transfer funds from one of your accounts to another
- ✔ Apply for a loan or credit card
- ✔ Reorder checks
- ✔ Communicate with the bank after-hours

The details of the specific online banking services available to you depend on the combination of what services your bank offers and the capabilities of the software that you use to access those services. You may not be able to do all the things on this list, but odds are that you can do most of them. You may even find that your bank offers other online services and handy features such as online calculators that help you estimate monthly loan payments for various amounts, terms, and interest rates.

You need to check with your bank to find out about the online banking services that it offers. Then you need to decide which software you want to use to access those online banking services. Depending on your bank's offerings, you may be able to access your accounts on the Web, use personal finance manager (PFM) software, or employ bank-branded software.

Keep in mind that you're not choosing between a right or wrong way to do online banking; you just look at the options that your bank supports and then pick the ones that best meet your needs and the way you manage your finances. What works best for me may not suit you at all. So, without further ado, I show you the advantages and disadvantages of each approach to online banking.

Smaller banks can compete with the largest banks for online banking turf

Online banking used to be the exclusive domain of the large mega-bazillion dollar banks, because the costs for a bank to develop and install online banking used to be measured in the millions of dollars. Today the cost is in the tens of thousands of dollars. The lower costs are tied directly to the fact that some companies are working together behind the scenes to provide banks with online banking technologies that banks then offer to people like you and me.

With this lower cost comes the ability for smaller financial institutions, especially community banks and credit unions, to get into the act and offer online banking services to their customers. Now, online banking has become much more affordable for most banks — and a downright bargain for consumers. As a banking customer, you don't have to look only to the gigantic banks if you want online banking services; you can now choose from a wide array of banks of various sizes.

Advantages of Web-based online banking

The primary advantage of Web-based online banking is convenience. I'm not talking about just the standard conveniences that any form of online banking offers, such as being able to check balances and view lists of transactions anytime you like. Web-based banking gets extra points for convenience because the access that most people have to the Internet is growing. Internet access is available at the smallest of companies, in airports, at home, at your local library, and in the ever-popular cyber-cafés. With Web-based banking, all you need is Internet access and a Web browser to access your bank account. Your bank account becomes all the more accessible, anywhere, at any time, nearly every day; therefore, banking is all the more convenient. You can see why experts believe that the number of consumers banking online may grow to somewhere between 8 and 10 million users in the next few years.

The following list shows you a few other advantages that Web-based online banking offers over traditional banking:

- ✔ **Widespread computer support:** The Internet is a great equalizer. For years, big computer companies like IBM, Apple, and DEC were all fighting to get you to buy and use their particular brand of computer. In those days, before the advent of a common way to share information, sending e-mail from an IBM mainframe in St. Louis to a supplier's DEC in Boston simply wasn't a viable option. Getting different brands and kinds of computers connected to each other and getting them to share and play nice together took a computer science degree and the patience of Job.

Along came the Internet. Poof! Computers (and the people they run) suddenly had a common way to share e-mail, files, and other information — regardless of operating system, type of computer, or whatever other mitigating factors you can think of. Just grab a Web browser or a similar tool to share data over the Internet and you're in business.

The Internet has grown so much that you can use a Web browser on a personal computer in your home or office to access information on other computers located across the world. If your bank offers Web-based online banking, your banking information is available to you securely anywhere you have access to the Internet. (I talk all about security in Part IV.)

✔ **No special software to install and use:** One of the biggest advantages of Web-based banking compared to other forms of online banking is that you don't need to install and run any special software. All you need is Internet access and a standard Web browser — the same Web browser you use to view any other World Wide Web content. Granted, you need to make sure that your Web browser is a recent version that supports the latest security features (as outlined in Chapter 12), but you need to do that anyway in order to see all the latest stuff on the Web and use your Web browser safely when you shop at e-commerce sites. You almost certainly already have everything you need, but if you do need to upgrade your browser to a new version, the software that you need is available on the Internet for free.

For Web-based banking, you don't need to request any special software from your bank and you don't need to purchase a commercial personal finance manager program. Also, you don't need to get a new version of your software in order to take advantage of any new online banking features offered by your bank. The bank can add new services and make changes to its Web site at any time. You automatically see the new-and-improved features the next time you access the bank's Web site, without making the slightest change on your system.

✔ **Sheer simplicity:** Web-based banking is almost always the simplest way to learn how to use online banking — because, of course, you already know how to use a Web browser. Unlike PFM software, Web-based banking doesn't force you to increase the amount of record keeping that you do to track your finances. You don't have to set up and meticulously maintain account registers and categorize each transaction. Instead, you can just pop onto the Internet and check your account balance anytime you want to. Many people don't have the time and interest required to keep up with a PFM program, so the simplicity of Web-based banking is its strongest allure.

✔ **Enables online bill paying:** Paying bills with the computer is super-convenient. (See Chapter 5 for more online bill-payment info.) You need to spend a little up-front time to set up your payees; then you can pay each bill with a few mouse clicks. Sure, you may want to watch the first set of payments closely to make sure that they arrive on time, but soon enough, you learn to trust online bill payment. After you set up everything and begin using online bill payment regularly, you'll be amazed at how much it streamlines the process of paying bills.

Once or twice a month, you just grab your stack of bills and jump online to pay bills. You log on to your bank's online banking site with your secret password and go to the *quick-pay* screen (or whatever your bank calls its online bill-payment function). Select who gets paid, the amount that you want to pay them, and the date that the payment should arrive. That's it — the bill is paid. I just wish that *making* money was as easy as paying it out.

✔ **Connects you to the bank's e-mail for easy interaction with your bank:** I don't know about you, but I don't have much time between 8:00 a.m. and 5:00 p.m. to talk to the bank. Most banks offer e-mail, online loan applications, and several other housekeeping services through a Web site, which means that you can jot a note to the bank at 2:00 a.m. or request a new account kit at 5:05 p.m., just after the bank closes.

Disadvantages of Web-based online banking

Using the Web to access online banking presents far more benefits than drawbacks, in my opinion. Web-based online banking isn't the way to go for everybody, however. The few disadvantages aren't worth the hassle for some, while others barely notice these drawbacks as they bask in the convenience. (It all depends on who you are and what you need.) Take a look:

✔ **Web-based online banking doesn't help you track expense categories.** If you need to track every financial transaction, such as separating business expenses from personal expenses, you may need a PFM (personal finance manager) software package. (See Part III for extensive coverage of various PFMs and their expense-tracking capabilities.)

✔ **You must have access to the Internet and the Web.** Many companies still don't allow you to access the Web from your desk at work. And in some parts of the country, you can't access the Internet with a local call. If you plan to do much online banking under those conditions, you may be better off banking online through a PFM program or bank-branded software that connects to your bank via a private data network.

✔ **Web-based banking is slower than software running on your computer.** Web-based banking must not only retrieve your banking data, but also all the rest of the online banking environment, by downloading it from your bank's Web site. You have to wait while the text and graphics of each Web page make their way across the Internet to your Web browser. How long you have to wait depends on the speed of your modem or Internet connection and on the speed or traffic congestion at the series of connections between your computer and the bank. If you access the Internet using a dial-up connection over a slow modem, the wait for each Web page can be significant — and very frustrating! For maximum performance, online banking software running on your computer can't be beat. PFM programs and bank-branded software reside on your computer and exchange only raw account data over the Internet, so the impact of a slow connection is minimized.

Advantages of online banking with PFM software

A common thread connects the people who use personal finance manager software packages: a strong addiction. After you form the habit of using a PFM program as a regular part of your financial planning routine, giving it up becomes very hard. Current versions of PFM software, such as Quicken 99, Money 99, and Managing Your Money all include online banking features in addition to the other personal finance manager features that make these programs so popular among their many users. As a result, you can have all the normal online banking advantages (such as instant online account balance updates, access to up-to-date lists of transactions, convenient online bill payments, and e-mail communication with your bank) available from within your PFM software.

In some cases, the only way to access online banking at your bank may be to use the PFM software that the bank supports. That used to be a fairly common situation, but it's becoming increasingly rare as more and more banks add Web-based banking to their online banking repertoire. If all you want is basic online banking, you can probably find these functions at your bank's Web site without resorting to the extra effort of working with a PFM program. The best reason to use a PFM is because you also want to use its other features (besides online banking). If you're the kind of person who likes to use personal finance manager software, the addition of online banking to a PFM program can be a very powerful combination.

The following examples show you the advantages of using a PFM for online banking:

✔ **The ability to track detailed information:** Most people who use personal finance manager software do so in order to take advantage of the software's ability to track detailed information about each and every transaction. You can categorize each transaction and use those categories to generate detailed reports and graphs showing facts such as how much interest income you earned and how much you spent on business expenses, groceries, and the like. Your PFM software becomes a rich source of information that you can use to analyze and manage all your finances.

✔ **The availability of budgeting and financial planning tools:** All the popular PFM programs include powerful tools for developing budgets and tracking your actual income and expenses against your budget projections. Typically, PFM software also includes other planning tools, such as calculators that help you estimate loan costs, compare leases, and project retirement income. Occasionally, you may find similar calculators on a bank's Web site, but the Web-based calculators are rarely as comprehensive as what you find in a PFM program, and you don't find Web sites that can begin to compare to a PFM program for budgeting and analysis.

✔ **Easy tax preparation:** Entering your financial information into a PFM program really pays off at about 11:00 p.m. on April 15, if at no other time during the year. For those of us who do put off taxes, filling out tax forms can be a major undertaking, and the fees and penalties for wrong information can be significant. If you use a PFM program diligently all year long, preparing for your taxes is very, very easy. PFM software can manage detailed information about your paycheck, mortgage, charitable contributions, and so on. All the major PFM software packages mentioned in this book allow you to *seamlessly* export data to tax planning software like TurboTax. Even if you don't choose to use tax preparation software, your PFM program can provide you with reports that organize and summarize all the information that you need to fill out your taxes, assuming that you entered the data throughout the year.

✔ **Paperwork management for the small business owner:** If you have a small business (one or two people) and use a PFM program to manage your financial activities, having the ability to see where every dollar comes from and goes is very powerful. The burden of keeping up with the paperwork (especially all the tax filings) can be a major undertaking, and without any help, gathering up all your receipts, canceled checks, and related paraphernalia can be a challenge. A PFM program's categories allow you to enter a transaction one time and be able to review your account information time and time again.

✔ **Online banking integrated with other financial management features:** Obviously, if you use PFM software to track and manage your finances, you gain plenty of advantages by using the same software for online banking. This combination provides not only convenience, but also the synergy that's possible between online banking features and other features of the PFM software, such as:

- **Automated data entry:** With a PFM program you can view your online account balance and list of transactions on-screen, but the PFM software can also download that data and automatically enter it into your PFM program's account register. This feature allows you to keep your account registers up-to-date without having to type each transaction into the software manually. If you have more than a few transactions to record each month, the time savings can be significant — as is the reduced chance of introducing typographical errors into your financial records. If you want the advantages of a PFM program but can't face all the tedious data-entry chores required to maintain it, the automated data-entry feature makes working with PFM software practical.

- **Simplified account reconciliation:** You probably dread the chore of comparing your account records to the statement that you receive from the bank and reconciling any differences that you find. (If you're trying to keep a manual checkbook register in this day of ATM withdrawals and debit card purchases, you probably find a lot of discrepancies to reconcile.) However, if you keep your account records in a PFM program and update them with online banking, reconciliation is a snap. In fact, the PFM software does most of the work for you automatically each time you check your account balance online and download transactions from the bank. You simply confirm the transactions that match your entries in your PFM account register and click your mouse to add any new transactions to the register. The end-of-month reconciliation to your paper account statement from the bank takes only a minute or two and becomes nothing more than a quick confirmation.

- **Integrated access to online bill payment:** Online bill payment is a tremendous convenience when you use it from your bank's Web site, but it's even more convenient when you use online bill payment from within your PFM program. PFM software gives you more ways to initiate an online payment — and some methods are almost totally automatic. You can initiate online bill payments by filling in an on-screen form that may be very similar to the one that you use in Web-based banking.

You can also initiate an online bill payment by entering the transaction into your PFM program's account register. The PFM software can remind you to make payments according to a predefined schedule, and you can configure the PFM software to make scheduled payments automatically on certain dates. After you reconcile a credit card account balance to the monthly statement, your PFM software may offer to automatically generate an online bill payment to the credit card company. Bill payment can't get any easier than this! No matter how you initiate online payments, your PFM software automatically sends the online bill payments to the bank for processing the next time you log on.

✔ **Faster operation:** PFM software resides on your hard disk and runs entirely on your personal computer. As a result, using PFM software is much faster than using Web-based banking; you don't have to wait for Web pages to download over the Internet. Even when you have to connect to the Internet or a private data network to receive online banking data from your bank, the PFM software needs to download only the raw data, not all the graphics and supporting screens that are required for Web-based banking. Because PFM software can accomplish online banking by transferring a minimum of data between computers, the effects of a slow modem or Internet connection are minimized. In fact, if you do your online banking from within a PFM, you can get by with using an Internet connection that's too slow to be practical for Web-based banking.

✔ **All online banking consolidated in one convenient location:** After you start using online banking, you may want to use it for all your bank accounts, credit card accounts, brokerage accounts, and anything else that you possibly can. If you use Web-based banking for all these tasks, you probably need to access different Web sites for each financial institution, and each one has its own look and feel. If all your institutions support the same PFM software, you can access all of them from the same program, using the same familiar screens and dialog boxes. The PFM software may even help you keep track of the separate user IDs and passwords for each bank and enter them for you automatically.

✔ **The ability to work when you're not connected to the Internet:** Because PFM software is a stand-alone program running on your personal computer, you can use it even when you're not connected to the Internet. Unlike Web-based banking, which is totally reliant on an active Internet connection, the PFM software can operate independently to provide you with access to all your account information at any time and in any place. As a result, you can review last month's spending patterns or work up a new budget using PFM software on your laptop computer during a cross-country airline flight or at the beach, far from a phone or Internet connection. Of course, you can't update your account information until you reestablish an online connection, but you can work with all the information stored on your computer and new information that you enter manually.

Disadvantages of online banking with PFM software

Although using PFM software to do online banking can be very helpful, PFM programs aren't for everybody. PFM software can be a powerful tool for tracking your finances and actively managing your financial affairs, but it requires a lot of care and feeding to keep the information in the PFM program complete and up-to-date. For many people, the benefits of PFM software just aren't worth the time and effort required to maintain the software and the numerous account registers.

Before you decide to start using PFM software, you need to carefully consider your personal money management style and whether you're willing and able to devote time to working with the PFM program. As you think about using PFM software, you need to consider the following points:

✔ **You have to use the same computer all the time.** The core feature of PFM software packages is the register list of transactions that you build and maintain over time. As a result, you have to use the PFM software on the computer where the data files containing all that transaction data are stored, and nowhere else. Although you could install multiple copies of the software on different computers, you would find it very hard to keep multiple copies of your register data up-to-date. For example, if I pay bills using my PFM software on my home computer, those transactions aren't listed in the register that I view using the computer on my desk at work unless I schlepp a copy of all the PFM's data files around with me — and believe me, that's a royal pain!

✔ **You experience a steeper software learning curve.** The long list of powerful features available in a PFM software package means that you need to learn how to use a lot of stuff. PFM software designers work hard to make the programs intuitive and easy to use, and the result is a good balance between power and simplicity. Still, if you're looking for the quickest, easiest way to do online banking, you're probably better off with Web-based banking than with a PFM program.

✔ **PFMs require more time and effort to keep your data current.** PFM software is all about keeping track of detailed information about your transactions. You can't really take advantage of all the fancy reports and graphs, analysis tools, and tax preparation features of the software unless you diligently enter all your transactions into the program and assign them to the appropriate categories. If you deal with enough transactions each month that you need a software program to help you organize them, then entering all that data takes some time. Automatically entering data that you download using online banking can help, but you still have to be willing to spend some time with your PFM software on a regular basis. Web-based banking, on the other hand, requires no such commitment; it remains just as useful even if you skip a month or more between visits to your bank's Web site.

✔ **Your bank must support your specific brand of PFM software.** In order to use PFM software for online banking access to your accounts at your bank, the bank must first install special computer systems and software to support your particular brand of PFM software. Not all banks have taken the necessary steps to support PFM software. And even if your bank does support PFM software, your bank may not support the brand of software that you want to use. In that case, you have no choice but to change your software selection, or your bank.

✔ **PFMs sometimes require software upgrades.** Every year or so, each of the leading PFM software companies introduces a new version of its software with extra bells and whistles. Although updating your PFM software isn't a huge expense, that money does add up.

Advantages and disadvantages of bank-branded online banking software

Making meaningful generalizations about the advantages and disadvantages of the many proprietary bank-branded software packages available for online banking is hard to do. Some packages are very limited, special-purpose programs, while others are full-fledged PFM programs with feature lists to rival the leading commercial PFM packages. Most bank-branded software falls somewhere in the vast space between the two extremes. You need to contact your bank and get a description of the features that are included in the software that the bank supplies. Consider these points, based on the characteristics of a typical bank-branded online banking program:

- ✔ **No Internet connection required:** Bank-branded online banking software often uses a private data network to establish the connection between your computer and the bank. This is an attractive alternative for people who can't use Web-based banking because they don't have easy access to a reliable Internet connection. The private data network may also be less susceptible to slowdowns and busy signals due to heavy Internet traffic during peak times. And some people believe that private data networks offer better security than a public network like the Internet.

- ✔ **Software dedicated to your bank:** Bank-branded software is, by its very nature, tied to the online banking services of one particular bank. This characteristic can be an advantage because you usually don't have to adjust confusing settings to make the software work with your bank — everything is preprogrammed into the software by the bank. This same point can be a disadvantage if you ever want to do online banking with another bank; none of the software, data files, or your experience learning to use the program are transferable to another bank.

- ✔ **Faster than Web-based banking:** Bank-branded software is almost always stand-alone software that you install and run on your personal computer. As such, it's probably faster than Web-based banking, where you download the text and graphics of multiple Web pages over an Internet connection. Also, like PFM programs, you may be able to run the program and use some of its features without having a live connection to the Internet or to the bank. Of course, you can't update online banking account balances when you're not connected to the bank, but you may be able to view previously downloaded transactions and use other features of the software.

- ✔ **Software may become outdated:** Originally, individual banks developed their own online banking software because they had no other practical way to provide online banking services to their customers. Bank-branded software available today probably descended from those efforts. Because many people in the online banking world are turning away from proprietary software and toward Web-based banking, bank-branded software has a fair chance of being phased out soon.

Establishing Your Online Banking Access

Despite how comfortable you may feel accessing the Internet, even you, the most savvy Internet surfer, can get a bit apprehensive about banking online. But as a matter of fact, getting set up for online banking really isn't that painful. I show you in this section just how painless and risk-free it is — assuming that your bank offers online banking.

Although you encounter different details for the enrollment process, depending on whether you use Web-based banking or PFM software, the basic process can be summarized in three simple steps:

1. **Apply for online banking service from your bank.**

   You need to fill out a form of some kind to formally request online banking services from your bank. (The bank doesn't usually activate your accounts for online access until you request this service.) Two things determine how fast and simple this part of the enrollment process is: the method that you use to access online banking, and your bank's policies.

2. **Receive a user ID and a password.**

   After your accounts are activated for online access, the bank gives you access codes that you use to identify yourself to the online banking system and unlock access to your accounts each time you start an online banking session. Each bank may have a different method of sending these access codes to you. Hint: Be prepared to wait a few days to use them for the first time.

3. **Complete the enrollment process.**

   For Web-based banking, your next steps may be to log on to your bank's online banking Web site and start using the services. But be prepared for an extra step or two the first time you log on. If you use PFM software, you have more setup to do in order to configure your program and accounts for online banking access.

These three steps give you the general idea. The following sections go into more detail so that you know what to expect when you sign up for online banking from your bank.

Filling out the enrollment forms

Your first step is to enroll in your bank's online banking service. In other words, tell the bank that you want to access your accounts with your computer. Remember that even though online banking is available for your accounts at the bank, nearly all banks leave that feature turned off until you specifically request that it be activated.

Online banking enrollment procedures vary from bank to bank and some are more stringent than others. The most important consideration for your bank when it signs up any customer is that the bank "knows the customer." The challenge for the bank is to find a way to identify you, the customer, without requiring you to meet someone at your bank face-to-face; after all, an online connection doesn't allow your banker to verify who you are by looking at a driver's license or some other form of identification. Before activating online access to your bank accounts, a bank employee needs to confirm that you are, indeed, the owner or authorized user of the accounts in question. Usually this confirmation of identity consists of your answering a few simple personal questions.

As part of the process of verifying your identity during online banking enrollment, your bank checks information that you supply on the enrollment form against the information in the bank's files. Your application for online banking can be rejected if the information doesn't match. Mismatches can be caused by typographical errors on the application or in the bank's records, or by the fact that you changed your phone number, for example, and neglected to inform the bank of your new number. Of course, you don't think of that when you put the new number on the application, do you?

Many banks let you apply online by filling out an on-screen form. The two leading PFM programs, Quicken and Microsoft Money, both have the capability to submit application information online. Many Web-based banking sites accept online applications as well. Even if you can't complete the application form online, you may be able to print an application that's available at your bank's Web site. If you print out a form, just fill it out with a pen or pencil, and then mail or fax it back to the bank. If enrollment forms aren't available via computer, you can always give the bank a call or visit a branch.

While you're searching for the enrollment form, keep an eye out for the online banking agreement, which is probably available from the same place. Like all bank agreements, it's normally dry and hard to read, but you really need to familiarize yourself with the terms of the agreement just the same.

After the bank receives your online banking enrollment form, the bank staff reviews it for completeness and verifies your identity and the accounts you have at the bank. If everything checks out, the bank assigns you a set of access codes that serve as your key to access online banking. If you're applying for online banking through your PFM software, your bank also sends you information that you have to enter into your PFM software in order to activate online banking access to your account.

Receiving your online banking ID or password from your bank

After you enroll in your bank's online banking system, the bank gives you a special identification number and a password that you will use to access your online account. Depending on whether you use Web-based banking or PFM software to do your online banking, the steps that you take to get your password may be different. The following sections cover the possible actions that you may need to take:

Getting a password for Web-based banking

After the bank activates your accounts for Web-based online banking access, all you need to get started is the access codes that you use to identify yourself to the online banking system. Normally, you're assigned two access codes: The first one is probably an account number (perhaps your primary bank account number or the number from your ATM card) or a user ID (such as your name, e-mail address, social security number, or something you select) that identifies you to the online banking system. The second access code is either a password or a personal identification number (PIN), which is your secret key that confirms your identity and unlocks access to your accounts. (For the sake of simplicity, I use the terms *user ID* and *password,* although your bank may call them something else.) The bank may send your access codes to you electronically, but more typically, you have to wait for them to arrive in the mail.

The following list describes the different ways that banks can send your user ID and password to you, depending on your bank's policies and operating procedures. Unfortunately, you don't get to choose the method. Often, your user ID and password arrive separately, and they may even come through different delivery channels. Banks typically take extra precautions to protect the security of your password because it's supposed to be your secret key.

- **Your bank may provide your user ID or password to you directly online.** In this case, you get your user ID and password on the same Web site where you sign up for online banking service. Currently, few banks deliver passwords this way. To use this type of enrollment you must be able to verify online who you are to the bank, which is very hard in the anonymous world of the Internet. One way that banks can accomplish this is to include questions that are unique to your banking relationship and that only you know the answers to. For example, you may be asked to enter the ending balance of your checking account as shown on your last bank statement.

✔ **Your bank can e-mail your user ID or a temporary password to you.**
Like the Web site delivery option mentioned earlier, this delivery
technique is also relatively rare because of concerns about security. It's
not that the bank fears that your e-mail will be intercepted and read;
the bank is more concerned about being able to confirm that the e-mail
address belongs to the authorized owner of the account that you're
trying to access.

✔ **You can call your bank and ask for your user ID and a temporary
password.** In some cases, the customer service unit that supports
online banking can give you your access codes after asking you some
questions to verify your identity. Don't be too upset if they refuse,
though, because bank policies (and bank regulators' requirements)
often prohibit giving out passwords on the phone.

✔ **Most likely, your bank will mail your user ID and password to you.**
This method causes a delay of a few days as the bank prints the letter
and sends it through the postal delivery system, but it ensures a high
level of security. By mailing the online access codes to the home
address listed on your account records — the same address that your
bank uses for sending you monthly account statements — the bank can
be reasonably sure that the user ID and password reach the owner of
the account — you.

If you ever receive a user ID or password that you didn't specifically request,
contact your bank immediately. Receiving such information may indicate
that someone tried to gain access to your accounts by impersonating you
online and requesting online banking privileges. Mailing access codes to the
account owner's address is designed to foil such attempts.

Getting a password for online banking with PFM software

After you apply for online banking with the PFM software that your bank
supports, you need to wait for an information packet to arrive in the mail
before you can go online. The information packet includes a temporary
password that you can use to access your bank's online banking service,
and also contains information about your accounts that you need when you
set up your PFM software to access your accounts online. You usually don't
get a separate user ID to enter when you access online banking with your
PFM software because the PFM program handles that part of the identification process for you.

Unlike some Web-based banking systems, conventional mail is the only
delivery option for the information packet from your bank (at least, none
that I've heard of have alternate methods). You just have to wait for the
package to arrive via old-fashioned postal mail. For security reasons, the
bank may send your password in a separate envelope, timed to arrive a day
or so apart from the rest of the information packet.

Completing the enrollment process

When you have all the necessary information to begin using online banking, all that remains for you to do is enter the information into your software (Web browser or PFM program) and connect with your bank for the first time. The following sections show you how.

Completing the connection to Web-based banking

The process of logging on to any online banking Web site is pretty standard, regardless of which bank you use or what online banking features it offers. Your bank's Web pages may look different from other bank sites in appearance, but most online banking sites function pretty much the same.

The following steps show you the general process for logging on to most banks' online banking Web sites:

1. **Go to the bank's Web site and look for a Log On or Go On Line button and click it.**

   You can find your bank's Web address in literature from the bank, by using an Internet search engine, or by looking in the *Banking Online For Dummies Internet Directory,* located in the second half of this book.

   You may not find a button on the first page of your bank's Web site that leads directly to the online banking log-on page; you may have to go to a page that introduces the service first before you find the link. Also, banks commonly label the button or graphic that leads to the online banking area with the bank's marketing catchphrase for online banking. Look for a name such as Account Link, PC Bank, Home ATM, PC Teller, Web Banker, Personal Accounts, or something similar.

2. **Enter your user ID and password.**

   In the boxes provided on-screen, type in the user ID and password that you received from the bank. Figure 4-1 shows an online banking log-on page, asking for a username and password. Make sure that you enter the access codes carefully, paying particular attention to exact spelling and capitalization. Be especially careful as you type the password because you probably can't see your keystrokes appear on-screen for visual confirmation. Asterisks usually appear on-screen in the password field to hide your password from prying eyes. (Of course, then the password is also hidden from you — so type carefully.)

   Remember to watch for an indication that your browser is connected to a secure Web site for online banking. The padlock symbol in the status bar at the bottom of your Web browser window indicates that SSL encryption is active. (See Chapters 11 and 12 for more about encryption.) Your browser may also display a message box alerting you when you enter and leave a secure area of the Web. Most banks switch to a secure server before displaying the log-on page so that your user ID and password are encrypted when you enter them.

3. **Click the Click To Start button to complete the logon and go online.**

For the bank site shown in Figure 4-1, you click OK. Other banks may label the corresponding button Click To Start, Log On, Enter, or something else.

4. **If prompted to do so, create a new password by typing the new password twice; then click the button to proceed.**

Many banks require you to change your password immediately upon entering the online banking area for the first time. If so, the next screen that you see prompts you to enter a new password of your choice. You probably need to retype your new password a second time for confirmation. After typing the password, you need to click an on-screen button to record it. The button may be labeled OK, Continue, Save, or something equally obvious.

After you create your new password, you enter the online banking area of your bank's Web site. In this area, you can check your account balance, make online bill payments, and use the other online banking services offered by your bank.

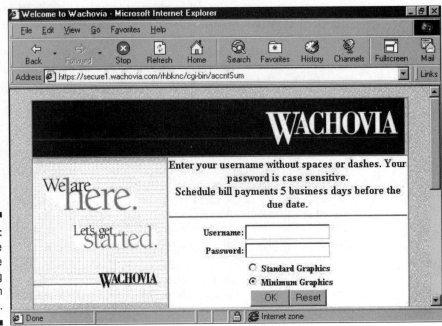

Figure 4-1:
A sample
online
banking
sign-on
screen.

Choose carefully when you create your new online banking password. Try to pick something that is easy to remember but hard for someone else to guess. Names of pets and family members are too easy to guess, as are birthdays. Random letter and number sequences are hard to guess, but they can also be hard to remember. One technique that seems to work well is to pick two unrelated words and join them with one or more numbers or punctuation characters. You end up with a password something like this: `weigh?clip6`. Personal identification numbers (PINs), on the other hand, are usually restricted to numbers, so you don't have as many choices. Try to use as many digits as allowed and avoid using parts of your social security number, address, telephone number, birthday, and other easily guessed numbers as your PIN.

Setting up PFM programs for online banking access

With PFM software, you have a few more steps to complete the enrollment process. After you receive the information packet, you need to go to the Online area of your PFM program and attend to some set-up chores. The details vary considerably, depending on which PFM software you use, but the general procedure goes something like this:

1. **Configure your PFM software to connect to the bank, either through the Internet or through a private data network.**

   This process can be as simple as confirming that you want to use the same Internet connection that you use for Web browsing or as complicated as a detailed modem configuration. Fortunately, the PFM programs normally use wizards to lead you through the set-up process so that all you need to do is answer a series of simple questions.

2. **Identify and configure the accounts that you want to use with online banking.**

   When you activate the PFM software's online banking feature for an account, you usually need to enter more information than what is required for a typical account definition. You need to enter things like account numbers and bank routing numbers, and you need to activate the online banking feature and link the account to your financial institution.

   I cover the specific steps for activating online banking in each of the major PFM programs in the individual chapters about those programs in Part III of this book. Likewise, I cover the steps for connecting to the bank for an online banking session in each of the programs. You find Quicken instructions in Chapter 7, Money instructions in Chapter 8, and Managing Your Money instructions in Chapter 9.

You may wonder why you must enter significantly more information into a PFM program in order to activate online banking than you must enter to activate Web-based online banking. The reason that PFM software requires a lot of information (compared to setting up online banking on your bank's Web site) is because the software is designed to work with the online banking services of many different banks. In fact, you can have online banking services active simultaneously for several different accounts from different financial institutions within the same PFM software. So naturally, you need to provide all the information that the software needs to identify the specific bank that you're dealing with for each account, the account numbers for the accounts that you want to access, and your social security number or other ID number that the software can use to identify you to the bank. In contrast, when you set up Web-based banking at a bank's Web site, you're communicating directly with the bank, so you don't have to enter any bank identification info (and probably no account numbers, either).

3. **Initiate an online banking session from within your PFM software to connect to the bank for your first online banking session.**

   After you set up everything, you can start using the online banking features of your PFM software. Again, the specific steps that you follow will vary depending on which PFM program you use. I cover those steps in detail in the chapters about individual PFM programs in Part III.

4. **Enter the password that you received from the bank and continue the log-on procedure as appropriate for your PFM program.**

5. **Create a new password by typing it twice; then press Enter to continue with the log-on process.**

   This step isn't always required, but most banks force you to change your password the first time you access a newly activated online banking account. All the PFM programs include a password change feature that appears automatically if the bank requires a new password.

6. **Complete the online banking session using the normal procedures for your PFM software.**

   Watch the magic happen as your PFM software logs on to your bank's online banking system and automatically retrieves updated information about your accounts. Refer to the chapters on the individual PFM programs for detailed information on how to use the various online banking features.

Understanding Basic Online Banking Features

With online banking, you can now address nearly all the transactions that you used to complete during a trip to the bank — except cash withdrawals. You can check your balances, transfer funds, review your statement, and even pay bills. The features are equally accessible and beneficial whether you're using Web-based banking or a PFM software package to access your accounts.

Show me the money! — reviewing balances

When you log on to do some online banking, you probably want to check how much money is in your account. (I show you how to log on to your bank's Web site earlier in this chapter.) Finding basic account information is a fairly simple matter. Some banks give you the type of information shown in Figure 4-2 as soon as you log on; others make you click a button like Account Summary or Check All Balances before displaying a similar screen.

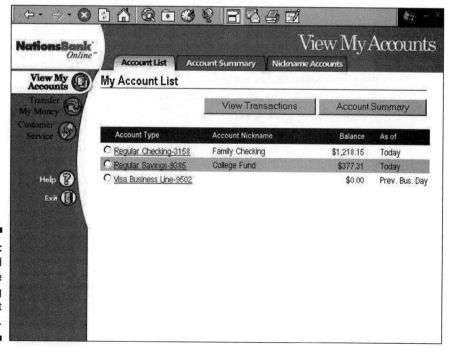

Figure 4-2: Web-based online banking account summary.

With PFM software packages, you can get similar results — viewing updated account balances — with just a few more mouse clicks. You need to run the PFM software and go to its Online area; then update your account information by logging on to your bank, which I describe earlier in this chapter. The detailed steps that you go through to conduct an online session depend on which PFM software you use. After getting the updated balance information from your bank, the PFM software displays your account balance (and more) in a window such as the one shown in Figure 4-3.

When viewing your account balances, you may be surprised to see that the bank shows more than one balance for each account. Banks maintain different types of balances, and the following sections give brief explanations of them. The two types of account balances are *ledger balance* and *available balance*. Figure 4-4 shows a sample Web-based online account balance summary. The two account balances shown in Figure 4-4 differ: The available balance accounts for several transactions that the bank knows are coming, and the other balance (the ledger balance) shows the exact monetary status of your account. When the bank knows that a transaction is coming, it sets aside the money until the actual transaction occurs and the money actually leaves your account, which accounts for the difference.

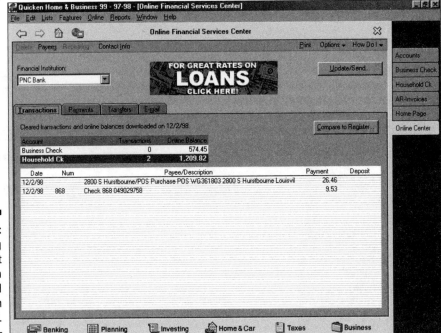

Figure 4-3:
Viewing
account
balances in
a PFM
program
(Quicken).

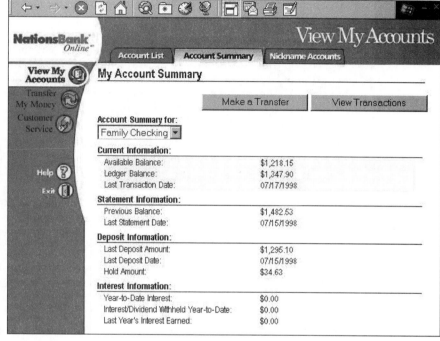

Ledger or statement balance

Every active bank account has a starting balance at the start of each bank business day, called the *ledger* or *statement balance*. A bank business day is any Monday through Friday (excluding holidays that the bank observes, like New Year's Day, the Fourth of July, and so on). The bank determines the ledger balance amount the night before, after processing all your deposits, withdrawals, checks, debit card transactions, and so on.

Available balance

The *available balance* is your ledger balance, minus any transactions that your bank knows about (and has set aside money to complete) but hasn't actually posted to your account. Bankers call this process of setting aside funds to cover a transaction a *memo post*. Upon learning about a pending transaction, the banker inserts a memo in your account and puts the money on hold. Later, when the transaction actually occurs and the money leaves your account (or enters your account — memo posts can include deposits as well as withdrawals), the banker removes the memo and replaces it with the permanent transaction record. Of course, all this is done electronically; no banker is sitting around with quill pen in hand, posting your transactions in a paper ledger book.

The following kinds of transactions commonly result in memo posts that affect your available balance:

- ✔ **ATM withdrawals:** These withdrawals also include fees that have occurred in the last few days or so, but which the bank's bookkeeping department hasn't yet processed. If you withdraw money at another bank's ATM, the moment that you pull money out of that bank's ATM, an automated memo post occurs at your bank, setting aside the full amount of the ATM withdrawal (plus any of those darn fees).

- ✔ **Pre-authorized transactions:** These transactions appear as a memo post at the start of the day when they are presented to your account. Then, at the end of the day, the bank processes the pre-authorized transactions along with all the other transactions for the day, and the bank pulls money out of your account. You may set up pre-authorized transactions for your auto or life insurance premium payments. During the one day that each of these transactions is being processed, these types of memo posts contribute to the difference between your ledger and available balances.

- ✔ **Debit card transactions:** The moment that you use your debit card and your purchase amount is approved, a memo post occurs. If you want to look into debit cards further, take a moment to review the "How debit card transactions affect your online balance" sidebar. It's around here somewhere.

- ✔ **Credits applied to your debit card:** When you return an item that you purchased with a debit card, the merchant issues a credit, effectively returning money to your account. These credits are handled with memo posts that work the same way as when you make a purchase with your debit card. Returning an item for credit causes your available balance to be higher than your ledger balance until the transaction posts to your account.

- ✔ **Direct deposit of your payroll check:** Payroll deposits normally become available on the morning of your payday and get recorded as a memo post. In this case, the money is in your account but the transaction doesn't post to your account until that night.

Figuring out when transactions appear online

You may understand the different account balances that you see when you're banking online, but odds are that you still don't have a reliable estimate of your current balance if you don't know when your latest transactions will be added to your online balance statement.

How debit card transactions affect your online balance

Debit cards look like credit cards, but they work like checks. Debit card transactions are one of the more popular types of transactions that affect your bank account balances. Understanding how debit cards work, therefore, can help you use online banking more reliably.

Many banks offer debit cards, which immediately take money from your checking account instead of billing you for your purchases at the end of the month as credit cards do. Another common term for debit card is *check card*. Visa offers the Visa Check card and MasterCard offers the MasterMoney card. Debit cards are issued by your financial institution and they often do double duty as ATM cards.

For consumers who make many purchases and like to pay as they go instead of accumulating credit card bills, a debit card works great. A debit card enables you to pay for your purchases with money from your checking account without the hassle of getting a check approved. When debit card transactions post to your account, your online or paper statements usually list the name of the merchant, which helps you to easily identify the category for a transaction (in your PFM program) instead of having to look up the check number and identify the merchant in your paper register.

A debit card reduces the number of paper checks that banks must process and replaces them with highly automated electronic transactions. Also, banks normally get a part of the fee that every merchant pays to the companies that handle processing for card payments. In case you were wondering: Yep, banks love 'em.

Debit cards can make balancing your online banking balances a little tricky, but not impossible. When you go to the store and pay for groceries with your debit card, the transaction follows the same course as when you use a credit card. Instead of getting an approval from your credit card issuer, though, the debit card process gets an approval from your bank that the money is available to spend. When the bank authorizes the purchase, it places a hold on enough money in your account to cover the transaction when it finally gets to the bank (a *memo post*) — usually within two to three days.

All online banking systems update their transactions in one of the following two ways:

  ✔ **Real-time processing:** If your bank uses real-time processing, you can see the results of your online banking transactions (money transfers, ATM withdrawals, deposits, and so on) as soon as you complete them.

  Real-time processing is possible when your bank hooks its online banking system directly to the system that tracks transactions from all parts of the bank, including the tellers, ATMs, and any other banking system that the bank offers. For example, suppose that my checking account balance is $250 at the start of the day. When I go out to lunch, I use my debit card to pay for a $10 lunch. If I want to, as soon as I get back to my desk, I can log on to my online banking service and see an available balance of $240 (assuming that my wife didn't use her ATM or debit card).

(Note that memo posts are usually what you see affecting the available balance in your account during the course of the day when your bank uses real-time processing. The actual transaction posts still occur in batches overnight.)

✔ **Batch processing:** If your bank uses batch processing, it updates balances only once a day. The bank's online banking system probably isn't linked directly to the computer system that manages the flow of memo posts that occur during the day. This means that my payment for a $10 lunch at noon doesn't show up on my account registers until the next morning.

The following list shows you the steps that a bank takes when it uses batch processing:

1. **Throughout the day, online banking customers like you and me interact with the online banking server through the Internet.**

   We can check balances and execute funds-transfer and bill-payment requests, just as customers on real-time systems can. The bank holds these requests during the day on the online banking server, which manages all the online banking information for the bank.

2. **At the end of the banking day (which is usually defined by an arbitrary cutoff time such as 4:00 p.m.), the online banking server sends all transaction requests, in one "batch" of information, to the bank's computer system.**

   The computer system then processes those requests, along with all the other banking transactions.

3. **Overnight, the bank processes all the checks, deposits, ATM withdrawals, debit card purchases, and other debits and credits for every customer and determines new balances.**

4. **After the bank (well, its computer system) finishes processing account information for all its customers, the bank updates the online banking server with the new balances and account statement details for its online banking customers.**

5. **The information is available early the next day for customers to review.**

   At this point, the process starts all over again, with any transactions that arrived after the cutoff time carried forward to the new day. (See Figure 4-5 for a flowchart that shows the entire batch process.)

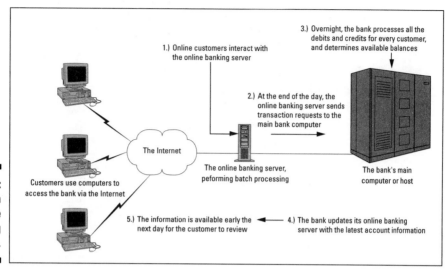

1.) Online customers interact with the online banking server

2.) At the end of the day, the online banking server sends transaction requests to the main bank computer

3.) Overnight, the bank processes all the debits and credits for every customer, and determines available balances

The Internet

The online banking server, peforming batch processing

The bank's main computer or host

Customers use computers to access the bank via the Internet

5.) The information is available early the next day for the customer to review

4.) The bank updates its online banking server with the latest account information

Figure 4-5:
The batch online banking process.

Real-time and batch processing aren't related to the kind of online banking service that your bank offers (Web-based banking or support for PFM software). Switching the type of online banking service that you use isn't likely to affect the type of processing that your payments go through.

Reviewing statements

Another element of your account that you may want to check via online banking is whether a particular transaction has (or hasn't) cleared your account. After all, for most of us, the most important factor is whether we have a comfortable-looking balance *after* deducting the mortgage payment. By checking the transactions listed in your online statement, you can see which transactions have cleared the bank and do a quick-and-easy reconciliation to answer the question, "How much money can I spend?"

The exact functions and steps vary by bank and according to whether you access your accounts via Web-based banking or PFM software, but reviewing online statements is easy no matter where you bank (provided that your bank supports online banking, of course). The following steps show you the general process for checking your statement with a typical Web-based banking system:

1. **Display the account list or summary page — the one showing your account balances.**

   If you're not already viewing the page that lists your accounts and their balances, you need to log on to your bank's Web-based banking site and go (or return) to that page. (Refer to Figure 4-3.) This process may be familiar if you've done this before.

2. **Select the account that you want to review, and click the View Transactions button.**

   Your bank may use a different label for the View Transactions button, or you may need to click a link instead of a button.

3. **If applicable, define the range of information that you want to review and then click the View button**.

   Some banks offer options for defining the range of information that you want to display and the order in which it appears. For example, the banking site shown in Figure 4-6 lets users see account activity since their last statement, or for any number of days up to 60. You may also be able to elect to review your entire last statement or select transactions based on search criteria such as a range of dates, check numbers, or transaction amounts. Although you may have options for the way that you want to sort this information, the information is normally presented in chronological order. After you select the sort options, click the View button to submit your request for transaction data.

   Some banks skip the sort options and go straight to the next step by simply displaying the list of transactions in default order.

4. **View the results.**

   The bank's online banking software retrieves the requested information from the bank's computer system and displays it in your Web browser for review. The statement screen shown in Figure 4-7 shows all the transactions within a requested seven-day period.

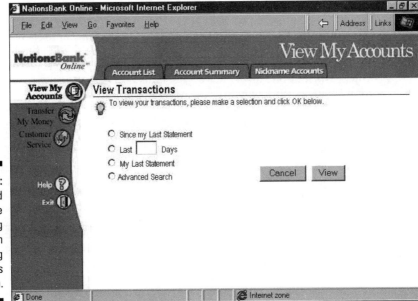

Figure 4-6:
Web-based online banking transaction viewing options screen.

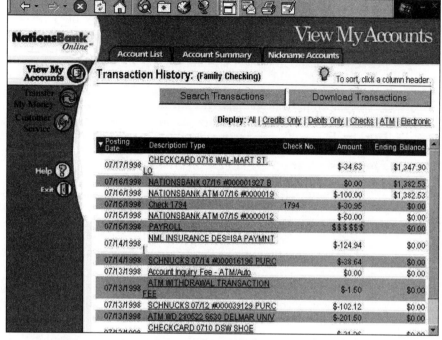

Figure 4-7:
Web-based
online
banking
transaction
history
screen.

You can do the same thing with any of the PFM software packages, but the
steps that you take to view an on-screen list of recent transactions will vary
depending on the PFM program you use. You can find those steps detailed in
Chapters 7, 8, and 9.

One important difference between the PFM programs and Web-based
banking is that you don't have to be connected to the bank to view your
online statement and transaction details. The PFM software automatically
downloads all the transaction details from your bank when you connect to
the bank to update your account balances, and then stores that information
on your hard drive. You can then view the balances or the transaction
details at your leisure, even after you close the connection to your bank.

Transferring funds

Transferring funds from one account to another is one of the simplest
transactions that you can perform with online banking. Maybe you realize
that you don't have enough money in checking (because you just compared
the amount of money that you have in your checking account to the amount
that you know you need in order to pay bills in the coming week), and you
need to transfer money from a savings account or money market account
into your checking account.

Or, perhaps you want to transfer money into a special account once a month
as you save toward a certain goal, such as a college fund for your children.
That's easy, too. In fact, many banks let you set up preauthorized transfers
that automatically move a certain amount of money from one of your
accounts to another account on the same date each month.

Like most of the online banking activities that I cover in this chapter, the
specific steps that you take to transfer funds between accounts vary depending on how your bank has designed its Web-based banking site or
which PFM software you use. For more detailed instructions on transferring
funds with Web-based banking, see Chapter 6. I cover transferring money
with each of the popular PFM programs in Chapters 7, 8, and 9.

To give you an idea of just how easy it is to transfer money between accounts using online banking, consider the following steps, which outline the
procedure that you follow with a typical Web-based banking system:

1. **Make sure that you're logged on to your bank's Web-based banking
   site.**

   Usually, the best approach is to start from the account summary screen
   that lists your account balances. However, you can start this procedure
   from any screen that offers a link to the transfer feature.

2. **Find the link to your bank's online funds transfer option and click it.**

   If you bank with NationsBank, for example, you select the Transfer My
   Money option, as shown in Figure 4-8.

3. **Select the account from which you want to transfer the money.**

   On the screen shown in Figure 4-8, you can choose the Transfer Money
   From list box and scroll down the list to find the account that you want.

4. **Select the account to which you want to transfer the money.**

   Figure 4-8 also shows the Transfer Money To list box, in which you can
   scroll up or down to find the desired account.

5. **Enter the amount of money that you want to transfer.**

   Click the Transfer Amount text box; then enter the dollars and cents
   amount that you want to transfer.

6. **Press Enter or click the appropriate button to execute the transfer.**

   On the NationsBank transfer screen, you need to click the Send button
   to send your transfer information to the bank. The online banking
   software at your bank processes your request and moves money from
   one account to another per your instructions. If your bank uses real-
   time updates (as discussed in the "Figuring out when transactions
   appear online" section earlier in this chapter), you can see the effect of
   the transfer on your account balances immediately. Otherwise, the
   transfer shows up at the beginning of the next business day.

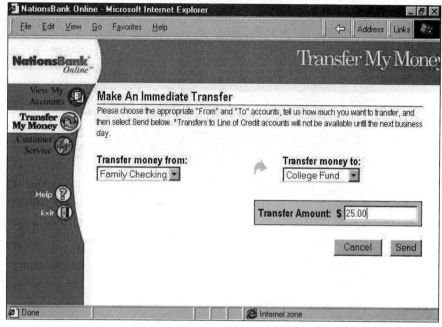

Figure 4-8:
A Web-
based
money
transfer
screen.

Remember to look for confirmation of the transfer before you exit the money transfer screen or close your Web browser. Most (but not all) online banking systems generate a confirmation number for a transfer transaction. If your bank does so, the confirmation number usually appears automatically when your transfer is complete, as shown in Figure 4-9. You can use this confirmation number to refer back to the transaction if you have questions later. Even if your bank doesn't generate a confirmation number, you can usually double-check the amounts and accounts involved in the transfer in some way before finalizing the transaction. Also, it's a good idea to check that the ending amounts are what you want them to be after the transfer by simply checking the new account balances.

Some people are concerned that the ability to transfer money between accounts with online banking can somehow enable a thief to move money from your account to his. It's *not* going to happen! You can't move money out of someone else's account unless you are authorized to make transactions on that account. To get approval to access anyone's account for any reason, you must be a *signer* (someone who can sign for money in the account). Online banking doesn't change that policy.

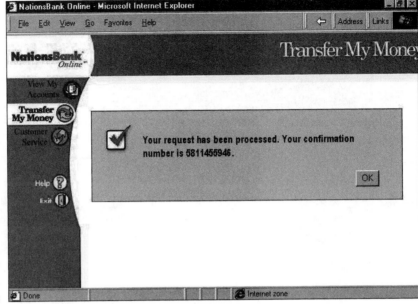

Figure 4-9:
A
confirmation
number
appears
automatically
after you
complete
your
transfer.

Communicating with your bank via e-mail

Among all the hoopla over online banking, one feature that often gets overlooked is the ability to handle many routine communications with your bank via e-mail. Just about every online banking system, whether Web-based or through PFM software, includes this handy feature. You can frequently find easy-to-use on-screen forms that facilitate handling routine requests such as ordering checks. For more specialized communications, a few mouse clicks open a window where you can type in a question or message and then send it on its way to the bank's customer service department with another mouse click or two. The bank can also send you messages, which you receive automatically the next time you log on for an online banking session.

Communicating with your bank via e-mail is not an earth-shaking development, but it does add to the convenience of using online banking, because you're able to use certain features at your convenience, not just when the bank is open.

Actually, you don't have to sign up for online banking in order to send e-mail messages to your bank. All you need is an Internet connection and any standard e-mail program (and, of course, the e-mail address of the appropriate person or department at your bank). The advantage of having e-mail capabilities built into an online banking system is that the e-mail messages that you exchange with your bank often benefit from some of the security precautions incorporated into the online banking system. (Oh, and your messages are automatically addressed to the proper department at the bank, too.)

Chapter 5

Paying Bills Online

· ·

In This Chapter

▶ Understanding the basics of online bill payment

▶ Setting up payees and scheduling payments

▶ Tracking the three paths for a bill payment

▶ Recognizing the difference between the pay date and the due date

▶ Counting on the bill-payment guarantee

▶ Figuring out the float issue

▶ Verifying that your payments reached the payee

· ·

*I*f you're like me, you probably have a list of things that you hate to do. For many people, that list includes preparing taxes, spring cleaning, having dinner with the in-laws (that's not *really* on my list, though), and, of course, paying bills each month. A few years ago, paying bills came off my list of dreaded chores when my bank introduced online banking. Online bill payment has transformed a terribly boring process that had consumed several hours each month into a task that is simpler, is less of a hassle, and now takes less than half the time. I can't imagine how I got along without the convenience of online bill payment.

Before online banking was available, here's what I would have to do after my electric bill arrived in the mail: I tore the payment stub off the bill, wrote out a check, found and addressed an envelope, put the check and payment stub in the envelope, stuck a stamp on the envelope, and then dropped the payment in the mail. Today, using online banking, I simply enter a few instructions into my computer, and my bank takes care of getting the payment to the electric company. This chapter shows you all the details of paying bills online so that you can start saving time, too. I cover bill payment from a generic standpoint in this chapter — each service will vary slightly, but the basics will be the same for all of them.

Understanding How Online Bill Payment Works

Online bill payment may seem like a complicated and somewhat mysterious process, but it's really just a simple service that your bank offers (for an appropriate fee, of course). Online bill payment is a prominent feature of many banks' Web-based banking sites, and online bill-payment capabilities are included in the popular PFM programs as well. I acquaint you with more of the details of online bill payment later in this chapter, but first, I give you an overview of the way online bill payments work. Using an online bill-payment service to pay your bills is analogous to an executive dictating letters to a secretary. The executive tells the secretary whom the letter is to and dictates its contents. The secretary takes it from there by attending to all the details of typing, proofreading, spell checking, printing, filing, and mailing the letter.

Online bill payment works the same way. You use your online connection to your bank to tell the bank whom you want to pay, how much, and when. The bank (or a contractor that provides the service for the bank) then takes care of all the details required to issue the payment on your behalf and get it to its destination. Online bill payment is just that simple.

It's important to understand that online bill payment (issuing payments on your behalf) is a separate service from online banking (online access to account balances, statements, and the ability to transfer funds between your own accounts). Online bill payment is often marketed along with online banking, and it's usually found on the same Web site and in the same PFM program as online banking, but it's a separate service nonetheless. You can have online banking access to an account without being able to make online bill payments from that account, and vice versa. Of course, online banking and online bill-payment services work together very well, and you can achieve maximum convenience if you have both.

What makes online bill payment possible is the convenience, efficiency, and security of online communications with a personal computer. If it weren't for the convenience of being able to send instructions to your bank from your personal computer, a bill-payment service wouldn't be practical. That's because, without that online communications link, you would have to do as much work to send instructions to the bill-payment service as you would to send the payment directly to whomever you are paying — and what's the point in that? Also, the same technology that keeps your online banking data communications safe and secure makes it possible to ensure the privacy of payment instructions you send to the online bill-payment service and to validate your authorization to make those payments from your bank account. (See Chapters 11 and 12 for more information about the security issues involved in both online banking and online bill payment.)

Of course, for online bill payment to work, the bank needs specific authorization to draw funds from your checking account to pay those bills for you. After all, you won't be submitting a paper document (a check) with your signature on it to authorize each payment. A fairly simple mechanism is available to grant the bank this authorization; it's essentially the same kind of arrangement that enables you to authorize automatic withdrawals from your bank account to pay bills such as insurance premiums and utility bills. You need to go through a sign-up procedure to activate online bill payment, and much of that procedure is to authorize the bank to withdraw funds from your account in order to make payments on your behalf.

After you sign up for the online banking service, using it to pay bills is easy. Just log on to your bank's Web-based banking site or fire up your PFM software and then go to the bill-payment screen. Enter the information that the bank will need to make the payment. In addition to the standard stuff on the face of a regular check (such as the payee's name, the date, and the amount of the payment), you need to provide some information that normally appears on the envelope and on the payment stub that you send along with the payments that you make manually. You need to supply the payee's full address and phone number and an account number or other identification that the payee will use to determine whose account the payment should be credited to.

Normally, you enter this information about the payee on a separate screen from the one where you enter the payment amount and date. The process is called *setting up a payee record,* and you usually have to do it only once for each payee. If you want to send another payment to the same payee (such as paying next month's bill), you can select the payee from a list of payees you've already defined. (See the sections "Entering payee information" and "Scheduling online bill payments," later in this chapter.)

After you enter the information for an online bill payment, click a button or two to send it on its way to the bank for processing. If you are logged on to your bank's Web-based banking site, the payment is submitted immediately. If you use PFM software, you can create your online bill payments offline and then transmit them to the bank the next time you connect to the bank for an online banking session. See Chapter 6 for more on using online bill payment at a bank Web site. For information on online bill payment with the popular PFM packages, see Chapters 7, 8, and 9.

After you send the online bill-payment instructions to your bank, the bank makes the payment at the scheduled time. Often, the online bill-payment service provider makes the payment by doing almost exactly the same thing you would do: writing out a check and mailing it. However, the bank may also pay the payee with an electronic funds transfer or a check drawn on one of the bank's accounts. The point is that you don't have to be concerned with the details, the bank takes care of the process for you. By using online bill payment, you don't have to sign checks, stuff envelopes, or buy postage; and you don't need to check the calendar to make sure that certain bill payments are mailed on certain days. The bank does all that for you for a monthly fee.

Getting to Know the Elements of a Bill Payment

If you experience a little déjà vu when you enter your first online banking bill payment, it's okay. Online banking bill payments use all the same data that you need when you're writing a traditional paper check, along with a few more pieces of important information. Figure 5-1 shows a paper check generated from the online banking system that I use. It looks a little different from a written paper check because it doesn't bear a normal signature and because it includes more complete information than a typical check. You can compare the information on the check in Figure 5-1 with the data that you enter to create an online bill payment.

Your name and address   Your account number with the payee

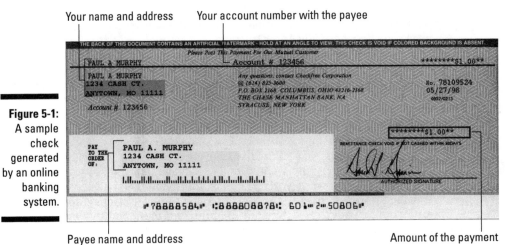

Figure 5-1: A sample check generated by an online banking system.

Payee name and address   Amount of the payment

Figure 5-2 shows an online bill-payment screen, which closely resembles a traditional paper check. You see all the familiar data, plus an added item for payment category.

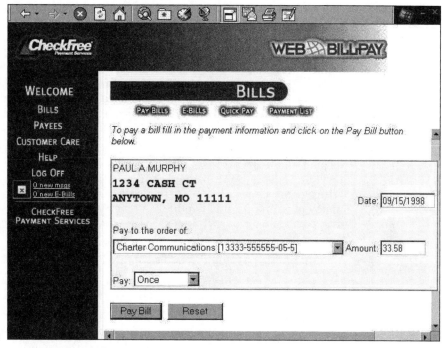

Figure 5-2:
A typical
screen for
entering
online bill
payments.

The following list explains all the categories of data that you need to include in your online bill payment:

✔ **The payee:** The person or company that you are paying. You can pay just about anyone with an online bill payment — from utility companies and mortgage lenders to department stores and even the kid down the street who mows your lawn.

✔ **Bank account:** The account from which the money is drawn to pay this bill. You may not see this field, or only one account may be listed. You usually need to set up online bill payment from each account separately. Having online bill payment active on one of your accounts doesn't necessarily mean that you can use online bill payment to pay bills from your other accounts at the bank. Also, it's not unusual for banks to support online bill payment from only one account per customer. Remember that sufficient funds must be available in the account to cover the payment requested!

✔ **Payee's address:** The address to which the payment is sent when you're paying with a traditional check through the mail. You can find this information on the bill that you receive from the payee.

✔ **The date:** The date that you want your bank to make your payment. You can schedule payments to be made immediately, in a week or two, or a couple of months in the future. Depending on the way your online banking system is set up, you may need to specify the date that you want the transaction processed, or the date that you want it to arrive at the payee. Understanding the difference is important so that you can specify a date that will get your payment to the payee before the due date for the bill. I cover this distinction in excruciating detail in the section "Knowing the Difference between the Pay Date and the Due Date."

✔ **Your account number with the payee:** The information (usually your account number) that the payee can use to identify the payment so that it will be applied to the proper account (just as you provide when you write a paper check). If you are just paying a friend or sending some money to your kids, this number is not a big deal. If you are sending your payment to a department store, however, the correct account number becomes a critical issue.

✔ **Amount of this payment:** Need I say more?

✔ **Your payment category:** An opportunity to categorize the payment, if you are using personal financial manager software to track expenses. I cover this feature in greater detail in Part III.

✔ **Your memo:** A field available for adding any additional information that may help you identify the transaction. Usually, the memo is just for your information, but some banks print the memo on the check if they send a paper check to pay the bill. For example, if you're paying a lawn care service, you may use the memo field to indicate that the payment is for "Spring fertilizer application" as opposed to being for weekly mowing service.

Entering payee information

Issuing instructions for an online bill payment is a two-step process:

1. **Enter the information about a *payee,* the person or company to which you want to send payments.**

2. **Create a payment to send to that payee.**

Usually, these are two separate steps that you perform by completing two separate on-screen forms. Some online bill-payment systems seem to merge the two steps by starting you out on the screen where you create a payment and automatically popping up a payee data entry screen when you start to enter the payee name.

Whether you get online bill-payment service through your PFM software or at your bank's Web site, the system usually gives you the option to create and maintain a list of payees that you can refer back to and pay on a regular basis. That way you don't have to reenter the payee's information each time you create a payment. Most Web-based banking sites will store your payee list, along with your account data, on the computer server at the bank so that it will be available to you anytime you log on to the site.

You can also create a list of payees, as well as manage all your online banking functions, with any of the popular personal financial manager software packages, such as Quicken by Intuit, Microsoft Money, and Managing Your Money by MECA Software. Each of these software packages effortlessly manages your lists of payees, and I explain each program in more detail in Part III.

Your list of payees can include just about anyone who has a mailing address. Most payees are either individuals or companies, including the following:

- Bank that holds your student loans
- Cable TV company
- Credit card account
- Doctor
- Electric company
- Health club
- Landlord
- Lawn care company
- Mortgage company
- Newspaper carrier
- Phone company
- Relatives to whom you owe money

You get the idea. You can use online bill payment to pay almost any company or person that you could pay by mailing a check. In fact, about the only exceptions are some kinds of taxes and court-ordered payments. (But even that bureaucratic red tape is gradually changing.)

Creating payees is very simple in both Web-based and software-based online banking. If you have enough information to pay a bill with a pen and a regular check, you have enough information to create a record for your payee. Follow these steps to create a payee:

1. **Log on to your bank's Web-based banking site, or launch your PFM software, and then navigate to the online bill-payment area.**

   The specific screens and button clicks required to get access to the online bill-payment portion of your software will vary, but it should be relatively easy to find.

2. **Create the payee record.**

   Whether you are in one of the personal financial manager software packages (such as Quicken or Money) or you are using a Web-based bill-payment feature, find the icon or button for Payees. From there, select the option to Add a New Payee. A screen appears so that you can fill in information about your payee. Figure 5-3 shows a typical on-screen form for defining a payee — this one is from a Web-based system, namely the CheckFree Web BillPay service.

   For larger payees (such as the phone company), the bank or online banking software vendor may already have records with all the vital information about the payee, including where to send your payment. Web-based online banking systems usually have extensive records for many payees. If you see your payee listed already, select the payee and move on to Step 4.

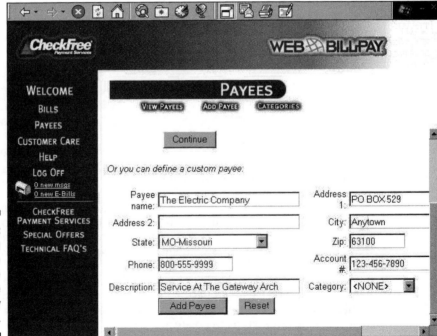

Figure 5-3:
Creating
a payee
with the
CheckFree
Web BillPay
service.

3. **Enter the basic payee information.**

   Start by entering the simple stuff such as the payee name, address, city, state, zip code, and phone number.

   All this information is on your bill, even the customer support phone number. You may need to peruse the fine print on your bill to find some of the information, but it should be there. Don't forget to include the area code in any phone number that you enter. Also, don't forget to double- and triple-check the information as you enter it. A small mistake, such as an incorrect zip code, could cause your payments to this payee to be sent to the wrong place.

4. **Enter your account information.**

   After you have entered your payee information, all that's left to do is enter your account number. *This step is very important!* If the payee is your best friend, an account number may not be necessary. However, large corporations process bazillions of payments every day, and the only way they know who you are is by using the account information that you list in your payee record. Your name and address will appear on the payment as well, but that is *not* enough to ensure that the payment will be credited to your account. You must include the correct account number as well.

   On the other hand, if you are sending a payment to a friend, a family member, or a very small business, you may not have an account number to enter here. In that case, you can just enter your name, or something else that will help identify the payment.

5. **Fill in any miscellaneous information.**

   Depending on the software or service that you're using, you may also have the opportunity to add more information in a description or memo field. If you have such a field, use it. This is a great place to add supporting information so that the person who processes the payment knows what to do with it.

6. **Click the Save button (or equivalent) to save your payee information.**

   Give the information one final check for accuracy before you record the payee information.

The basic process of setting up a payee is common across all online banking software and services. The individual steps may vary, depending on the design of your bank's Web site or the PFM software you use. See Part III for more detailed examples of creating payees for online bill payment in specific software programs.

TIP

Update your payee records

Creating and maintaining your list of payees is an ongoing process. Most people set up their payees the first time they make an online bill payment and don't go back to review them.

I highly recommend that you review your payee address information two or three times a year. It's not unusual for some payees, such as national retail stores, credit card companies, and utilities, to change the payment address from time to time. This change can happen, for example, if they change companies or banks that they use to process the payments or if they set up a regional bill-processing center closer to your home town.

I compare the information in my payee database to the information on my latest bills a few times a year to make sure that everything is still current. The payee's address may change and even account numbers can change, particularly if the payee has merged with another company or undergone some other organizational change. I can count on one hand the number of times that inaccurate information has been a problem in the last six years. In some instances, my bank automatically updated some payee information based on data provided to it by a particular payee. But, because this is my money, I still prefer to keep an eye on my payee data.

Scheduling online bill payments

By using online banking, you can check your account balances, transfer funds between eligible accounts, and set up bill-payment requests any time you have access to your computer. However, bill-payment transactions, like most normal banking activities, can actually be completed only during normal banking hours. Typically, the bank sets a cutoff time for submitting new transactions in order to allow time to process all the transactions that came in during the day and update all its records and systems overnight, including clearing transactions with other banks. At my bank, for example, the bill-payment cutoff time is 5 p.m. Any online bill payments that you submit after the cutoff time will be processed as if they were entered the following business day.

There are two types of payments:

- **Single payments:** Are made only once, or they change in amount each month. Your phone bill is probably an example of a bill that varies each month depending on how many long-distance phone calls you make. The simplest way to handle these single payments is to just set up a payment each time you receive the bill.

✔ **Recurring payments:** Allow you to pay the same payee the same amount of money on a regularly scheduled date. This feature is great for making payments on your auto loan, mortgage, and other payments that are the same from month to month. You enter instructions for recurring payments only once, and the bank repeats the payments each month (or week, or whatever) according to your instructions. Recurring payments continue automatically until you stop them or until you reach a predetermined number of payments or a specified date.

It's also important to know that you can set up both single and recurring payments well in advance. You can enter instructions today for online bill payments that may not be processed and sent to the payee for several days or weeks. This schedule allows you to hold on to your money as long as possible without the risk of forgetting to make the payment just before its due date.

Making single payments

After you create your list of payees (as I describe in the section "Entering payee information"), you're ready to schedule bill payments. Payments fall into two categories: single payments and recurring payments. Single payments are necessary for bills that change in amount each month (for example, the electric bill).

Some online banking software packages, such as Quicken, require a two-step process to schedule the payment itself. The first step creates the bill-payment request, and the second step sends that request to the bank. However, you can't assume that just because you created the payment, it was sent to the bank. You must initiate the second step — connecting to the bank to submit payments and update account information. In contrast, you must be connected to the Internet in order to use Web-based online banking and bill payment. As a result, the payments that you enter on your bank's Web site will automatically go to the bank as soon as you press Send or a similar button. Check with your bank's online banking customer service department or the software vendor if you're not sure about the steps to follow with your software.

The following steps show how to schedule a payment and pay the bill:

1. **Log on to your bank's Web-based banking site or launch your PFM software, and then navigate to the online bill-payment area.**

   The specific screens and button clicks required to get access to the online bill-payment portion vary with the software, but it should be relatively easy to find.

2. Click the Schedule a Payment button.

The exact steps required to get to this point vary depending on the design of your bank's Web site or your PFM software. After you reach the screen where you can define a payment, the on-screen form will probably look similar to a paper check. Figure 5-4 shows a typical on-screen form.

3. Select the account from which to draw the money to pay the bill.

You perform this step only if you have several checking accounts enabled for online banking. If you have enabled only one account for bill payment, you can skip this step.

Some online bill-payment systems allow you to designate only one checking account as the source of money for your bill payments. This is not a big deal, because you can simply transfer money to the bill-payment account if you need (and, of course, have) money in another account.

4. Select the payee for this bill from your list of payees.

For example, your payee can be your electric company. You can select the electric company by scrolling through a list, or you may be able to type in the first few characters of the payee's name and the software will find the payee and fill in the rest of the payee name for you.

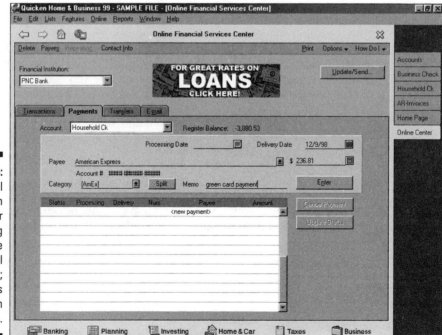

Figure 5-4:
A typical on-screen form for scheduling an online bill payment; this one is from Quicken.

5. **Enter the amount of the payment.**

Obviously, you want to be careful when entering the amount and double-check that it's correct. Watch the placement of the decimal point!

6. **Enter the date that you want to schedule the payment to be made.**

You can schedule the payment to occur immediately, or on some date in the future. Make sure that you understand how your bank or PFM software interprets this date — either as the payment's processing date, or as the date that the payment should reach the payee — and adjust the date appropriately in relation to the bill's due date. If your software uses a payment due date, you'll probably want to schedule the payment to be due a couple of days before the bill's actual due date, just to be safe. If your bank uses a processing date, don't forget to leave about five days between the day that you schedule the payment to be made and the bill's due date to allow ample time for processing the payment and mailing it to the payee.

7. **Send the payment request.**

When the request is ready, click the Send, Submit, Enter, or Record Check button that starts the payment on its way. If you are using PFM software, this will simply record the payment on your computer. Don't forget to complete the process by connecting to the bank and submitting your payment requests.

Making recurring payments

If you make the same payment for the same amount each month to the same payee, you probably want to set up a recurring payment. Recurring payments work exactly like single payments except that you need to supply two additional pieces of information: how often to make the payments and how many payments to make.

Suppose that you want to use recurring payments to make the payments on your auto loan. You need to make the payments on the 15th of each month, and you have 36 payments left to pay off the loan.

Although slightly different with each software or Web-based bill-paying service, recurring payments offer a payment scheduling option. This feature allows you to set up the frequency of payment and the number of times you want the payment to be repeated.

To set up a recurring payment, you can probably follow the same steps that you would use to create a single payment. Set up the payee for your auto loan, for example, and then create the first payment scheduled for the 15th of next month. Before you submit the payment as a single payment, look for a button or check box on the payment form that enables you to schedule subsequent recurring payments. Clicking that button usually opens another window (see Figure 5-5) where you can set the frequency of the recurring payment (monthly, weekly, annually, and so on) and the length of time the payments should continue. (You may specify a fixed number of payments or a date when payments should stop.) In the case of the auto loan, you would specify the monthly frequency and a duration of 36 payments. After you supply all the information for the recurring payment, submit it for processing.

The bank will make the first payment, just like making a single payment. Then the bank will automatically repeat that payment each month for 36 months without any further action on your part. You won't even have to think about your auto loan payment again (except to make sure that you have enough money in the account to cover the payment each month).

Setting up payments in advance

Most online bill-payment systems allow you to set up payments up to a year in advance. You can schedule payments for bills such as annual and semiannual insurance premium payments, association dues payments, and other payments that won't come due until several months into the future. This feature is great for those bills that are so easy to forget because you receive them so far in advance of the date they are due. You can enter the payment instructions as soon as you get the bill and be assured that the payment won't be sent until the appropriate time.

Figure 5-5:
A typical screen for defining the frequency and duration of a recurring payment.

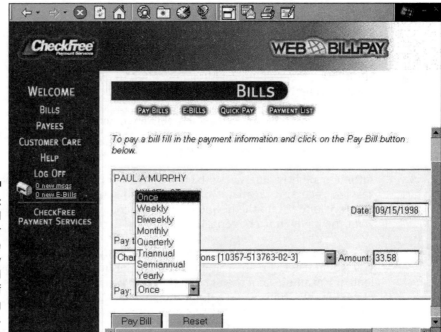

The actual steps for paying a bill in advance are exactly the same as the steps for entering a one-time payment (as I explain in the "Making single payments" section). You simply enter a payment date that is further in the future than your usual monthly payment. The computer and the bank don't really care which date the payment goes out as long as the money is in your account to fund the bill-payment request.

Discovering the Three Paths for a Bill Payment

After the bank receives your payment request, it stores that request until the payment's scheduled pay date. (The pay date is the day that you ask the bank to start the payment on its way to the payee.) Just after the cutoff time at the end of the bank business day, the bank processes all the bill-payment requests that were scheduled for that day and transmits them to a third party that actually processes your bill-payment request. (Very few banks process their own payments, and most banks rely on a reputable third party to complete the process.)

Your payment takes one of three paths to reach the payee: a check drawn on your account, a check drawn on the bank, or an electronic payment. The path that your payment takes depends on the type of third-party processing arrangements that your bank has in place. Figure 5-6 shows the three possible paths that a payment can take from the bank to the payee.

In the early days of online bill payment, nearly all payments were made with individual paper checks drawn on customer accounts. A lot of payments are still made this way — especially payments to small companies and individuals. However, the banks and third-party payment companies that handle bill payments are moving more and more of those payments onto the other payment paths.

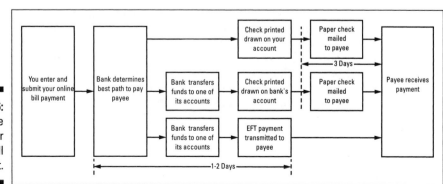

Figure 5-6:
The three paths for a bill payment.

Online bill-payment processors handle thousands of payments every day from customers across the country. Naturally, on any given day, a number of different customers send payments to some of the same payees, especially the big national credit card companies, utility companies, mortgage lenders, long-distance phone companies, and many others. As the bill-payment handling technology has improved, the payment-processing companies have been able to improve the efficiency of their systems by grouping payments from multiple customers to the same payee and paying them with a single check.

The third-party payment companies worked with the payees receiving a large number of payments to establish a way to further streamline the process by transmitting payments electronically. After all, what could be better? By using electronic payments, payees can process payments more efficiently and get their money faster, while the bill-processing vendor reduces postage costs and provides a better level of service. The next sections further explain these three payment options.

Option 1: A check drawn on your account

Of the three paths that your online bill payment can take on its way to your payee, perhaps the simplest to understand is a check drawn on your account. The bank simply prints a check on your behalf and mails it to the payee. The check looks a little different from your typical handwritten check because it includes some extra payee address information and lacks your signature. (Instead, it carries a notation that your signature is on file.) But despite the cosmetic differences, it works just like a normal check.

In this case, the bank does not first inquire whether your account has sufficient funds to cover the requested payment; it just prints the check and mails it for you. The account number at the bottom of the check is your checking account number. If the money is not in your account when the check works its way back through the channel from the payee to the payee's bank and is presented to your bank for payment, the check reacts like any other check drawn on insufficient funds — it bounces!

Payments made with individual checks typically take five business days (or more) to go through the processing, printing, and postal mail delivery and finally reach the payee. At the end of the month, online bill payments that were paid by checks drawn on your account will show up on your bank statement just like any other check. If you get your canceled paper checks returned to you in your statement envelope, these checks will arrive along with all the rest of your handwritten checks.

When I first began to pay my bills by computer, I was curious to know what really happens to my payments. So I just sent myself a test check! I did this by setting myself up as a payee and scheduling a $1 payment. Just for fun, I filled out the memo and account fields so that I could see what the payees see when they get my check. You may want to try this trick yourself when you start banking online. It's a great way to see how long payments take to reach a payee.

Option 2: A check drawn on the bank

The second path that your payment can take on its way to the payee requires the bank to transfer the funds needed to pay your bill from your account to one of the bank's accounts. Then the bank will make the payment on your behalf by writing a check from one of the bank's accounts.

First, the bank confirms that the funds for your payment are available; then the funds are transferred into the bank's bill-payment disbursement account. Within 24 hours of that transfer, a check is printed and mailed to the payee along with your name and account number so that your account will be credited with the payment. The check is drawn on the bank's bill-payment disbursement account.

This process does raise the issue of the bank's *float*, because the money sits in the bank's disbursement accounts instead of your account while the check floats through the mail and back through the check processing system. I address float a little later in this chapter, in the "Staying Afloat: The Float Issue" section.

Payments that follow this path eliminate the chance of checks being returned for insufficient funds, and the process does allow the bank or bill-processor to achieve some efficiencies. However, the time between the date that processing begins and the date that your payment gets posted to your account isn't usually much shorter than the time required to handle an individual check drawn on your account. The spread between pay date and due date is still about five business days.

When you get your account statement at the end of the month (or view it online), payments made by this method won't usually be listed in the same way as your regular checks. Instead, these payments will probably be grouped with ATM withdrawals, online banking transfers, and automatic drafts (such as insurance premium payments).

Option 3: Electronic payment

A payment that can be made electronically is known in the banking industry as an *EFT* (Electronic Funds Transfer). EFTs are, by far, the most efficient way to handle your online bill payments. Consequently, the bill-payment processors are working hard to get as many online payments as possible traveling to the payees along this path. If you make a bill payment to any large utility companies, department stores, credit card companies, oil companies, or other businesses that receive payments from across the country, chances are good that the payments are going electronically.

The only problem with EFTs is that the payee must set up its computer system to receive the electronic payments and get those payments properly credited to the correct customer accounts. It's not a simple setup that every mom-and-pop operation can afford. In the past, payment by EFT was the exclusive realm of big corporations that handle large volumes of payments. Still, several thousand companies are capable of receiving payments electronically today. As online banking and online bill payment have grown in popularity, regional payees are now establishing the ability to receive payments electronically. Costs to the payees are coming down to the point where a volume of only a few hundred payments a month can justify the cost of receiving payments electronically.

For you, the online bill-payment customer, the advantage of EFTs is that the payments following that route don't usually take five business days to get posted with the payee. On the day that you schedule the payment, money to cover the payment is withdrawn from your account and placed into a bill-payment disbursement account until it is electronically transmitted to the payee. That process usually occurs within one business day. Because the payment is going directly into the payee's computer system, the payment is often posted to your account immediately upon receipt.

As a result of the efficiency of EFTs, some of my payments get posted within 48 hours. For example, I scheduled a payment on my wife's American Express card on a Monday before the 5 p.m. cutoff. When I checked the status of the American Express account the following Wednesday morning (less than 48 hours later), the money was posted to her account. Not all payments are processed in less than 48 hours, however. As I checked with other vendors, I discovered that electronic payments sometimes took from three to five days to be posted. The payment time all depends on the relationship that the payee has with the bill-payment processing company.

Because EFTs occur electronically, you won't get a canceled check in your account statement envelope at the end of the month. But the transaction will show up on both the paper and online versions of your account statement. If your statement groups transactions by type, look for online bill payments that are made by EFT among other electronic transactions (ATM withdrawals, online banking transfers, and automatic drafts), not among the list of paper checks.

What happens after your payment follows its path

After your payment reaches the payee, it goes through some processing and handling before the payee posts your payment to your account. When you pay bills the traditional way, you probably must include a tear-off portion of the bill or a return coupon with your payment. This payment stub that accompanies your check helps to identify you and facilitates handling your payment and getting it posted to the correct account. (Most large payees contract out payment processing and the payment-processing companies use systems that rely on that payment stub for routine handling of your payment.)

Because an online bill-payment check sent from your bank doesn't include that payment stub, the check is processed on an *exception* basis, which means that it gets set aside for special (often manual) handling instead of going through the standard process. This factor may delay the posting of the payment to your account by anywhere from a day or two up to a couple of weeks. Much to my surprise, I have experienced very few significant delays with the posting of payments that I know are sent this way.

Contact your payees and let them know you are using online bill payment and that your payments will arrive without the usual payment stub. Ask if you should send your payments to a different address from the payment address on your bill. Often, if your payment is going to be handled as an exception anyway, you can expedite the process by sending it to a separate address where the payee handles payments that don't fit the usual mold.

Knowing the Difference between the Pay Date and the Due Date

When you're creating online bill payments, it's very important to understand the difference between a payment's pay date and its due date:

- ✔ **Due date:** Is the date when your bill is due — the date when the payment must arrive at the payee's office and be applied to your account.

- ✔ **Pay date:** Is the date on which your bill-payment transaction is scheduled to occur — in other words, the date on which the bank will start processing your payment. (Remember that you can create payments weeks or months in advance. The bank will hold them until their scheduled pay date before sending the payment on to the payee.)

Depending on your PFM software or the bank's Web-site setup, you may specify either the pay date or the due date when you create your online bill payments. It's critical for you to know whether the date that you enter when you define an online bill payment is the pay date or the due date for that payment.

For example, most Web-based banking sites ask you to specify the pay date for each payment you create. As long as you're entering a payment before your bank's cutoff time, you can schedule the payment to be processed on the same day that you enter it or on any date in the next year. It's up to you to make sure that you allow enough time between the pay date and the due date.

In Quicken, on the other hand, you enter the anticipated due date for each online bill payment instead of the pay date. In other words, you specify the date when you want the payment to arrive at your payee, not the date when you want your bank to begin processing the payment. The software keeps track of the lead time (the minimum time between pay date and due date) for each payee, depending on whether payments go to that payee by postal mail or EFT, and automatically schedules each payment's pay date for the correct number of days in advance of the due date that you specify. Quicken enforces its lead times by requiring you to enter a due date at least that far after the date when you create each online bill payment.

Most banks suggest that you allow no less than five business days between your pay date and due date. I agree wholeheartedly! For example, if your student loan payment is due on the 8th of the month, set the pay date to be the 1st of the month. This schedule allows five *business days* and the week-end to process your payment.

For the record, a bank business day is a day that the bank is open for business *and processes* payments. Bank business days are usually Monday through Friday except for holidays such as Christmas, New Year's Day, Labor Day, and the other biggies — such as the vernal equinox, Alan Greenspan's birthday, and the anniversary of that great banking time-saver, the Susan B. Anthony dollar.

The window of five business days gives the bank or its bill-payment processing vendor enough time to process your payment instructions, print a check, and send it on its way to your payee. The five-day schedule allows about two days for payment processing at the bank and three days for a paper check to travel through the postal mail system. Normally, that's enough time, but you should remember that postal mail isn't guaranteed and may take longer than three days (sometimes much longer). If you know from past experience that payments to a particular payee are handled by EFTs, you may be able to schedule payments a little closer to the due date because electronic transfers are much more reliable and faster than paper checks delivered by postal mail. (Software such as Quicken will automatically adjust lead times for payees that are paid by EFT.)

 Actually, scheduling your payment to arrive a day or two before the due date is a good idea — in order to allow time for the payment to go through the payee's internal processing and get posted to your account before the due date.

Banking on the Bill-Payment Guarantee

Many banks offer a five-business-day guarantee for online bill payments, but be aware that not all banks make this offer. Here's how the guarantee works: If you schedule your pay date five business days or more before the due date, the bank will cover any late fees or penalties if the payment does not get processed and credited to your account by the payee on or before the due date. Most banks limit the amount per incident to $50, but some are higher. This guarantee creates a significant incentive for the bill-payment processing company and the bank to process your payments in the fastest and most efficient manner possible. Think of the irony: The bank is paying the fee for a change.

The guarantee also helps the banks and bill-payment processing companies identify payees that may not be processing payments as efficiently as they should. The banks and the bill-payment processing companies then work with the payee to streamline their procedures and help prevent further trouble. In the six years that I have been making online bill payments, I have had to resolve only one discrepancy, and my bank made good on the guarantee. I have seen a few instances of breakdowns in the bill-payment chain, but once again, the bank stepped in and stood by its customers.

Staying Afloat: The Float Issue

In the online banking world, *float* is considered to be the amount of interest that a consumer can earn on his or her money as bill payments float through the mail and bill-payment system. You already enjoy float when you write out a paper check and drop it in the mail. Your check goes through the mail to your payee, gets deposited in the payee's bank, and finally works its way back through the banking system to your bank and is presented for payment. Only then does the money actually come out of your account. This process usually takes several days, during which time your money stays in your accounts and potentially earns interest.

If your bank uses a bill-payment system that pays the bill with a check drawn on the bank (see the previous, "Option 2: A check drawn on the bank"), the bank transfers money from your account and places it into one of the bank's accounts on the day that you instruct the bank to pay a bill on your behalf. The bank actually cuts a check from its account. As the payment proceeds from the bank to the payee and then back to the bank, the money remains in one of the bank's accounts earning interest — for the bank.

By the way, float isn't an issue on payments that are made by electronic funds transfer (EFT). Even though the bank may transfer funds out of your account into one of the bank's accounts, the funds get transferred out of the bank's account just as quickly and are sent directly to the payee's account. It all happens electronically with no delay to generate float, whereas a paper check moves through the mail and back through the banking system.

The idea of the bank, instead of the customer, getting the advantage of the float really bothers many people. However, given the amount of money most consumers are dealing with, the effect of losing the float on online bill payments is negligible. It just doesn't add up to enough money to be worth worrying about it. If you're concerned enough to do the math, I help you with that in the "Chalk talk" sidebar.

Letting the bank benefit from the float can actually have some positive side effects for the online bill-payment customer. One consideration is that, because the bank has already verified the availability of the funds in your account and transferred them into an account controlled by the bank, the bank can guarantee the payee that the check is good. That guarantee reduces bad-check collection worries and costs for the payee and gives the bank clout in negotiations with the payee about setting up EFT systems and other procedures that improve the efficiency of the payment process. That clout translates into improved service for online bill-payment customers like you and me.

Letting the bank keep the float on some payments also helps offset some of the bank's costs related to online bill payment and thus should help keep costs down. Finally, through the magic of overnight couriers, banks have a very sophisticated and efficient system for moving checks back to the bank for payment. The system is getting faster all the time, which reduces the amount of float on everyone's checks, including the banks'.

Chalk talk

Don't avoid using online banking simply because of loss of float. Calculate exactly what float really costs you in lost interest.

Assume that you make $1,000 in bill payments each month. You have an interest-bearing checking account paying 2.5 percent annually, and none of your payments are made by EFT (where, by definition, there is no float). In reality, banks use electronic payment methods (rather than cutting a paper check) to pay the payee for about four of every ten online bill payments that people make.

A 2.5 percent annual interest rate spread over 365 days equals a daily interest rate of .00006849 percent. Multiply that amount times the typical float of seven days (five days for the money to get to the payee and another two days for the check to float back through the check-clearing process). Interest on $1,000 at

2.5 percent for seven days is exactly $0.4794. Be a generous person, and round it up to 48 cents. The bottom line is that you need to pay more than $2,000 worth of bills per month online before your loss of float reaches $1 a month.

Yes, on an aggregate basis, banks can accumulate an appreciable amount of interest by processing online bill payments for thousands of customers. If you are managing a business with accounts payable ranging from $50,000 to $100,000 per month, you may have reason to be concerned about who gets the advantage of the float. But when you manage your personal funds by using online banking, don't give it a second thought. For most people, the convenience of online bill paying is far more valuable than the *pennies* a month that they lose to float.

Confirming That Your Payments Reach the Payee

Many consumers are reluctant to make online bill payments because they fear that they will have no way of tracking what happened in the bill-payment process. The truth is that you have several ways to confirm that your bank sent out your payments and that the payee received and processed them.

You may want to monitor your online bill payments closely for the first month or two that you use an online bill-payment service. By using the techniques outlined below to track a few payments through the process from beginning to end, you will build faith in the system so that you can rely on your experience and understanding and have the confidence that your payments will arrive on time.

Remember the traditional bill-payment process? You mail a check with a payment coupon, and the payee receives and deposits the check. Depending on your bank's policies, after the check clears your bank, you receive a canceled check with your statement. In some cases, only the image or a small copy of the canceled check is included with your statement. Nonetheless, you have something that confirms that the payment was processed and your account was properly credited.

If your bank makes your payment using a check drawn on your account (see the previous "Option 1: A check drawn on your account" section), you get a canceled check back for your online bill payments, just like you do when you make payments with handwritten checks. For online bill payments made using one of the other options, either a check drawn on the bank's account or an EFT, you won't have canceled checks, but you can still confirm that your payments have been made as scheduled. You can break up the confirmation process into two steps: first, confirming that the payment occurred, and second, confirming that the payment was applied to your account.

Confirming that the payment went out

There may not be a canceled check for each online bill payment in the envelope with your paper checking account statement, but there is a line-item entry on the statement for each of those payments, showing that the transactions were completed. Not only that, the entries for online bill payments are often more complete than the entries for traditional paper checks. For example, the line-item entries for online bill payments and other electronic transfers typically include all the following:

- ✔ The date that the bill payment was processed
- ✔ The amount of the bill payment
- ✔ The name of the payee

Notice that last item in the list: the name of the payee. That information makes it much easier to locate a payment on your statement than trying to identify payments solely by check numbers and amounts. Even though the entry on your statement is not a canceled check, it is everything you need to confirm that the transaction occurred. In addition, some banks also list a transaction reference number for each payment — a sort of electronic check number that you can use as a backup reference if you ever need to contact your bank's customer service department with any inquiries. And don't forget — because this is online banking and you can see your checking account statement any day of the month, your bill payment should show up in your online account statement the day after it is processed.

Confirming that the payment was applied to your account

Now that your checking account statement confirms that the payment request was sent out, what can you do to confirm that the payee processed it? First, you can call the payee and inquire about the account's balance and payment activity. Many companies let you call their computer to check on your accounts by using a Touch-Tone telephone. Also, many companies are moving toward using online statements. For example, American Express customers can access their account data by using America Online or by using the Quicken or Microsoft Money software. With your American Express information updated daily, you can easily see when your payment was credited to your account.

Normally, five business days is enough for the bank to process your payment and get it to the payee. Most payees process incoming payments promptly and post the payment to your account within a day or so after receiving it, but occasionally it might take an extra day or two for your payment to show up on your account. Give the whole process seven to ten business days before you begin to worry that the payment has been delayed. If you still can't confirm that your payment has been credited to your account after two weeks have elapsed, call your bank and begin to trace the transaction. But please, wait at least five business days after sending the payment before you ask the bank to start an inquiry.

The second opportunity to confirm whether your payment was received and applied to your account occurs when your next statement from the payee arrives in the mail. Although waiting for the statement may delay the process a bit, the statement usually arrives within a week or two of the payment due date. If a breakdown occurred in the payment processing and the payee hasn't processed the payment, you can call the situation to your bank's attention and still have time to correct the problem before your bill is more than 30 days past due.

Part III
Using Online Banking Tools

"Let me guess - checking your balance again, right?"

In this part . . .

This part gives you all the essentials that you need in order to use the most popular tools for online banking. You gain an understanding of Web-based banking and the three major personal finance manager software packages (Quicken, Microsoft Money, and Managing Your Money). You also find plenty of information to help you use the online banking capabilities of some popular business accounting programs for your business banking needs.

Chapter 6

Web-Based Online Banking

*W*eb-based online banking has been looming on the horizon for years. Until fairly recently, though, only a handful of leading-edge banks and a few completely virtual banks offered Web-based online banking products and services. But in late 1997 and early 1998, the tide turned, and the banking community finally accepted banking online via the Internet and the Web.

Traditionally, banks are very conservative organizations, so it's not surprising that many of them were reluctant to take the lead in implementing a new technology such as Web-based banking. However, now that the banking community has accepted Web-based banking, many banks seem to be in a race to make sure that they are not the last to adopt Web-based banking as a mainstream banking service. Web sites that support online banking are popping up like mushrooms after a spring rain. Nearly all the big banks now offer online banking on the Web, and a legion of smaller banks, savings and loans, and credit unions are rushing to join them.

The odds are good that your bank already offers Web-based banking. If not, your bank is probably working on plans to implement online banking services on the Web in the near future. This chapter, along with Chapters 4 and 5, gives you some idea of what to expect from a typical Web site that supports online banking and online bill payment. Furthermore, this chapter outlines some of the alternatives to Web-based banking from your bank.

Connecting to Your Bank via the Web

Most banks have Web sites these days. You can probably find the address (URL) of your bank's Web site on just about every piece of correspondence and advertising material that you get from the bank. The trend these days is to list the bank's Web address right along with the other contact information, such as telephone and fax numbers. All you need in order to visit a Web site is your computer, an Internet connection, a Web browser, and the address of the Web site that you seek. You've got all that, right?

So the question isn't whether you can visit your bank's Web site, but rather what you find there and how many things you can do. Of course, some banks have not yet started supporting online banking, so you may find a Web site that is little more than an advertisement for the bank — an online version of those colorful brochures that are displayed in the bank lobby and handed out to new customers. But suppose your bank is one of the many banks that does support Web-based online banking. How, then, do you go about using this exciting new technology?

Well, that's hard to say. At least, it's hard to give precise, detailed instructions that apply to more than one individual bank's Web-based banking site.

Chapter 4 outlines the way that online banking works and provides a good general idea of the processes involved in signing up for online banking and doing things like checking your account balance, viewing an online statement, and transferring funds between accounts. The information in Chapter 4 applies to just about every online banking service — at least, in general terms.

However, every bank designs its own individual Web site, and that Web site looks and functions just a little bit differently from every other bank's Web site. No two are exactly alike. The logos and other graphics, the color schemes, the catchy names for the various banking services, and the exact arrangement of Web pages and the links that you use to navigate to them all vary from one bank's Web site to the next. As a result, it isn't possible to precisely describe the steps that you follow to access any of your bank's Web-based banking features. The screens that you see and the links that you click to get access to your account balances are different from the screens that I see and the links that I click when I perform the equivalent task at my bank's Web site.

Still, observing the procedures for accessing online banking features at one bank's Web site can be instructive, even if you can't duplicate the exact procedure at your bank's Web site. What you do find is that most banks use similar procedures for delivering similar services. (Not the same, mind you, but similar.) The details may be different, but the overall process is fundamentally the same. So in this chapter I show you some step-by-step procedures for using online banking and online bill-payment services at particular banks in the hope that they serve as instructive examples. You should be able to get similar results at your bank's Web-based banking site, but the exact procedure that you use to do so undoubtedly differs in some details.

Web-based banking at your bank

In this section, I examine the steps required to log on to one bank's Web-based banking site and check the current balance on your accounts.

Normally, you need to sign up for the online banking service before you can access your accounts, but in this case, signing up isn't necessary because the bank automatically sent all its customers a letter containing the user ID and password that they need to access the bank's Web-based banking service. (The bank is trying to promote the online banking service in much the same way that it promotes ATM use by sending an ATM card to just about every account holder.)

The exact arrangement of the Web pages, the names of the hyperlinks, and the sequence of steps in this example are particular to one bank's Web site. You need to follow slightly different steps to accomplish the same things on your bank's Web site. I chose PNC Bank's Web site for this example simply because it was convenient for me when I created the figures for this chapter. You need to choose an institution for Web-based banking based on your own needs.

With your user ID and password in hand, you're ready to get started. Here are the steps:

1. **Establish an Internet connection and launch your Web browser software.**

   Use whatever procedures you normally use to get started browsing the Web. Often, all you need to do is choose your Web browser from the Windows 95/98 Start menu.

2. **Go to your bank's Web site — visit the main, home page to start.**

   Type the bank's Web address into the address box at the top of the Web browser window and then press Enter. (In this example, I entered www.pncbank.com.) The bank's home page loads in your Web browser as shown in Figure 6-1.

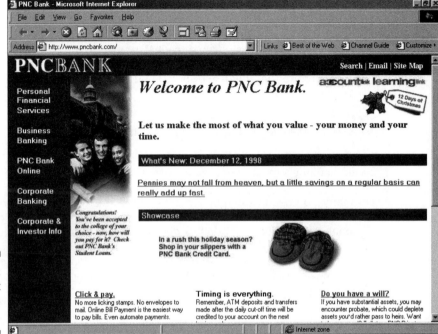

Figure 6-1:
Start at
the bank's
home page.

If your system is set up to automatically connect to the Internet as needed, you can combine the first two steps by opening the Start menu, choosing Run, typing the bank's Web address into the Run dialog box, and then clicking OK. Windows 95/98 automatically launches your Web browser and attempts to load the requested Web page.

3. **Click the link that takes you to the Web-based banking area of the bank's Web site.**

PNC Bank calls its Web-based banking service Account Link. You can access it directly from the home page by clicking the Account Link graphic near the top of the page.

Because the Web-based banking area uses special security precautions, your browser probably alerts you that you are about to view pages over a secure connection.

4. **Click OK to close the Security Alert dialog box.**

Your browser loads the log-on page of your bank's Web-based banking area. Note the padlock symbol in the browser's status bar in Figure 6-2. That indicates that the browser is using SSL to encrypt communications between you and your bank. (See Chapter 12 for a full explanation of SSL and security precautions.)

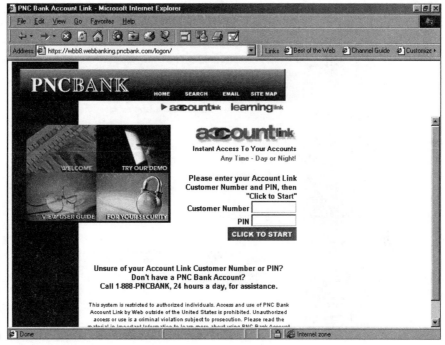

Figure 6-2:
The padlock
symbol
shows you
that SSL is
encrypting
your data.

Save the address of this page in your Favorites list (if you use Windows 95/98 and Internet Explorer) or bookmark it (if you use Netscape Navigator) so that you can bypass the bank's home page and go directly to the log-on page for Web-based banking in the future. Of course, you'll probably want to stop by the bank's home page once in a while to check for news of new services and such.

5. Enter your user ID and password in the Customer Number and PIN text boxes respectively. (Refer to Figure 6-2.)

Type in the identification numbers that the bank gave you. In most cases, the user ID is something familiar, such as your social security number, account number, or perhaps an abbreviated form of your name. Depending on what sort of identification scheme your bank uses, the password may be an alphanumeric password or a numeric PIN like you use to validate your ATM card.

6. Click the Click To Start button.

This step completes your logon to the Web-based banking site and allows you access to your account information. Your account list appears in the browser window, as shown in Figure 6-3.

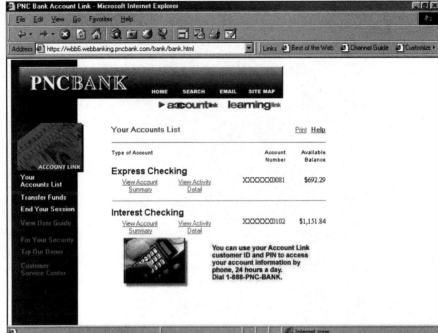

Figure 6-3:
Checking
your
account
balance is
usually your
first action
when you
log on for a
Web-based
banking
session.

Some banks force you to change your password the first time you access your online banking accounts. If so, you may have to go through an extra step or two here to create your new password (or PIN).

Even if your bank doesn't force you to change your password the first time you log on, you may want to change it yourself to create a password that is easier to remember. Most Web-based banking systems enable you to set your own password. At the PNC Bank site, you can change your PIN by clicking the Customer Service Center link on the left side of the screen and following the prompts and links.

To return to this page from any other screen in the Web-based banking site, you can click the Your Accounts List link on the left side of the page.

After you gain access to your account information, you probably want to check out more detailed information about one of your accounts. These are the steps for viewing online statement details:

1. **Start by displaying the account list.**

2. **Click the View Activity Detail link for the account that you want to view.**

The Web-based banking system displays the Activity Detail By Date page as shown in Figure 6-4. You can use the scroll bars in your browser to scroll through the list and view information about different recent transactions.

The default sort order for the list of transactions is by date. If you prefer to see the transactions grouped by type (deposits, checks, and transfers each grouped together), click the View By Type link to display the list of transactions sorted in that order.

To view details about another account, return to the account list (click the Your Accounts List link on the left side of the page) and then click the View Activity Detail link for that account.

Besides viewing your account balances and an online statement, the other main thing that you can do at most online banking sites is transfer funds from one account to another (assuming that you have more than one account at the same bank and have activated online banking access to them). Here are the steps for performing a transfer at the PNC Bank site:

1. **Start by displaying one of your account pages.**

    Actually, you can initiate a transfer from any page after logging on to view your account information.

Figure 6-4:
View transaction details on this online statement.

2. Click the Transfer Funds link in the bar on left side of the screen.

The Web-based banking system displays the Transfer Funds screen (shown in Figure 6-5).

3. Select the account *from* which you want to transfer funds.

Click the Transfer Funds From drop-down list box and select the appropriate account from the list by clicking it.

4. Select the account *to* which you want to transfer funds.

Make your selection from the Transfer Funds To drop-down list box.

5. Enter the amount of money that you want to transfer.

Type the amount in the Amount to Transfer text box.

6. Click the Transfer button.

The Web-based banking system displays another screen summarizing your selections. It's basically the transfer form with the information filled in.

7. Click the Confirm button.

If the transfer settings are correct, click the Confirm button to confirm the transfer. The system then displays a confirmation screen showing that the transfer was completed.

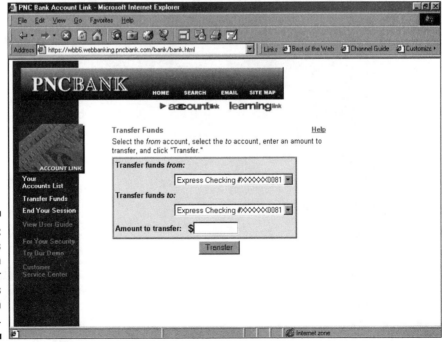

Figure 6-5:
Use this simple form to transfer funds between accounts.

When you are through with your online banking session, don't forget to click the End Your Session link at the left side of the screen and then click OK in the dialog box that appears to confirm the action. This sequence closes your accounts and removes your account information from your browser window in an orderly fashion instead of just shutting your browser window and breaking your Internet connection.

Paying bills via Web-based online banking

In addition to the account balances, online statements, and funds transfers that are the hallmark of online banking services, the other major feature of many Web-based banking sites is online bill payment — the ability to send instructions to your bank to make payments on your behalf.

Using Web-based banking to pay your bills gives you tremendous control, flexibility, and convenience. You almost certainly want to take advantage of the online bill-payment service if it's offered by your bank as part of its Web-based banking services.

However, you need to remember that online bill payment is normally a separate service from online banking (access to information about your accounts). Your bank may offer online banking at its Web site but not offer online bill payment. The bank may support online bill payment for users of PFM software, but not for Web-based banking users. And even if the bank does offer online bill payment, activating the service probably requires a separate sign-up process (and a separate monthly fee).

Some banks incorporate online bill payment into their other Web-based banking services. After you get signed up for the service, it is seamlessly integrated into the rest of the Web-based banking system. After you log on to the bank's Web-based banking site, you can navigate back and forth between viewing account balances and paying bills by simply clicking a link, much like the Transfer Funds procedure described in the preceding section.

At some banks, the online bill-payment service is almost totally separate from the online banking services. To access online bill payment, you must follow links to a separate area of the Web-based banking site and complete a separate log-on procedure before you can create payees and enter bill payments.

The specific steps and procedures that you use to access the online bill-payment features of your bank's Web-based banking site vary depending on the design of the Web site. However, despite differences in details, those steps and procedures are basically the same as the ones that I describe in Chapter 5.

Investigating Other Web-Based Online Banking Benefits

To round out your online banking experience, try a few of the other features that you can get through your Web-based online banking connection. Many banks that offer Web-based online banking also offer investing services, online loans, and special access to credit card information. Your online bank may offer some or all of these extras. If your bank doesn't offer the online extras that you're looking for, however, the convenience of the Web enables you to jump from one financial services company to another very easily to find the extra features that you want. If your bank doesn't offer investment services, you can go to an online brokerage that does. If you have a credit card issued by another bank or credit card company, you may be able to go to that bank's Web site to get access to your account there.

Investing your money via computer

Web-based online investing offers you the ability to do the following from your computer:

- Buy and sell stocks, bonds, and mutual funds
- Research investment ideas and help pick the right information from historical stock information
- Discuss investment ideas and decisions with other Internet users

Online banking and online investing have several things in common, too:

- You can use the same hardware and software you use for Web-based banking to do Web-based investing.
- You need to set up accounts with a company that manages your accounts and completes your transaction requests (or stock trades, in the case of online investing).
- Like banks, many companies offer deeply discounted products and services for Web-based users.

The big difference between online banking and online investing is that when you transfer money to your savings account, the money will definitely be there when you come back for it. Unfortunately, that is not always the case with investments.

The focus of this book is online banking, not investing. Online investing is a related but separate subject, so I'm not going to explore the topic in any detail on these pages. It's enough to note that online investing is a related financial activity that you can do online and that it complements online banking very nicely. For more information about online investing, you may want to get a copy of *Investing Online For Dummies,* by Kathleen Sindell (published by IDG Books Worldwide, Inc.).

You can also glean plenty of info about online investing by visiting some of the more popular online investing Web sites that I list in the *Banking Online For Dummies Internet Directory,* located in the second half of this book.

Some banks offer online investment services alongside their online banking services, and other banks plan to add investment services soon. On the other side of the coin, some brokerages offer checking accounts and other services reminiscent of banks, in addition to their investment services — and a growing number of these brokerages offer their services online. One such example of the growing number of aggressive online investing sites is the Charles Schwab home page (www.schwab.com) shown in Figure 6-6. Schwab has one of the more complete sites, providing links to a plentitude of great investing information and resources. You can also check stock quotes, the value of your portfolio, and so on, and even trade online after you finish your research.

Applying for loans

Banks love to make loans, so it should come as no surprise that many Web-based online banks offer online loan applications. The next time you need a loan, be sure to check out your bank's Web site for this convenient way to apply for a loan.

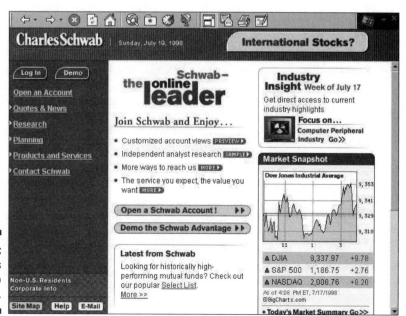

Figure 6-6:
The Charles Schwab home page.

Before you finalize that loan, however, you may want to make sure that you're getting a good interest rate. You can compare the going rates for a mortgage, car loan, or RV loan on that new personal watercraft at the Bank Rate Monitor Web site (www.bankrate.com), shown in Figure 6-7.

Accessing your credit card information

Access to credit card bills and data is already available through several select banks and from several major credit card companies such as Discover and American Express. Online access to your credit card account works just like online access to your checking account. You can view the current account balance and see a list of recent transactions. In addition, you may be able to see information about your next payment — the minimum payment amount and the date it is due.

If you travel regularly and often lose receipts (like I do), you can really benefit from being able to check your credit card data online whenever you choose. Also, online access to your credit card account provides a good way to monitor your available credit line if your account is close to its limit.

When your bank offers online credit card data, you can look forward to seeing all the information that you see on your regular statement, but you see it on your computer. Figure 6-8 is a great example of what credit card information users at Huntington Bank can see online.

How many banks are you working with?

With the Web, you can visit a large number of banks without having to get out of your chair. So which bank or banks do you work with?

The speed and convenience of online banking make it possible for you to go to a different bank for each banking service you need. However, just because you can use several different banks doesn't mean that you should. In most cases, your best bet is to do as much business with one bank as possible.

Banks are really focused on the total relationship with a customer and, like any other business when it comes to sales, they want to have all of your business. The more accounts and other business that you have with a bank, the more likely they are to waive fees, offer a better interest rate on a loan, or offer other incentives for you to do business with the bank. So if you have a car loan, home loan, retirement plan, investments, credit card, and a checking account, you're usually better off keeping them all at the same bank.

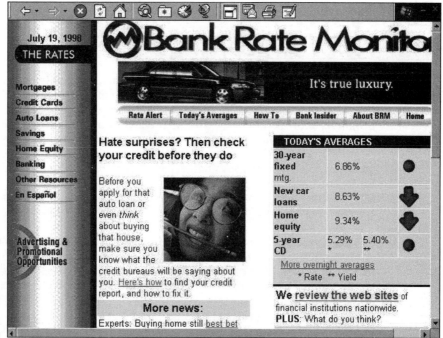

Figure 6-7:
The Bank
Rate
Monitor
home page.

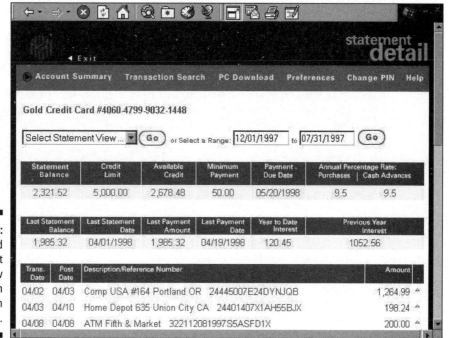

Figure 6-8:
Credit card
account
review
screen from
Huntington
Bank.

Sharing Web-Based Banking Data with Your PFM Software

Almost 20 million families in North America use personal finance manager (PFM) software, such as Quicken or Money, to manage household finances. (See Chapters 7, 8, and 9 for more detailed information on PFMs.) PFM programs allow you to track your financial information by attaching a category to every entry in your computer checkbook register. If you keep your PFM software up-to-date by entering all your transactions, you can get an accurate picture of your financial status from the software at any time. When you need to prepare for taxes or calculate what would happen to your budget if you bought a new house, you can run a report in which all your transactions are neatly summarized and subtotaled by category.

PFMs are great tools, but they require plenty of care and feeding to enter all the data for every check, deposit, and other transaction. What many PFM users really want from online banking is the ability to transfer data from the bank's online banking system directly into the PFM software, and thus automate the chore of entering data about all those transactions. The leading PFM programs can all access online banking data at the bank and use it to update the PFM program's data — provided that the bank specifically supports such a connection with your particular brand of software.

If your bank doesn't directly support a particular PFM program, you may still be able to transfer data from your bank's Web-based banking system into your PFM software. Importing this kind of data into PFMs is possible, but the process is not convenient and foolproof enough to qualify as an "easy" task.

Your task, should you decide to accept it, is to find a way to extract information about your accounts and transactions from your bank's Web-based banking site and put it into your PFM software without retyping all that information. (This tape will self-destruct in ten seconds.) This task doesn't quite qualify as a *Mission: Impossible* assignment, but it does require some extra effort. You probably have to get to know QIF files, although you may be able to use one of the newer techniques, such as Microsoft Money's Active Statement or Quicken's Web Connect, to transfer data.

Getting the most from QIF files

The primary method for sharing data between Web-based banking sites and PFM programs is the QIF file. The folks at Quicken were the first to develop a standard file format for transferring data into and out of PFM programs. This format is called a Quicken Information File, or QIF, but most of the other PFM programs can use the same file format for exchanging data.

Many software packages and Web-based online banking sites allow you to use a QIF file to either import or export data. If your bank's Web-based banking site supports QIF file download, you simply find the QIF file download page (such as the one shown in Figure 6-9) on your bank's Web site and then follow the directions to download the file to your computer and save it on your hard disk. The instructions for downloading are different on each site, but they are usually easy to follow. After you have your account data saved in a QIF file, you can open up your PFM software and go through the procedure for importing that data into the program. Again, the procedure is different for each program, but you should be able to find detailed instructions in the program's manual or help files.

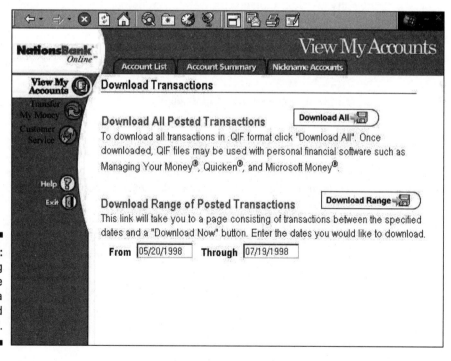

Figure 6-9:
Requesting
a QIF file
from a
Web-based
online bank.

One of the challenges in using QIF files is how to deal with duplicate entries. When you create a QIF file from account data that you download from your bank's Web-based banking site, you may have limited control over what transactions are included in the file. When you import the contents of the QIF file into your PFM program, some of the transactions may duplicate transactions that you have entered manually or transactions that you had imported previously. Usually, you have no choice except to manually review your account registers in your PFM program and delete the duplicate entries that you find, which is a tedious and confusing process at best.

Active Statement activates Money 99

In this age of ultra-competitive software developers, the team at Microsoft that manages the Microsoft Money PFM product has built a small Web-based program, called Active Statement, that allows you to import data from a bank's Web site into your Microsoft Money PFM software package — and not worry about duplicating entries.

Your bank must offer this feature by installing it as part of the online banking software that manages its Web-based banking system. If your bank offers this feature on your online banking Web site, you can use it just like a regular download feature. Here's how:

1. **Run your Money 99 program and open your Money data file.**

2. **Use your Web browser to log on to your bank's Web-based banking site and display your accounts.**

   You need to connect to the Internet, launch your Web browser, go to your bank's Web site, and then log on to the online banking area to get access to your accounts.

3. **Navigate to the page on your bank's Web site where the Active Statement feature is offered and click the Open Active Statement button.**

   The button is usually located on your account summary screen. When you click the button, the Web-based banking software creates a file containing transaction information from your account and transfers it to your computer.

4. **When Money 99 is up and running, it receives the statement information automatically.**

   The Money 99 software automatically reconciles and enters transactions into your Money account register. It automatically detects and deletes duplicate transactions.

For more information on the Microsoft Money 99 PFM program, see Chapter 8.

Web Connect connects to Quicken 99

Not to be outdone, Intuit has announced its Web Connect feature, which provides the capability to download data from your bank's Web-based online banking system directly into your Quicken 99 software. Web Connect offers approximately the same functionality for Quicken 99 users as Active Statement does for Money 99 users.

Like Active Statement, the Web Connect feature must be supported by your bank and installed on its Web site. If the feature is available, you see a button or link on your account information page at your bank's Web-based banking site. Clicking that button in your Web browser while the Quicken 99 software is running automatically transfers transaction data from the bank's Web-based banking system into your Quicken program. The transaction data appears in Quicken's Online Center, where you can review and edit it if necessary before adding it to your Quicken account register. That process is essentially the same as the procedure that you use to handle transaction data that Quicken downloads from a direct connection to your bank. (See Chapter 7 for details on Quicken's online banking account updates.)

What to Do If Your Bank Doesn't Offer Web-Based Online Banking

Although the list of banks that offer Web-based online banking is long and growing fast, many banks still don't offer Web-based online banking. If your bank isn't online yet, what can you do? Believe it or not, you can do several things to help organize your personal finances and get ready for online banking ahead of time.

Opting for a PFM program

PFM programs are great tools for managing your household finances. You can track income, expenses, payees, and a host of other financial facts and figures. They include powerful budgeting and financial planning tools, as well as online banking and online bill-payment features.

If your bank doesn't offer online banking, you can use Quicken or Microsoft Money to keep tabs on your finances and to get some limited online capabilities by paying bills through a bill-payment-only service. I cover Quicken, Microsoft Money, and Managing Your Money by MECA Software in Chapters 7, 8, and 9, respectively.

If the power of PFM software appeals to you, you can use a PFM program to organize your finances and, at the same time, get ready for the day when you can bank online and automatically transfer data from your bank to your PFM program.

Checking out CheckFree's Web BillPay service

If you want to pay bills online but you don't see a PFM program in your future, you can always pay bills from the Internet. CheckFree is a third-party firm that many banks use to process online banking bill-payment requests. CheckFree provides many other payment-related services, but for the purposes of these discussions, I concentrate on its role as the leader in the online payments business.

Mostly, CheckFree markets its services to banks and large corporations. However, CheckFree also offers a Web-based bill-payment service directly to end users. The service works with just about any bank account in the country that provides check-writing privileges, whether or not the bank itself offers any online banking or bill-payment services. So if your bank doesn't offer online banking or bill payment, you can sign up with CheckFree to get at least the bill-payment part. It costs about ten bucks a month and works very well.

The paper-based sign-up process is a little cumbersome because you have to supply a little more information to CheckFree than you would have to send to your own bank. After you sign up, you can log on to CheckFree's Web BillPay site and use it to enter online bill-payment instructions, just like you would at your bank's Web-based bill-payment facility. I used CheckFree as the example in much of the discussion of Web-based online bill-payment processes in Chapter 5. You can also get more information about CheckFree's services at its Web site: www.checkfree.com.

Trying telephone banking

If your bank doesn't offer online banking from your personal computer, you may want to see whether it offers another form of electronic banking — telephone or Voice Response Unit (VRU) banking and bill payment. Telephone banking doesn't have the power and versatility of online banking from your computer, but it can offer some of the same services:

> ✔ **Anytime access to banking services:** Like online banking, telephone banking is usually an automated service that is available 24 hours a day, 7 days a week, so that you can bank at your convenience instead of during the bank's regular business hours.

✔ **Account information:** You can usually access the same account balance information with telephone banking that you can access with Web-based banking. Most banks allow transfers between your accounts by phone.

✔ **Bill-payment features:** You can pay bills by pressing a few buttons on your Touch-Tone phone. Of course, it isn't practical to enter information about payees with a telephone keypad, but you can use a pre-defined list of payees established by your bank or you can fill out new payee forms and either fax or mail them to your bank. The bank takes a couple of days to establish your payees.

✔ **Access to a bank representative 24 hours a day:** Many banks staff customer service centers around the clock. If your bank doesn't, telephone banking enables you to leave a voice mail message.

Only the money isn't virtual at virtual banks

In contrast to the brick-and-mortar banks that offer online banking as an adjunct to their physical presence, a handful of banks, dubbed *virtual banks,* offer their banking products and services only over the Internet. Virtual banks offer some clear advantages but also pose some equally clear disadvantages. Depending on your total banking needs, virtual banks may be a good choice for you and your family.

The good news about virtual banks is that anyone can use them to bank online, even if your real bank doesn't yet offer online banking services. Also, with a lower cost structure, virtual banks attract more customers with higher yields on Certificates of Deposit (CDs) and lower interest rates on loans.

The biggest drawback to the virtual bank model is that if your virtual bank doesn't install a network of ATMs, you must use ATMs at other banks to get cash. ATM transactions at a "foreign" ATM (one owned by a different bank from the issuer of your ATM access card) typically incur two separate fees — one from your bank, and another from the bank that owns the ATM. The virtual bank may waive its ATM transaction fees in order to attract business, but that still leaves you liable for fees charged by the bank that owns the ATM you use. These fees can add up fast.

I know of many people who use a bank in their hometown for their day-to-day financial needs and a virtual bank for CDs and loans. The following sections describe a few of the best virtual banks that are currently online.

Net.B@nk

Net.B@nk serves almost 12,000 people around the country — not just in its home base of Atlanta. Net.B@nk offers online banking and bill payment, as well as online mortgages and investing. Net.B@nk has also set itself apart as the first true Internet bank to turn a profit. You can find Net.B@nk (and view all its products and services) at `www.netbank.com/`. See Figure 6-10 for a quick glimpse of the Net.B@nk home page.

First National Bank of the Internet

A growing trend among established banks is to create a virtual bank under the wing of their physical bank. It's a great economic formula for existing banks that want to attract more customers but don't want to lose existing customers to the convenience offered by responsive virtual banks. After all, after you have one bank set up, how much can it cost to add a second with no incremental brick-and-mortar costs? The costs of customer service functions are also divided over a larger customer base.

One example of this trend is the First National Bank of the Internet, shown in Figure 6-11, which is a subsidiary of the First National Bank of Cherokee in Woodstock, Georgia. You can find First National Bank of the Internet at `www.fnbinternet.com/`.

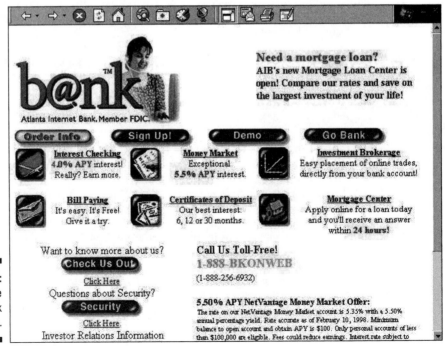

Figure 6-10: The Net.B@nk home page.

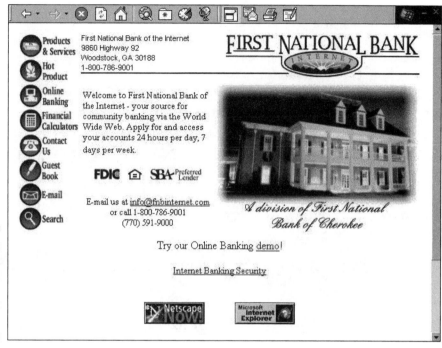

Figure 6-11:
The First
National
Bank of the
Internet
home page.

Security First Network Bank

About two years ago, Security First Network Bank (www.sfnb.com) opened as the first truly virtual bank in the country and proved that the concept of a virtual bank was viable. SFNB was born without the high-cost network of branches and ATM machines and the large number of tellers that are the hallmarks of a traditional bank. Security First Network Bank has just one physical branch in Atlanta (to meet legal requirements), but it serves customers all over the country. Its home page, shown in Figure 6-12, does a great job of making you feel like you're truly entering a branch.

SFNB was recently bought by the Royal Bank of Canada (RBC), which appears to be a good move for both RBC and the current SFNB customers, as it continues to offer a lower-cost banking for people outside of RBC's traditional market area of Canada.

Figure 6-12:
The
Security
First
Network
Bank home
page.

Banking online with AOL

America Online (AOL) is the world's most popular online service. (An *online service* is a company that offers information, also referred to as *content,* via a personal computer and a modem.) AOL is also an Internet service provider (ISP) providing Internet access in a user-friendly way especially targeted at online newcomers. In addition to being able to view content online, you can also send and receive e-mail, engage in online chats, and complete online transactions like buying books and music CDs. You see all sorts of headlines, weather, and shopping opportunities as soon as you log on to AOL, as shown in Figure 6-13.

Chances are, if you have purchased a computer in the last few years or have ever subscribed to a personal computer magazine, you have received an offer from America Online to give them a try.

America Online has more than 14 million customers who cover all types of computer experience levels. AOL is especially helpful for the first-time computer user looking for a kinder, gentler experience than jumping into the Internet with both feet. Everything you could possibly want to know about AOL is covered in *America Online For Dummies,* 5th Edition, by John Kaufeld (published by IDG Books Worldwide, Inc.).

Figure 6-13:
The AOL
Welcome
screen.

AOL versus the Internet: You make the call

AOL is both an online service, providing proprietary content to its subscribers, and an Internet service provider, furnishing access to the Internet and World Wide Web. But if most of the online banking activity is happening on the Web, why go through AOL instead of just getting Web access through an ISP? AOL has several advantages:

✔ **It's easier to install.** When you install the AOL software, preferably with the AOL CD, all the components that you need to run the AOL software and manage the modem connection with AOL are installed automatically with very little user knowledge required.

Easier installation used to be a very big issue because the process of just establishing a connection to the Internet, not to mention the browser software, was a major task. Now, several Internet service providers (ISPs) like MindSpring and the Microsoft Network have made great strides in creating an almost-foolproof installation and enrollment process. The contrast between setting up AOL and setting up Internet access with other ISPs isn't as great as it once was, but AOL is still the champ when it comes to fast, easy installation.

✔ **It can be easier to use.** If you are new to the online world, and the use of letters and symbols like http:// may as well be Greek to you, then AOL may be a good place to get started. I know many people who start with AOL and move on to the Internet later.

✔ **It offers convenience for travelers.** If you travel extensively on business, AOL is accessible via a local call in hundreds of U.S. cities and numerous locations around the world. AOL also offers 1-800 number access (for a reasonable, additional per-minute-of-use charge) for those times when you are way out in the boonies and need to go online for just a few minutes.

✔ **It may have something of interest that you can't find anywhere else online**. Many people enjoy the conversations in AOL chat rooms and message boards discussing finances, shopping, investments, and other topics. Because AOL has such a large number of users, the participation in online discussions and bulletin boards can be very interesting and sometimes even informative. Several personal finance resources and the BankNOW service (which I cover in the "Online banking with AOL BankNOW" section) are available on AOL.

The AOL Banking Center

Several dozen banks have entered into an agreement with AOL to offer online banking to their customers through the AOL service. You can find these banks at the AOL Banking Center shown in Figure 6-14, which you can reach by following a series of on-screen links or by clicking the Keyword button at the top of the AOL window, typing **Banking** in the dialog box that appears, and then pressing Enter. You can choose from one of the banks that appear on this screen, or you can click the red More Banks button just below the list to see more bank logos.

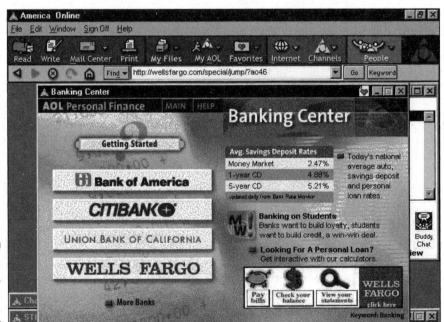

Figure 6-14:
The AOL
Banking
Center.

When you find your bank on the list, you can click it and find out more about its online banking offerings via AOL. You can also enter your bank's name, like **Wells Fargo**, as an AOL Keyword and go directly to that AOL screen. Figure 6-15 shows the Wells Fargo screen on AOL.

Online banking with AOL BankNOW

BankNOW (AOL Keyword: `BankNOW`) is a proprietary online banking service from AOL and a number of participating banks. The BankNOW software is a small program that you can download and run in conjunction with the AOL access software. After installation, BankNOW is designed to offer the following online banking functions from one simple screen (see Figure 6-16):

- Online statements and account balances
- Bill payment
- Funds transfer
- Maintain banking account registers

Several dozen banks originally signed up for AOL BankNOW when it was built a few years ago. At that time (ages ago in Internet years), the Web was not yet ready to conduct online banking tasks, and BankNOW was a very attractive way for the banks to reach customers online. Today, Web-based banking is a viable alternative that has the potential to reach even more customers than AOL. Consequently, BankNOW has diminished in relative importance as many banks have shifted their marketing emphasis to promote their individual Web sites and offer AOL BankNOW as an alternative.

If your bank offers AOL BankNOW, it's a great option for online banking, especially if you use AOL regularly.

AOL as your Internet connection

As I mention earlier, AOL is not just an online service, it's also an ISP, providing Internet access to its subscribers. So naturally, you can use AOL to access your bank's Web-based banking site. The AOL access software even includes a copy of Microsoft Internet Explorer, so if you have AOL, you have your Web browser all set up and ready to run.

To view a Web site on AOL, sign on to AOL and then enter any Internet address instead of a Keyword. The Web browser window comes to the foreground, and you're able to view your bank's Web site (or any other Web site, for that matter) just like you would if you were using another form of Internet access and a stand-alone Web browser.

Figure 6-15:
The Wells
Fargo AOL
screen.

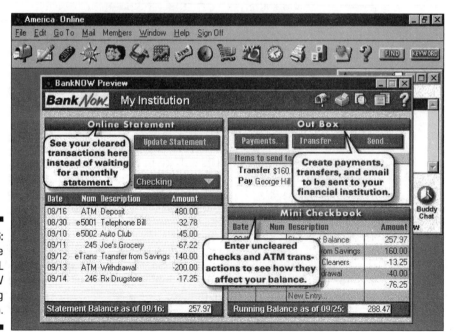

Figure 6-16:
A sample
AOL
BankNOW
banking
screen.

The AOL Personal Finance Channel

Much of the content on AOL is organized into interest groups called *channels*. The Personal Finance channel (Keyword: Personal Finance) is stocked to the rafters with information and links to just about anything you would want to know about finances. (See Figure 6-17.)

The Banking Center is a prominent part of the Personal Finance channel, but much more than links to bank Web sites and the BankNOW service is available. AOL has many other personal finance resources, such as the following:

✔ **Stock quotes:** AOL offers the simple service of providing quotes from markets all over the world. Simply go to the Quotes screen (Keyword: Quotes), select the symbol that you want to look up, select the investment exchange where the investment is traded, and click Look Up.

Figure 6-18 shows a sample AOL response displaying all the information that it can find about (in this case) IBM. If you don't know the symbol, you can put in the name of the company, and AOL helps you look up the correct symbol.

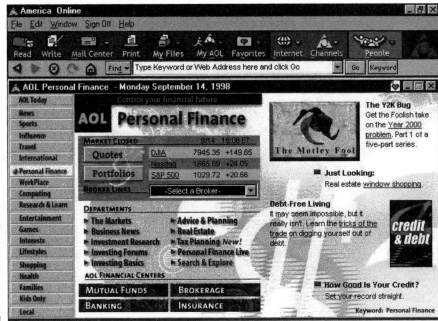

Figure 6-17: The AOL Personal Finance screen.

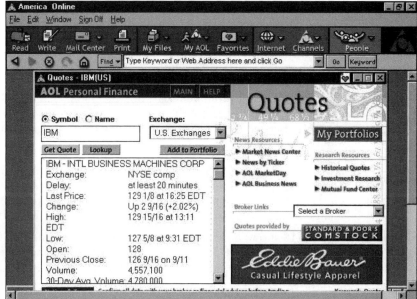

Figure 6-18:
AOL looks
up stock
quotes
for you.

> ✔ **Review performance numbers:** AOL offers current and historical
> stock, bond, and mutual fund information. Historical Quotes (Keyword:
> `Historical Quotes`) let you view stock and mutual fund graphs over
> various periods of time. (See Figure 6-19.)

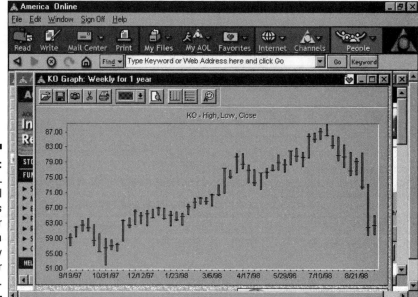

Figure 6-19:
The AOL
Historical
Quotes
graph for
Coca-Cola
on a weekly
basis over
52 weeks.

✔ **Review expert opinions and publications:** AOL provides access to several investment-oriented reports, publications, and experts (Keyword: Investment Research).

✔ **The Motley Fool:** So you want to know more about investing? Well, you may want to take a look at The Motley Fool (Keyword: Fool). "The Fool" is a lighthearted way to discover investing. The Motley Fool site (shown in Figure 6-20) creates some great online education for would-be investors. The Motley Fool is published in newspapers all over the country, and the AOL edition is just as fun and more in depth.

✔ **Online brokerage companies:** From the Brokerage Center (Keyword: Broker), you can open an online trading account with many different companies, as shown in Figure 6-21.

✔ **Online investing basics:** As the home to many first-time online users, AOL is also the home to many first-time investors. The AOL Brokerage Center has links for people looking to find out more about how the investing process works. You can see links in the lower-right corner of this screen, including How to Trade Online and Investing Basics.

Kathleen Sindell's *Investing Online For Dummies* (IDG Books Worldwide, Inc.), is also a great resource to discover even more about online investing.

Figure 6-20: The Motley Fool.

Figure 6-21:
The AOL
Brokerage
Center.

✔ **Portfolio management:** AOL offers you the option to set up portfolios and view them at any time of the day or night. When the market is open, you can see how your investments are doing (although the numbers are delayed by 20 minutes or so). With some of these recent market swings of 150 to 300 points a day, seeing your investments is very meaningful information to have. Setting up your portfolio is very easy.

✔ **Market news and indices:** The AOL Market News Center (Keyword: MNC) offers a one-screen snapshot of the investment market news of the day. This news includes graphs, short news stories, and market statistics. You can see market-related updates, including most active stocks, market gainers, and market losers.

✔ **Mortgages:** The biggest single purchase that most people make is a home. At the AOL Mortgage Center (Keyword: Mortgages), you can find plenty of information about mortgages, shop for the best deal in your area, and get preapproved right online. The Mortgage Center is full of information and links to mortgage companies offering online applications and rates.

✔ **Credit cards:** The AOL Credit & Debt Center (Keyword: Credit Debt) offers information on how to manage credit cards. Links from this AOL site take you to resources on the Web where you can keep a constant watch for the best credit card rates. For those folks who already have credit cards and may want to spend some time reducing their debt load, this site has several timely and informative resources.

Chapter 7

Online Banking with Quicken 99

*Q*uicken is the world's most popular personal finance manager (PFM) software package. The latest version of Intuit's flagship product, Quicken 99 enables you to track all sorts of financial information. You can keep track of everything from daily activity in your bank accounts and credit cards to outstanding balances on your loans. The program helps you stay on top of your retirement plan and other investments and even includes features such as a home inventory module. And of course, Quicken 99 includes online banking, online bill payment, and other online features — provided that your bank supports online connections to Quicken.

Quicken 99 is a very robust financial management tool, developed with more than 15 years of user feedback. What started out as a simple electronic checkbook register has evolved into a program that includes features to address just about any personal finance issue.

This chapter highlights the online portions of Quicken 99 — particularly the online banking and online bill-payment features. I won't attempt to cover the entire program and its many features in this limited space. (For more information about using Quicken 99, you can refer to Stephen Nelson's *Quicken 99 For Windows For Dummies,* IDG Books Worldwide, Inc.) This chapter explains how the program's main online features work, giving you a glimpse of how this software can help reduce the amount of time you spend on routine banking tasks, while at the same time offering more information to enable you to make better financial decisions.

Getting Around in Quicken

When you launch Quicken 99, the first thing that you see is your Quicken Home Page. (See Figure 7-1.) Although it isn't a Web page on the Internet, your Quicken Home Page shares many characteristics with a Web home page. The most notable feature of the Home Page is the underlined links to different pieces of your financial information managed by the Quicken software. Simply click a link to open a page displaying the associated account register or other information on the link topic.

The menu bar at the top of the screen is typical of most Windows programs. The Activity Bar along the bottom of the screen is also a menu bar of sorts. Simply point to an icon on the Activity Bar, and Quicken pops up a menu of related activities. Selecting an activity from one of the Activity Bar menus takes you to the related Quicken feature. The QuickTabs on the right side of the screen provide instant access to any of the account registers or other pages that you may have open in the Quicken window.

Figure 7-1:
The
Quicken
Home Page.

With Quicken, you can keep track of all your various financial accounts: checking accounts, savings accounts, money market accounts, credit card accounts, brokerage accounts, loan accounts, and much more. Each account has its own account register in Quicken where you can record transactions such as checks, ATM withdrawals, deposits, and transfers. To keep things familiar, Quicken account registers (shown in Figure 7-2) look very much like your paper check register.

As with all PFM software, a large part of Quicken's power is its ability to categorize your transactions and then generate charts, graphs, and reports with transactions grouped and subtotaled according to categories. Of course, that means that you must enter category information for each transaction, which can get tedious, but Quicken includes some features to make it easier.

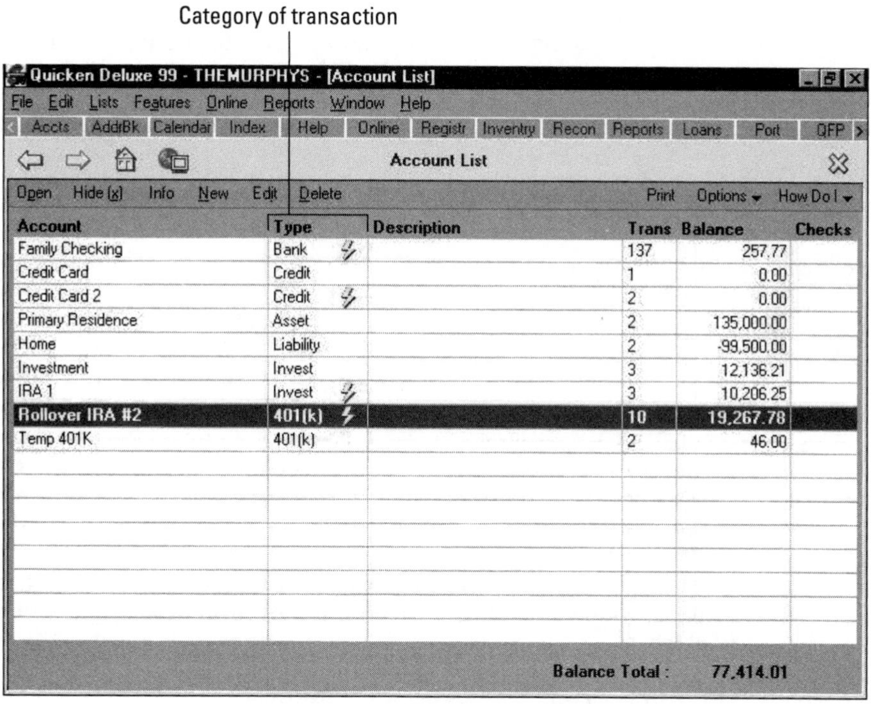

Category of transaction

Account	Type		Description	Trans	Balance	Checks
Family Checking	Bank	⚡		137	257.77	
Credit Card	Credit			1	0.00	
Credit Card 2	Credit	⚡		2	0.00	
Primary Residence	Asset			2	135,000.00	
Home	Liability			2	-99,500.00	
Investment	Invest			3	12,136.21	
IRA 1	Invest	⚡		3	10,206.25	
Rollover IRA #2	**401(k)**	⚡		**10**	**19,267.78**	
Temp 401K	401(k)			2	46.00	

Balance Total : 77,414.01

Figure 7-2:
A Quicken account register looks familiar.

Establishing Your Online Banking Relationship

Before you can use Quicken's online banking features, you need to sign up with your bank to get online access to your account data via the Quicken software. Of course, this assumes that your bank is one of several dozen major banks across the country that has installed the equipment and software necessary to support exchanging your account data through Quicken.

First, you need to have an account set up in Quicken for each account that you want to access online. This arrangement gives the data a home when it arrives at your computer. Then you need to complete an enrollment form to sign up for the online banking service from your bank. After you complete an enrollment form, your bank sends you a welcome kit that contains, among other things, a password and some information about your accounts that you need to plug into your Quicken software to enable you to access the bank.

Applying to your bank for online access

The application process for gaining online banking access to your accounts with Quicken varies somewhat, depending on your bank. However, most of the banks that support online banking with Quicken let you at least start the application process with an online connection from within the Quicken program. Of course, you need to be able to connect to the Internet with Quicken. Part of the normal installation process for Quicken includes configuring the program to use your Internet connection, so you should be all set. If you skipped that part of the installation, you can take care of the oversight now by choosing Online⇨Internet Connection⇨Setup and following the prompts.

After you have your Quicken program running and are able to connect to the Internet, follow these steps to initiate the enrollment process for online banking:

1. **Choose Online⇨Financial Institutions.**

    Quicken opens an Internet connection and then accesses the Quicken Internet site and downloads the most current list of participating financial institutions. The list appears in the Apply for Online Financial Services page, as shown in Figure 7-3.

Figure 7-3:
Quicken
automatically
updates its
list of
participating
financial
institutions.

2. **Select your financial institution from the Financial Institution Directory list on the left side of the Apply for Online Financial Services page.**

   Quicken displays information about your selection on the right side of the Apply for Online Financial Services page. Most banks list the Quicken online banking services that they support and the account data download options that you have.

   At this point, Quicken usually shows you a link to the bank's Web page. Click that link to go to the bank's Web site for more information.

3. **Click Apply Now.**

   An on-screen application form or other instruction page will appear in place of the Financial Institution information lists.

4. **Follow the on-screen instructions to fill out your bank's online banking application.**

   Different banks allow you to apply in different ways. Some banks let you fill out an application form online. Other banks require you to mail or fax a paper form to the bank. Still other banks allow you to apply by phone, which is a very fast way to get started. Many banks also have enrollment forms available in the branches.

If your bank is one of those that offers an on-screen application form, fill in the form, typing your name, address, and other requested information in the corresponding boxes. After you complete the form, double-check your entries and then click Submit to send the application information to the bank.

If your bank offers a telephone enrollment, call the bank at the phone number that's supplied. Otherwise, follow the instructions to obtain and submit a paper application form.

5. **Wait for your bank to send you a welcome kit in the mail.**

After you send in your application and the bank okays it, the bank sends you an enrollment kit, which can be anything from a single-page letter to an entire package of goodies. You also receive a password or personal identification number (PIN) that you use to gain access to your accounts from Quicken. Many banks send the password in a separate letter from the rest of the online banking welcome kit.

Unfortunately, you can't start Quicken for the first time, fill out your application, and access your financial records online all in one day. Usually, banks take anywhere from a few days to a week to verify your application and send you the enrollment kit so that you can go online. But while you're waiting, you can familiarize yourself with Quicken's many features, and you can work with the Quicken sample data to become proficient with the software before you have access to the real money and financial records. You can even set up your Quicken accounts — one for each bank account, credit card, and other account you want to track — and enter data from your last statement. You just can't make the online connection to update your accounts until the bank processes your enrollment and sends you that welcome kit.

Enabling your online accounts

When you receive the enrollment information and password from your bank, you have everything that you need to go online. You simply need to use that information to enable your online banking accounts. Although you can create a new account and enable it for online banking access in one consolidated operation, the much simpler choice is to create accounts ahead of time and then enable online access by following these steps:

1. **Run the Quicken program and choose Online⇨Online Financial Services Setup from the menu bar.**

The Get Started with Online Financial Services dialog box appears (as shown in Figure 7-4).

2. **Click Enable Accounts.**

The Select Financial Institution dialog box appears.

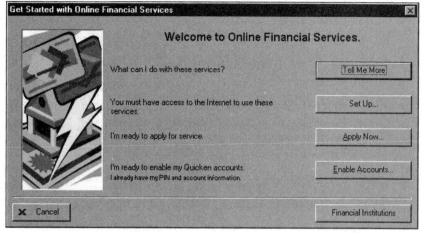

Figure 7-4:
The Online
Financial
Services
Setup
welcome
screen.

3. **Select your bank from the Financial Institution drop-down list box and then click Next.**

   The Online Account Setup dialog box appears, as shown in Figure 7-5.

4. **Click the Edit Existing Quicken Account radio button, select the account that you want to activate for online banking from the Account Name list box, and then click Next.**

   The Select Financial Institution dialog box appears with the first page of an EasyStep wizard displayed. The wizard prompts you to choose the online services that you want to use with this account.

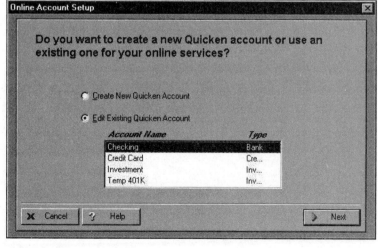

Figure 7-5:
Selecting
the account
that you
want to
enable for
online
access.

5. **Click Yes or No beside Online Account Access and click Yes or No beside Online Payment to indicate the online services that you want to be active for this account. Then Click Next.**

   The next page of the EasyStep wizard appears in the dialog box, asking you to enter the account information that you received from your bank. The bank name is already displayed. You may also see a number in the Routing Number text box.

6. **If necessary, enter the bank routing number that the bank supplied in your welcome kit into the Routing Number text box and then click Next.**

   The next page of the EasyStep wizard appears, asking for more information that you received from your bank. This time the wizard asks for the account number and type of account.

7. **Enter the account number that you received from your bank in the Account Number text box, select the account type from the Account Type drop-down list box, and then click Next.**

   The next page of the wizard appears, asking you to enter your customer ID number.

8. **Enter the customer ID number from your bank welcome kit into the Customer ID text box and then click Next.**

   The customer ID number is usually your social security number, but it may be another number that the bank assigned to you. Like the other account information, it's listed in the information that the bank sent you in its online banking welcome kit.

   The EasyStep wizard moves on to the Summary tab, as shown in Figure 7-6.

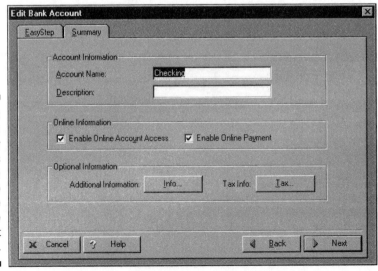

Figure 7-6:
The Summary tab gives you the chance to confirm the online account settings.

9. **Confirm the settings shown on the first page of the Summary tab and then click Next.**

The next page of the Summary tab appears, as shown in Figure 7-7.

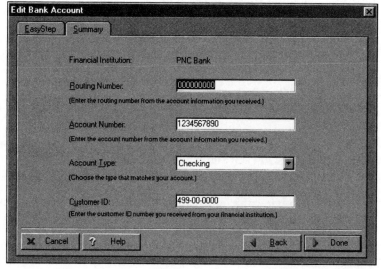

Figure 7-7:
Make sure
to double-
check the
account
number and
bank
routing
number.

10. **Verify the settings shown on the final page of the Summary tab and then click Done.**

Double-check all the settings before proceeding — paying particular attention to the bank routing number and the account number.

When you click the Done button, Quicken displays a final dialog box that asks whether you want to set up more accounts for online services.

11. **Choose Yes or No and then click Next.**

Choose Yes if you want to set up another account for online banking or online bill payment. Choose No if you're through setting up online access to your accounts. Depending on your choice, Quicken takes you back to the beginning of this procedure to start again defining another online account, or Quicken simply closes the dialog box and updates its account settings.

You're finally ready to begin using Quicken to access online information about your accounts.

Getting Online Account Updates

One of the greatest benefits of online banking with Quicken is the ability to use the connection between the Quicken program and your bank to enter into your computer that long list of bank transactions that appears on your paper monthly statement — without typing in the transactions line by line. The online banking connection enables you to download account balances and transaction data from your bank and automatically add them to your Quicken account registers. When you have all your account transactions in Quicken, you can supplement them with categories describing the purpose of the transactions.

After you enable your Quicken accounts for online access, you're ready to enter the world of online banking. All you have to do is initiate an update when you want Quicken to connect to the bank and get the latest account information. The Quicken software handles most of the details of making each connection to the bank, downloading account data, and sending any pending requests and transactions. Then after the online session is complete, you can review the information that Quicken received from your bank and begin the process of adding transaction data into your account registers.

The following steps show you how to go online to exchange account data with your bank:

1. **With Quicken running, choose <u>O</u>nline⇨Online <u>C</u>enter from the menu bar or point to the Banking icon on the Activity Bar and choose Online Transactions from the menu that appears.**

   The Online Financial Services Center page (Online Center, for short) appears with the Transactions tab selected. (See Figure 7-8.)

2. **Choose your bank from the Financial Institution drop-down list.**

   Quicken updates the Online Center page to reflect the accounts and online options available from the financial institution you selected. For example, if you have more than one account at the selected bank and have both online banking and online bill-payment services enabled, four tabs are visible: Transactions, Payments, Transfers, and E-mail. If, on the other hand, you don't have online bill payment enabled at any of the accounts at this bank, the Payments tab isn't visible.

3. **Click <u>U</u>pdate/Send.**

   The Instructions to Send dialog box appears, listing what the software is about to do. (See Figure 7-9.) Normally, two items appear in the list: "Download latest cleared transactions and balances" and "Bring my payment information up to date." Other items may also appear on the list if you have instructions for payments or transfers waiting to be sent to the bank.

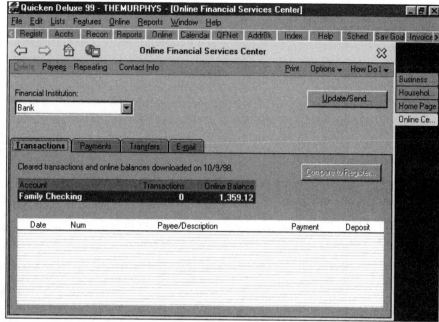

Figure 7-8:
The Online
Center is
your
mission
control
center for
online
connections
to your
bank.

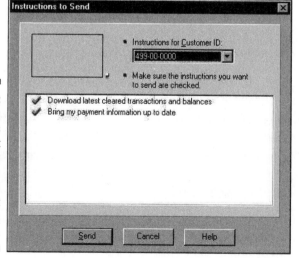

Figure 7-9:
This dialog
box shows
you what
Quicken is
about to do
in the
current
online
session.

4. **Review the list of instructions and, if necessary, click items to toggle the check marks on or off.**

   Select which instructions you want Quicken to execute during this online session with the bank. A check mark beside an item indicates that it will be processed during this session. If the check mark is missing, that item will not be processed during this online session.

5. **Type your PIN into the Enter Your PIN text box.**

This is the password or PIN that you received from your financial institution. Be sure to type it carefully because you won't be able to see what you type. Quicken displays asterisks in place of the characters that you type in order to hide your PIN from prying eyes that might read your PIN off the screen as you enter it.

6. **Click Send.**

This action starts the online banking session. Quicken normally runs on automatic pilot for the rest of the online session. You can just sit back and watch.

If this is the first time that you're accessing your online banking accounts with Quicken, the bank may require you to change your PIN. If so, Quicken opens a small dialog box where you can enter your new PIN and then retype it a second time for confirmation before clicking OK and continuing with the online session.

The Quicken software initiates an Internet connection and establishes a connection to your bank. Quicken manages the conversation between your computer and the bank's computer to download account information, including statement detail and account balances, and send any pending payment or transfer instructions to the bank. Quicken displays a series of message boxes with animated graphics to show you the progress of the online session.

After completing the online session with your bank, the Quicken software disconnects from the bank's computer. Depending on the preference settings that you established when you installed Quicken, the program may disconnect from the Internet immediately after the online session is finished or leave your Internet connection open for possible additional sessions.

Finally, Quicken displays the Online Transmission Summary dialog box (shown in Figure 7-10) and updates the information in the Online Center.

7. **Review the contents of the Online Transmission Summary dialog box and then click OK.**

The Online Transmission Summary dialog box is a very important screen to review after each online session. It contains a list of the actions that Quicken completed during the online session. If you have asked Quicken to do something, like send your car payment, the Online Transmission Summary dialog box confirms that the transaction was sent to the bank or alerts you to the fact that the request was *not* properly transmitted.

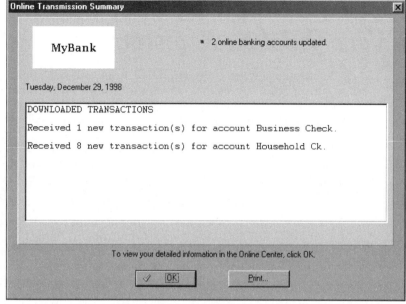

Figure 7-10:
The Online
Transmission
Summary
dialog box.

After the online session is over, Quicken updates the display in the Online Center page. The account balances shown in the Accounts list on the Transactions tab reflect the latest balances according to your bank records. If transaction details were available for download, the transactions are listed in the large list area of the Transactions tab. (I show you how to move that transaction data into the account register in the next section.)

The PIN Vault

With Quicken 99, you can track all sorts of online accounts, and each of those online accounts requires a password or PIN (personal identification number). If you have several accounts at different banks, remembering all the different PINs and entering them properly can be a challenge.

Quicken 99 includes a new feature, called the PIN Vault, to help manage multiple PINs. You can enter all the individual PINs for different accounts into the PIN Vault and then create one master password to protect the PIN vault. That way, you have to remember only one password. When you start an online session, Quicken prompts you for the password to the PIN Vault. If you enter the password correctly, Quicken automatically enters the individual PINs for you.

Accepting Online Transaction Data into Your Quicken Registers

When Quicken downloads transaction data from your bank during an online session, the program stores that data in the Online Center rather than automatically dumping it into your account register. Moving the transaction data into your account register requires a separate step in which Quicken compares the downloaded data to transactions already in your account register. This gives you the opportunity to check off the transactions that match and add the remaining transactions to the account register (after reviewing the transactions and editing them to add categories and other details if needed).

So bringing online transaction data into your account registers is a two-step process: First you download the transactions from the bank; then you move them to your account register. The "Getting Online Account Updates" section of this chapter explains the first part of the process. The following steps show you how to complete the process of bringing online transaction data from your bank into your Quicken account registers:

1. **From the Quicken menu bar, choose Online⇨Online Center.**

   Quicken displays the Online Financial Services Center page.

2. **To specify the account that you want to work with, select the bank from the Financial Institution drop-down list box in the upper left-hand corner of the screen and then click the account name in the list just below the Transactions tab.**

   Assuming that you have downloaded transactions for the selected account during a recently completed online session, Quicken displays a list of those transactions in the large list box on the Transactions tab. (See Figure 7-11.)

3. **Click Compare to Register.**

   Quicken opens an account register page displaying the account that you selected in Step 2 and superimposes the list of downloaded trans-actions on the bottom half of the account register. (See Figure 7-12.) Quicken automatically compares the downloaded transactions to the existing uncleared transactions in your account register and marks the downloaded transactions to designate which match and which are new.

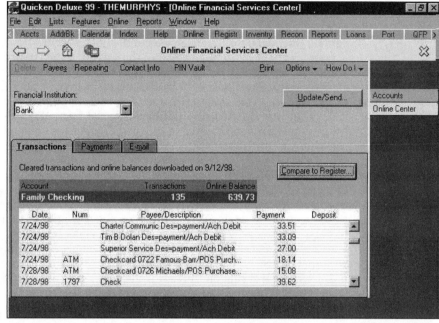

Figure 7-11:
Transactions
waiting for
review and
acceptance
into
Quicken.

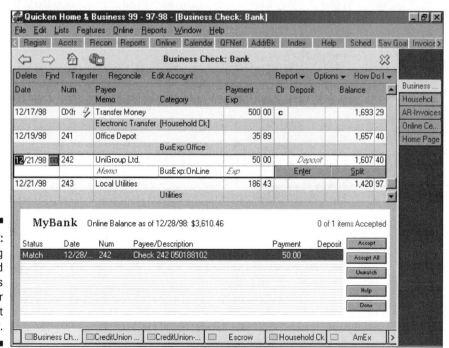

Figure 7-12:
Comparing
downloaded
transactions
to your
account
register.

4. **Click one of the downloaded transactions.**

   For any downloaded transaction that you select in the lower half of the screen, Quicken automatically selects the corresponding entry in the account register in the upper half of the screen. If the transaction that you selected matches an existing transaction in your account register, Quicken automatically selects that transaction in the upper half of the screen. If you selected a downloaded transaction marked New, Quicken inserts the new transaction into the account register. Either way, the transaction that you selected in the lower half of the screen is selected for editing in the upper half of the screen.

5. **Edit the transaction (if necessary) and then click Accept.**

   You can edit any part of the transaction in the account register. However, you don't usually need to change much. If a downloaded transaction is a check that's identified only by a check number, you may need to enter the payee. Quicken automatically assigns new transactions with a given payee to the same category as the previous transaction with that payee, so you don't usually need to change the category unless you're working on the first transaction with a payee. You may want to add a memo to remind yourself what a particular transaction was for, but that step is strictly optional.

   When you finish editing the entry, click Accept. Quicken updates the register entry and removes the accepted transaction from the list in the lower half of the screen.

6. **Repeat Steps 4 and 5 until you've accepted all the downloaded transactions.**

7. **Click Done.**

   Quicken returns to the Online Center page.

Transferring Funds between Online Accounts

If you have online banking access to more than one account at the same bank, you can use Quicken's online banking features to transfer funds between those accounts (provided, of course, that your bank supports online transfers). The process for transferring funds between online accounts is very simple. You initiate the transfer by filling out a simple on-screen form where you can record instructions to move a certain amount of money from one account to another. Then the next time that you connect to the bank for an online update, Quicken sends your instructions to the bank. Quicken also records the transfer as an entry in the appropriate account registers.

The whole process of transferring funds between online accounts requires only the following quick and easy steps:

1. **From the Quicken menu bar, choose Online⇨Online Center.**

   Quicken displays the Online Financial Services Center page.

2. **Select your bank from the Financial Institution drop-down list box.**

   Of course, if you have online accounts at more than one bank, you need to select the bank where the accounts are located that will be involved in the transfer.

   By the way, most banks allow you to do online transfers only between accounts at the same financial institution. Things are going on behind the scenes in the banking world to make interbank online transfers possible, but for now, you are probably limited to transferring between accounts at one financial institution.

3. **Click the Transfers tab.**

   Quicken displays an on-screen form (shown in Figure 7-13) where you can quickly indicate the accounts that you want to transfer money to and from, as well as the amount and the effective date.

   The Transfers tab isn't available in the Online Center if you don't have at least two online accounts enabled at the selected bank.

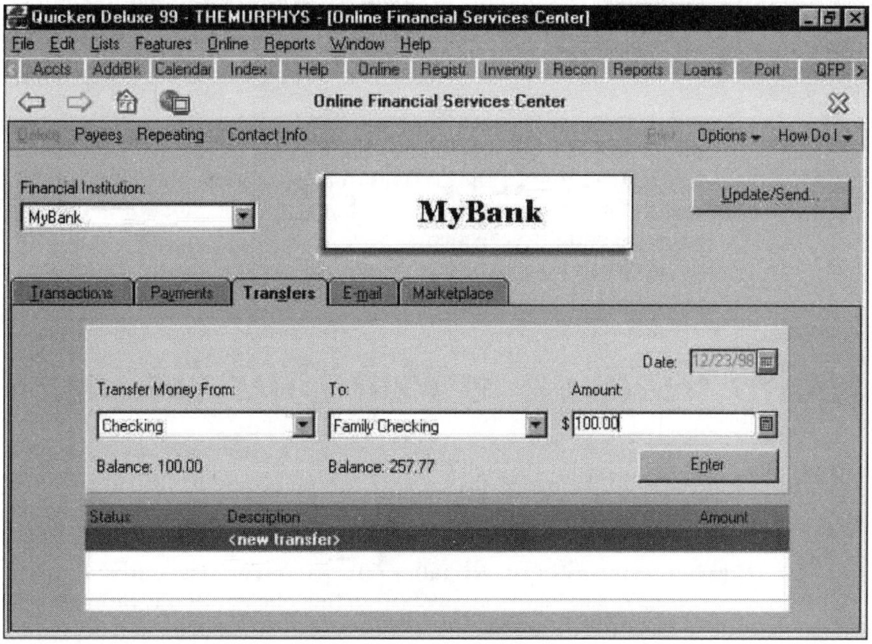

Figure 7-13:
Creating a transfer.

4. **In the Transfer Money From drop-down list box, select the account that is the source of the money that you want to transfer.**

5. **In the To drop-down list box, select the destination account where you want to deposit the money.**

Make sure that you don't confuse the *from* and *to* accounts. You don't want to transfer funds in the wrong direction by mistake.

6. **Enter the amount of the transfer in the Amount text box.**

7. **Click E_nter.**

This action records the transfer instructions. Quicken enters the transfer in the list below the form on the Transfers tab. Quicken also enters a transaction in each of the account registers affected by the transfer. A notation appears under the Update/Send button to indicate that an instruction is waiting to be sent to the bank.

At this point, you have recorded the transfer in Quicken, but your bank doesn't know anything about it yet. The transfer request doesn't get transmitted to the bank until the next time you connect to the bank for an online update.

8. **Click U_pdate/Send and follow through with the normal online update procedure to begin sending instructions to the bank.**

You can postpone this final step until you have completed preparing other transfers, online bill payments, and the like. Then you can send them all to the bank at one time. Just don't forget to send your instructions to the bank. The transfer request doesn't become effective until it reaches the bank.

Online transfers are usually subject to the bank's cutoff time rules. If you submit a transfer request to the bank before the bank's cutoff time, the bank processes the request at the end of the business day and transfers money between your accounts when the bank updates accounts overnight. However, if you submit your transfer request after the bank's cutoff time, the transfer doesn't become effective until the end of the following business day.

Using Quicken to Pay Bills Online

People have been entering bill payments into Quicken since it was first released. In the early days, everyone marveled at Quicken's ability to print a batch of paper checks. It meant that you didn't have to get writer's cramp paying your bills. By today's standards, printing paper checks seems almost quaint. Why bother with paper checks, envelopes, and stamps when you can pay your bills electronically with a few clicks of your mouse?

Like online banking, online bill payment is a service furnished by your bank. Before you can use online bill payment, you must sign up for the service with your bank and enable the online bill-payment feature of the appropriate accounts in your Quicken software. Most banks offer online bill payment as a separate service from online banking. You can order one service, or the other, or both. In Quicken, you can order, and enable, both services at the same time; you don't normally need to submit separate applications for the two online services.

If you haven't already read Chapter 5, you may want to do so before attempting to use the online bill-payment features of Quicken (or any other software). That chapter explains the fundamentals of the online bill-payment process. After you understand the basics of the online bill-payment process, finding out how to use the related features in Quicken is a snap.

Creating payees

Before you can pay a bill by using Quicken's online bill-payment feature, you need to enter some information about the payee — the person or company to whom you're sending money. Quicken makes it easy to create a list of payees so that each time you go to pay the person or company, all the important information is there, and all that's left to do is fill in the amount of a payment and send it on its way.

Personally, I like to create my list of payees before attempting to create payments to those payees. Some people enter the information for each payee the first time they pay a bill to that payee. (If you try to create a payment to an unknown payee, Quicken prompts you for the payee information that it needs and then stores that information in its Payee List.) To be honest, it really doesn't matter which way you do it. I just prefer to create payees ahead of time. The process of scheduling payments seems to go a little faster with fewer distractions that way.

Here are the steps for creating a new payee in Quicken's Online Payee List:

1. **From the Quicken menu bar, choose Lists⇨Online Payees.**

   Quicken displays the Online Payee List page, as shown in Figure 7-14. Notice that the list shows the Payee, Lead Time, and Account Number for each entry on the list.

2. **Click the New button in the toolbar at the top of the Online Payee List page.**

   Quicken opens the Set Up Online Payee dialog box, as shown in Figure 7-15.

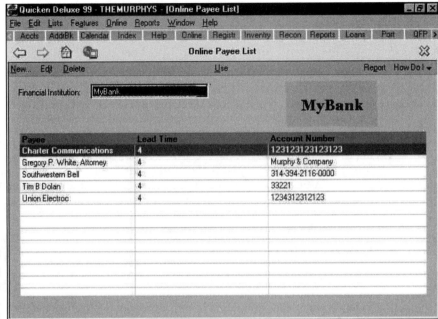

Figure 7-14:
The Online
Payee List.

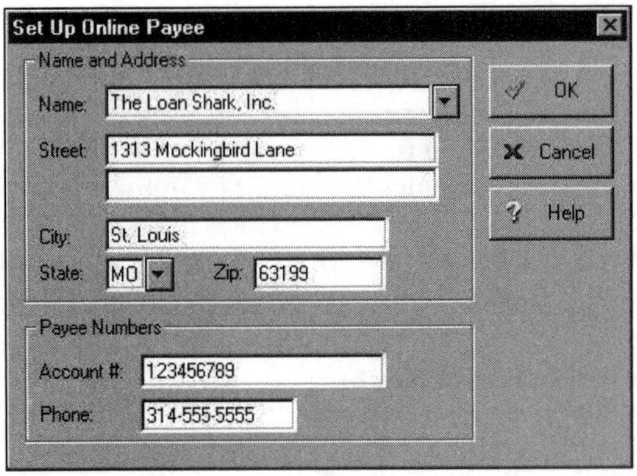

Figure 7-15:
Setting up
an online
payee.

3. Enter the requested information in the Set Up Online Payee dialog box.

You should be able to find all the information on a recent bill or state-ment from the payee. Be sure to enter the information carefully and double-check it for accuracy. Errors could cause your payments to this payee to be misdirected or credited to the wrong account.

4. **Click OK.**

   The Set Up Online Payee dialog box closes, and Quicken enters the new payee in the Online Payee List.

5. **Repeat Steps 2 through 4 for any other payees that you want to define.**

Scheduling online payments

Online bill payment is thoroughly integrated into the Quicken program. There are several different ways to define payment transactions in Quicken, and you can use just about any of them to define online bill payments as well. If you can enter a transaction for a paper check in Quicken, you can use the same technique to enter an online payment. As long as you're creating a payment from an account that's enabled for online bill payment, it usually takes nothing more than clicking a check box or selecting an option to tell Quicken to make the transaction an online payment rather than a paper check.

If you're already familiar with Quicken, you can use any of the following techniques to create online bill payments:

✔ From the menu bar, choose Features⟹Bills⟹Write Checks to open the Write Checks page, which looks like a paper check. Select the account to use by clicking the appropriate account tab at the bottom of the screen. Simply fill out the check like a regular check, making sure to choose an online payee in the Pay To The Order Of drop-down list box. To make it an online payment, click the Online Payment check box. Click Record Check to record your payment.

✔ From the menu bar, choose Features⟹Reminders⟹Financial Calendar to open the Financial Calendar page. Select an online payee in the list box on the right side of the calendar; then drag and drop the payee name onto the date when you want to schedule the payment. Quicken opens a New Transaction dialog box in which you can enter information to define the payment. To make it an online payment, select Online Pmt in the Type of Transaction drop-down list box. Click OK to record the payment.

✔ Open the account register for the account that you want to use to pay the bill. Press Ctrl+N to create a new transaction on a blank line of the register. Normally you enter the Date, Payee, Payment amount, Memo, and Category. (Be sure to select an online payee in the Payee field.) To make it an online payment, select Send Online Payment in the NUM column. Click Enter to record the payment.

In addition to the preceding simple techniques for defining payment transactions, Quicken furnishes one payment creation technique that's unique to online bill payments. To create an online bill payment in the Online Center, follow these steps:

1. **From the Quicken menu bar, choose Online⇨Online Center.**

   Quicken opens to the Online Financial Services Center page.

2. **Select the desired bank from the Financial Institution drop-down list box.**

   Be sure to select a bank where you have an account enabled for online bill payment.

3. **Click the Payments tab.**

   Quicken displays the Payments form and list, as shown in Figure 7-16.

4. **Select the account from which you want to make the payment in the Account drop-down list box.**

5. **In the Payee field, type the name of a payee or select it from the drop-down list box.**

   Select a previously defined online payee or define the payee as you go.

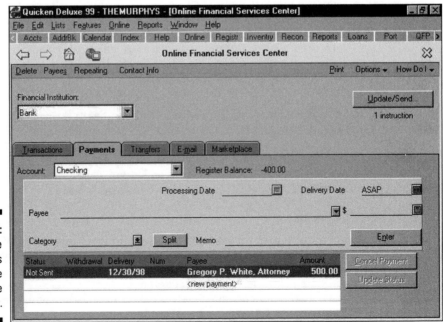

Figure 7-16:
The Payments tab in the Online Center.

6. **Enter the amount, category, and memo in their respective fields.**

7. **Enter the Delivery Date.**

   In Quicken, you specify the delivery date (due date), not the pay date, for online bill payments. The delivery date must be far enough in the future to allow at least two to four days of lead time for processing and delivery.

   The lead time required for different payees varies depending on whether the payee receives payments via electronic funds transfer or paper checks. You can verify the lead time for each of your payees in the Online Payee List.

8. **Click E<u>n</u>ter to record the payment.**

   Quicken adds the new payment to the list below the payment entry form on the Payments tab in the Online Center. Quicken also records the payment transaction in the appropriate account register.

When you create an online bill payment, Quicken records the payment in the account registers but doesn't automatically send the payment instructions to your bank. You must open the Online Center page and click Update/Send to initiate an online connection to your bank and transmit payment instructions and other data to your bank. You can wait until you have defined several online bill payments and transfers and then send them all at once, but you must be careful not to forget to send the payment instructions.

If you attempt to exit Quicken without first going online to send your pending online bill-payment instructions, Quicken alerts you to your oversight and gives you an opportunity to initiate an online session before you exit.

Paying bills online when your bank doesn't offer the service

If your bank doesn't offer online banking or online bill payment through Quicken in any way, shape, or form, you're not out of options. Quicken offers a bill-payment-only service that at least automates the process of paying bills. This service, called Intuit Online Payment and furnished by CheckFree, enables you to use online bill payment to pay your bills even though your bank doesn't offer bill-payment service. If you don't find your financial institution listed when you begin the online banking sign-up process, you can select the Intuit Online Payment option instead.

The good news is that all you need is a checking account with a bank that's recognized by the Federal Reserve System — which you probably have already. Simply enroll in the CheckFree service that's right for you. An application process is part of the enrollment, and the service needs a canceled check from you so that it can get all your account numbers, routing numbers, and the exact name of your bank. When you're ready to go, CheckFree sends you an enrollment letter, and you can begin to pay bills online.

The bad news is that you pay a little bit more for a bill-payment-only service like CheckFree than if you use your bank for online banking and bill payment.

Exploring Other Quicken 99 Features

Without a doubt, the online features of Quicken 99 are very robust and offer great convenience and time savings. Quicken also includes many features that make managing your finances easy — so easy that you'll want to use them all the time, instead of using any old-fashioned budgeting methods that you may have.

The Account List feature

The Account List is a simple and fast way to get a quick look at the balances in all your accounts. Because Quicken keeps track of your assets like checking and savings account balances, portfolio balances, and liabilities, including loans and credit cards, you can quickly see your net worth.

Accessing the Account List is really easy. Just point to the Banking icon in the Activity Bar and choose Account List from the pop-up menu. Quicken opens a page listing every account that you have set up. Clicking a particular account takes you directly to the account register, where you review details about the account.

Alerts

Quicken does a great job of helping you manage all your account balances. With proper feeding of updated information, Quicken can alert you when certain financial milestones are passed. For example, you can set alerts to notify you when account balances get too high or too low, when credit card accounts are nearing their credit limits, when you reach a certain check number (so that you remember to reorder checks), when monthly expense categories reach preset limits, and more.

In addition to setting up Quicken to alert you to specific account changes, you can set up investment alerts and other more general and less frequent alerts. Also, Quicken has left a place in the software to add future alert criteria. The first one that I have seen is a mortgage rate watcher to let you know when mortgage rates hit a certain rate.

The Financial Calendar

The Quicken Financial Calendar is one of the most useful parts of the entire software program. With one look at the calendar, you can graphically see where you stand with your transactions.

You can see your Financial Calendar by pointing to the Banking icon in the Activity Bar and choosing Financial Calendar from the pop-up menu that appears. Here are a couple highlights to take a look at:

✔ When you enter transactions, they appear on the calendar under the day you have them scheduled or the date they cleared your account.

✔ Click a date that has transactions listed to get a complete list of all transactions and links to more information about each transaction.

✔ Set up a bill payment by dragging a payee listed on the right side of the screen to the date on the calendar when you would like to send that payee a payment. A window opens up, in which you can enter all the information that you need to complete the transaction.

Features to manage investments

Quicken not only tracks bank accounts, credit card accounts, and the like; it can also keep track of your investment portfolio. In fact, Quicken is a fairly robust portfolio manager that can use your online connections to monitor stock prices and automatically update your portfolio value and calculate the return on your investments. Quicken even includes special features to make it easier to keep tabs on your retirement accounts, especially 401(k) plans and IRAs.

The WebEntry feature

One of the difficulties of using personal finance manager programs like Quicken is that you're pretty much tied to one computer where the program is loaded and your data files are stored. If you're away from that computer, recording transactions as you make them is often difficult.

WebEntry is a feature of Quicken that enables you to store transactions on a special Internet Web site while you're away from the computer where you normally use Quicken. The idea is that you can enter your transactions on the Web while you're on the road or at the office. When you return home, you can log on to the Internet and download your transactions into your Quicken account register.

Home inventories

In its never-ending effort to present a complete view of your financial position, Quicken offers the capability to track an inventory of your personal possessions. With the Inventory feature, you can keep track of everything you own, in case you need the list for insurance purposes. Also, as you attach value to each item in your inventory, Quicken adds up the amounts to create another asset account, which it includes in calculations of your net worth.

Quicken Financial Planner

The Quicken Financial Planner (QFP) is a tool to help you estimate your future financial needs. The QFP pulls data from your day-to-day financial activity found in the Quicken account registers and also steps you through an interview where you can input every aspect of your financial planning future. The full version of the QFP is a part of the Quicken Suite 99 package. An abbreviated version of the QFP is included as part of other packages like Quicken Deluxe 99.

Other online Quicken 99 financial resources

With Quicken, the financial data that you manage online is not limited to just your bank accounts. Quicken provides several other online resources to help you create and understand your total financial picture. For example, you can set up online banking connections that enable you to get account balances and download transactions for credit card accounts and brokerage accounts, and you can manage your investment portfolio with online stock price updates. You can even receive your bills online rather than by mail. With Quicken's built-in connection to the Web, you can receive all kinds of daily financial information at www.quicken.com, connect to mortgage.quicken.com to plan a mortgage and then actually apply for it online, shop for insurance online at www.insuremarket.com/, and use extensive tax-planning and preparation features, among other things.

Which Version of Quicken 99 Is Right for Me?

Quicken started out as a single software product. But, over the years, it has grown and diversified, with various sets of extra features and accessory programs bundled with the basic PFM program. Quicken is now available in five different versions. For your online banking purposes, all versions of Quicken offer the capability to pay bills and update account information online.

So which version of Quicken should you buy? That really depends on what else you want to do with it. The following list gives you a brief rundown of the many features of each version:

- **Quicken Basic 99:** If all you want to do is manage your finances, Quicken Basic 99 is the best choice. With Quicken Basic 99, you can manage bank and credit card data; pay bills online and offline; receive bills online; update your registers; create, customize, and view reports and graphs; use basic investment-tracking capabilities, including updating investment prices online; and more. Quicken Basic 99 is the base model, so all its features are included in all other versions of Quicken 99.

- **Quicken Deluxe 99:** Quicken Deluxe 99 is designed for people who have the need for the basic account-management features found in the Quicken Basic 99 package and need some additional financial-planning and tax tools as well. The additional features include a Debt Reduction planning tool to show you the most efficient way to pay off credit cards; Financial Alerts that watch all sorts of variable data, from the amount of money in your checking account to the current rate on a mortgage; What If scenarios that let you project long-term financial plans (such as retirement income) based on financial information that you enter; 401(k) plan tracking; a mutual-fund finder and stock screening tools; online investment information, including historical quotes; a Capital Gains Estimator to check the impact that selling investments will have on your taxes; an estate planning guide; and much more.

- **Quicken Home and Business 99:** If you're a small-business owner, Quicken Home and Business 99 is the software for you. This version was designed with feedback from individuals who have business transactions to manage but don't need an entire business accounting package. Quicken Home and Business is essentially Quicken Deluxe, plus some simple invoicing, accounts receivable, and accounts payable features. It's a great solution for many self-employed individuals.

- **Quicken Suite 99:** Quicken Suite 99 is really three complete software packages. It includes all the features of Quicken Deluxe 99 and adds a legal document preparation program with more than 100 legal documents that you can review, edit, and use for your own purposes, along with the Quicken Financial Planner, which enables you to review your future income and expense needs so that you can set up the best possible retirement savings plan.

- **Quicken Financial Center 99:** Quicken Financial Center 99 is also very similar to Quicken Deluxe 99, with a few tax-related additions, such as an on-screen tax library, on-screen IRS publications, video advice, and a tax Q&A.

Chapter 8

Online Banking with Microsoft Money 99

*M*icrosoft Money 99 is designed for managing and tracking home finances, and the program offers many other amenities besides. For example, a gizmo called the Lifetime Planner helps users plan for retirement, figure their children's college expenses, and find out how investments will increase in value over the years. Starting from a window called the Decisions Center, you can find ways to reduce your taxes, evaluate whether buying a home or renting is worthwhile, and decide what type of investments are best for you, given the risks that you're willing to take.

Overall, however, Money 99 is meant to help you track your personal finances, including investments. For each bank account and credit card that you have, you set up an account register. You record your transactions — deposits, withdrawals, account transfers, and checks — in the registers. Figure 8-1 shows a check being recorded in a checking account register. Notice the form at the bottom of the register for recording transactions — in this case, a check.

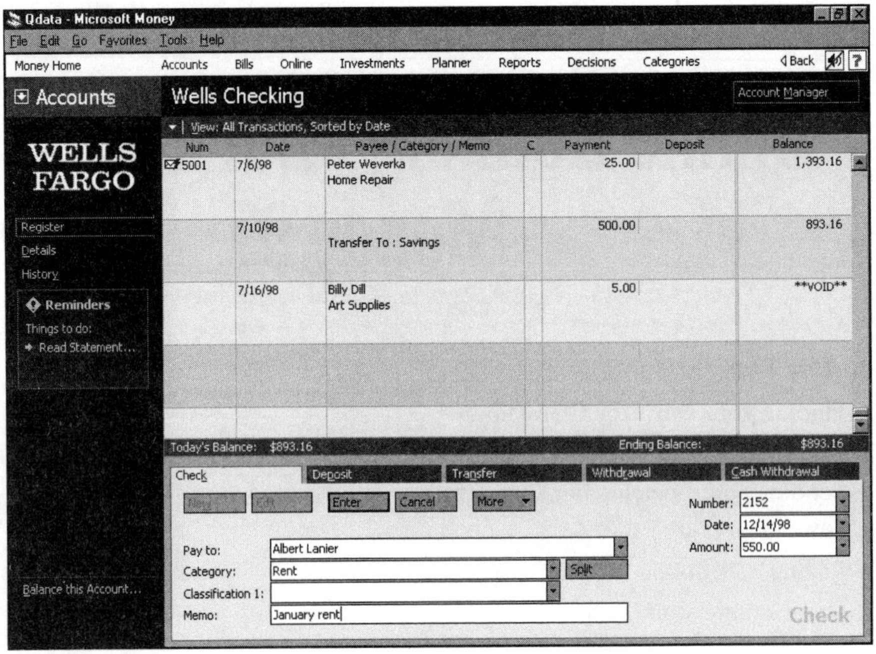

Figure 8-1:
You record
transactions
in registers
like this one.

When you record a transaction in a register, Money 99 gives you the opportunity to categorize it. In Figure 8-1, for example, the check is being assigned to the Rent category. By assigning each transaction to a category, you can discover a great deal about your spending habits and sources of income. You can generate a report or graph and find out how much you spent on clothing, dining, office supplies, or rent. You can find out how much you earned in interest income and how much you earned from different clients. You can even find out how much you are allowed to deduct for income tax purposes.

Navigating from Window to Window

When you start Money 99, you go straight to the Money Home window. The Money Home window lists the bills that you need to pay and gives you the opportunity to click a button to see information such as your monthly report (a report that shows your income and spending this month), your net worth, and your general financial condition.

Money offers nine windows in all, each designed to help you track your finances or investigate your financial health. To travel from window to window, click the buttons on the Navigation bar (which is the stripe along the top of the screen), or choose commands on the Go menu. Table 8-1 gives you a quick rundown of the purposes of the different Money 99 windows.

Table 8-1	The Various Money 99 Windows
Window	*What It's For*
Account Manager	Setting up new accounts and opening account registers so that you can record transactions
Bills & Deposits	Scheduling the bills that you pay regularly and getting the help of Money 99 to pay your bills on time
Online Financial Services	Signing up for the online services, paying bills over the Internet, finding out which transactions have cleared an account, downloading bank statements, and transferring money between accounts
Investments	Monitoring stocks, bonds, mutual funds, and other investment holdings
Planner	Drawing up a budget, planning for retirement, calculating the cost of a college education, and estimating how investments will grow
Reports & Charts	Generating reports and charts that show where you stand financially
Decisions Center	Offers articles, worksheets, and links to sites on the Internet where you can get advice for improving your finances
Categories & Payees	Lists your clients, customers, and vendors

Downloading Information from Your Bank

It goes without saying, but you can't bank online with Money 99 unless your bank offers online banking service to users of Money 99. After you find out whether your bank offers the service, your next step is to go on the Internet and download your bank's information to your computer. You can't bank online with Money 99 unless you've downloaded the information.

Follow these steps to download information about your bank to your computer:

1. **Choose Go⇨Online Finances or click the Online button on the Navigation bar.**

   You arrive at the Online Financial Services window.

2. **Click the down arrow in the upper-left corner of the window (next to the Online Financial Services title) and choose the financial institution that you want to bank online with.**

   Figure 8-2 shows how to choose a bank. The names of the banks on the list come from your account registers. If the bank that you want to go online with isn't on the list, either you entered its name incorrectly when you set up your bank account in Money 99 or you haven't set up an account in Money 99 for the bank account yet. (Be sure you've done these tasks correctly before you continue with this process.)

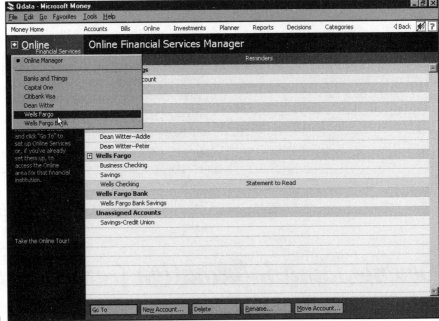

Figure 8-2:
Choosing a bank so that you can use its online services.

After you choose a bank, you land in the Get Connected! window. This is your launching point for reaching out to your bank in cyberspace.

3. **Click button 2, the Investigate Offerings button.**

   The first of several wizard dialog boxes appears.

4. **Click the Next button.**

5. **Make sure that the name of your bank appears in the dialog box, and if it doesn't, enter the correct name; then click the Next button.**

6. **Enter your password and user name in the Connection dialog box, and click OK to go on the Internet.**

   Assuming that Money recognizes your bank, you see a dialog box like the one shown in Figure 8-3. However, if the program can't recognize your bank, a message box opens to tell you that. Sorry, Charlie, you're out of luck, and you can't bank online.

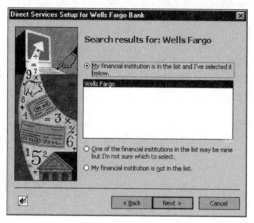

Figure 8-3:
If you can bank online, you see the name of your bank in this dialog box.

7. **Click the Next button.**

   Money downloads the information about your bank to your computer. As the dialog box warns, it can take a minute or two.

8. **Click the Finish button and disconnect from the Internet if you don't care to stay online any longer.**

   You return to the Get Connected! window.

9. **Click button 3, the Review Service Details button, to find out about the bank's online services, and then click Finish.**

   In the dialog box, you find information about how much online banking and online bill payment cost.

10. **Click button 4, the Read Signup Info button, to read how to sign up for online banking services, and then click the Finish button.**

You can click the Contact Information button in the Get Connected! window to find out where to call to sign up for services with your bank. As shown in Figure 8-4, the Contact Information window lists your bank's Internet address. Try clicking the Go To button to visit your bank's Web site and learn more about the online services.

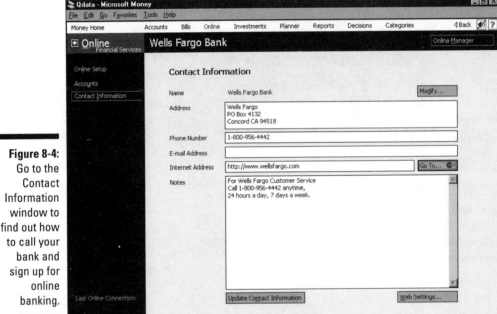

Figure 8-4:
Go to the Contact Information window to find out how to call your bank and sign up for online banking.

Activating an Account as an Online Bank Account

As you know, you must have been assigned a PIN (personal identification number) in order to access your bank account online. After your PIN number arrives in the mail along with a start-up kit, the next step is to activate your plain-Jane account so that you can take it online and bank or pay bills with it.

Follow these steps to set up a bank account so that it works online:

1. **Click the Online button on the Navigation bar to go to the Online Financial Services window.**

   You can also get there by choosing Go➪Online Services.

2. **Click the down arrow in the upper-left corner of the window and select the name of your bank.**

   You land in the Get Connected! window.

3. **Click button 5, Set Up Online Services.**

   The first of several wizard dialog boxes tells you that you are about to be asked for some details about the online account. All right already! Start asking.

4. **Click Next; make sure that the Yes, I Have This Information option button is selected in the next dialog box; and click Next.**

   As shown in Figure 8-5, the next wizard dialog box asks for some rather personal information about you. Make sure that you enter this information correctly. The information that you enter must match the information that the bank has if you want to go online.

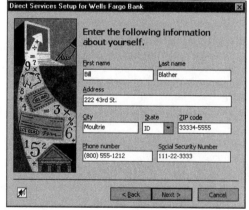

Figure 8-5: Enter your personal information carefully.

5. **Fill in the dialog box and click the Next button.**

6. **Enter your bank's Financial Institution ID number and click Next.**

   The start-up kit that you got in the mail from your bank should include this number.

7. **Select the account that you want to be an online account and click Next.**

   This dialog box is for naming which account is to receive online status. If you have more than one account with this bank, you have an opportunity to return to this dialog box and designate another account as an online account as well.

8. **Click the Direct Bill Payment check box, Direct Statements check box, or both check boxes, and click the Next button.**

   Here, you tell Money which service or services you want. Click the Direct Statements box for online banking; click the Direct Bill Payment box for online bill payment.

9. **In the Enter Account Information dialog box, enter your bank account number (if it isn't listed already), your account type, and your bank's routing number; and click Next.**

   The *routing number* is the first nine numbers in the lower-left corner of your checks. The start-up kit that the bank sent you should include the routing number.

10. **In this dialog box, click the Yes button if you want to set up more online accounts; click the No button if you are finished; then click Next.**

    Click the Yes button and you go back to the dialog box that you saw in Step 7, from which you can repeat Steps 7 through 9 to change another account to an online account.

11. **Click the Finish button in the Online Setup Complete dialog box.**

    You return to the Ready to Connect! window. Now button 5, formerly the Set Up Online Services button, has become the Change Direct Services button. And what's this? The Get Connected! window is now called the Ready to Connect! window. How about that!

Sending Instructions to the Bank

To bank online, you start by creating instructions in Money 99 concerning what you want to do. Then you send those instructions over the Internet to your bank. The following sections in this chapter explain how to prepare the instructions to your bank. These pages explain how to tell Money 99 which instructions to send and then how to actually send those instructions to your bank.

The Connect window is where you tell Money which instructions to send. All online transactions and online payments appear in the Connect window shown in Figure 8-6. The Connect window in Figure 8-6, for example, shows instructions for paying a bill and getting the latest balance for a savings and checking account.

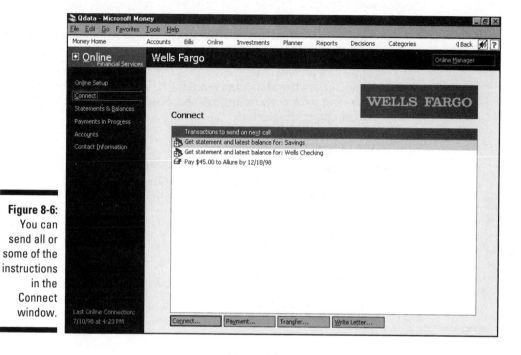

Figure 8-6:
You can
send all or
some of the
instructions
in the
Connect
window.

Follow these steps to reach the Connect window, tell Money 99 which transactions to send, and send the instructions:

1. **Click the Online button on the Navigation bar or choose Go⇨Online Finances.**

   The Online Financial Services window appears.

2. **If necessary, choose the name of a bank from the Online drop-down list in the upper-left corner of the window.**

   You have to do this step only if you bank online with more than one bank.

3. **Click the Connect button.**

   That's the Connect button on the left side of the window, the one below the Online Setup button, not the one on the bottom of the window.

   You see the list of online banking and bill-payment instructions. These are the instructions that you gave your bank for banking online. You don't have to send all the instructions at once.

4. **Tell Money 99 which instructions to send:**

   • **Send an instruction:** Make sure that a lightning bolt appears beside the instruction. If one doesn't appear, right-click the instruction and choose Send on Next Call from the shortcut menu.

- **Postpone sending an instruction:** Right-click the instruction and choose Don't Send on Next Call from the shortcut menu. Postponed instructions are "grayed out" on-screen.

- **Cancel an instruction:** Right-click the transaction and choose Remove from the shortcut menu. When you remove a transaction, it stays in your account register. It becomes a normal transaction, not an online transaction.

5. Click the Connect button.

This time click the Connect button on the bottom of the window instead of the one in the upper-left corner. The Call Your Financial Institution dialog box shown in Figure 8-7 appears.

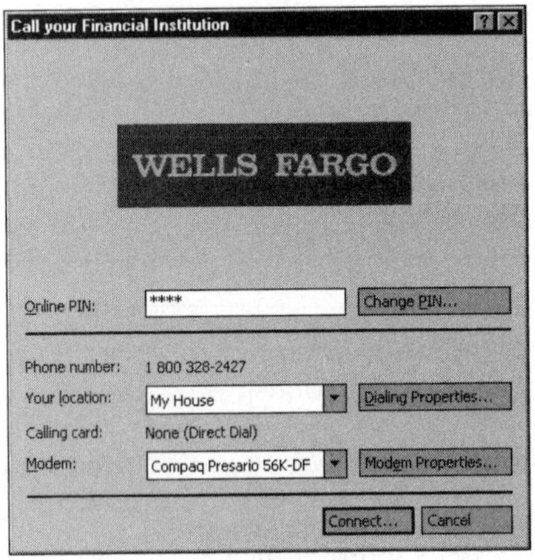

Figure 8-7:
Connecting
with the
bank so that
you can
bank in
cyberspace.

6. Enter your PIN and click the Connect button.

You see the Call Summary dialog box, the instructions are sent, and information is downloaded to your account.

7. Click Close when the download is finished.

You see the Statements & Balances window, which lists how many transactions downloaded and shows you your bank balance.

Reviewing and Reconciling Account Data from Your Bank

To get account data from your bank and reconcile the bank's records with yours, make sure that lightning bolts appear next to the Get statement and latest balance for instructions in the Connect window before you go online (refer to Figure 8-6). The previous section explains the Connect dialog box and how to send instructions. The `Get statement and latest balance for` instructions tell Money 99 to download account data from your bank. If no lightning bolt appears, right-click the instruction and choose Send on Next Call.

After you finish downloading data from your bank, follow these steps to review the data and, if you want, reconcile your records with the bank's:

1. **If necessary, click the Statements & Balances button in the Online Financial Services window to go to the Statements & Balances window.**

   This window lists the names of accounts, their current balances, and how many transactions were downloaded from the bank.

2. **Click the name of the account whose records you want to review and perhaps reconcile.**

3. **Click the Read Statement button.**

   The Statement dialog box shown in Figure 8-8 appears. Scroll down the list of transactions to see which ones have cleared the bank. You can see your account balance at the top of the dialog box.

   After you review the downloaded transactions, you may want to compare the bank's records to your own records. This way, you can be sure that the amounts in your register are the same as the bank's records. And you can fix discrepancies if Money finds any.

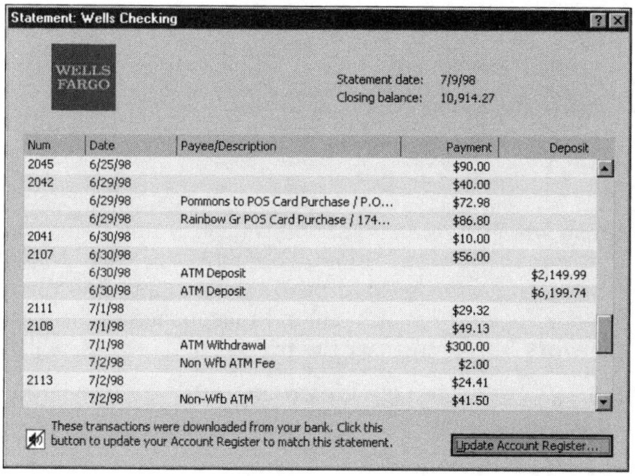

Figure 8-8: In the Statement dialog box, you can see which transactions have cleared the bank.

Statement: Wells Checking

WELLS FARGO

Statement date: 7/9/98
Closing balance: 10,914.27

Num	Date	Payee/Description	Payment	Deposit
2045	6/25/98		$90.00	
2042	6/29/98		$40.00	
	6/29/98	Pommons to POS Card Purchase / P.O...	$72.98	
	6/29/98	Rainbow Gr POS Card Purchase / 174...	$86.80	
2041	6/30/98		$10.00	
2107	6/30/98		$56.00	
	6/30/98	ATM Deposit		$2,149.99
	6/30/98	ATM Deposit		$6,199.74
2111	7/1/98		$29.32	
2108	7/1/98		$49.13	
	7/1/98	ATM Withdrawal	$300.00	
	7/2/98	Non Wfb ATM Fee	$2.00	
2113	7/2/98		$24.41	
	7/2/98	Non-Wfb ATM	$41.50	

These transactions were downloaded from your bank. Click this button to update your Account Register to match this statement.   Update Account Register...

4. **Click the Update Account Register button in the Statement dialog box. (Refer to Figure 8-8.)**

   Money compares the transactions that you entered in account registers to the transactions that were downloaded from the bank. If the program encounters what appears to be a discrepancy, you see one of the Update dialog boxes shown in Figure 8-9 or Figure 8-10.

5. **Correct the error in the Update dialog box and click Next to move on.**

   Depending on which Update dialog box you see, you take the following actions to correct the error:

   - **If you see** `The amounts are different. Are these the same transaction?` **(shown in Figure 8-9), do this:** You have a difference between your records and the bank's records. Click the Yes option button if you believe that the bank is correct (banks usually are about these things), or click No to enter the downloaded transaction and also keep the transaction in the register.

Figure 8-9: This Update dialog box appears when a transaction from your register and a downloaded transaction are a little bit different.

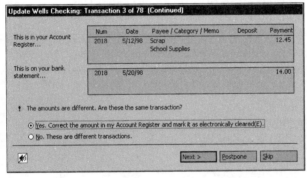

   - **If you see** `This transaction is on your bank statement but could not be found in your Account Register` **(shown in Figure 8-10), do this:** Money can't find the transaction in your account register. Fill in the transaction form, including the Category boxes, to enter the transaction in your register.

6. **Repeat Step 2, and keep clicking Next, until you have updated your account register.**

7. **Click the Finish button.**

Figure 8-10:
This Update
dialog box
appears
when you
forgot to
record a
transaction
and the
transaction
cleared the
bank.

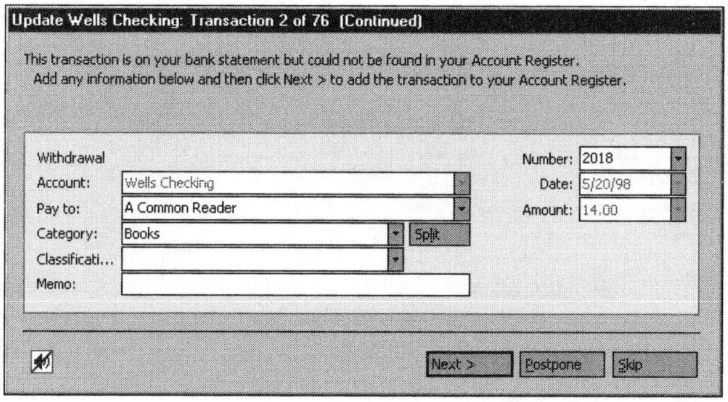

Transferring Money between Online Accounts

You can transfer money between accounts as long as both accounts are held at the same bank and both are approved for the online banking service. Follow these steps to give instructions to Money 99 to transfer money between accounts:

1. **Go to the Online Financial Services window.**

   To get there, click Online on the Navigation bar or choose Go⇨Online Finances.

2. **Click the down arrow beside the Online button and choose the name of your bank from the drop-down menu.**

3. **Click the Connect button.**

   The Connect window appears (refer to Figure 8-6).

4. **Click the Transfer button along the bottom of the window.**

   The Edit Transaction dialog box shown in Figure 8-11 appears. (I have no idea why they call the dialog box "Edit Transaction," because you use it to transfer money.)

5. **In the From drop-down list, choose the name of the account that the money comes from.**

6. **In the To drop-down list, choose the account that the money goes to.**

   On the drop-down lists, online accounts have lightning bolts next to their names.

Figure 8-11:
You can transfer money between online bank accounts as long as both are at the same bank.

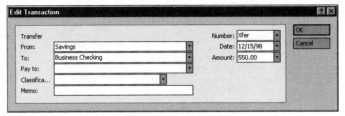

7. **Enter the date when you want the transfer to take place in the Date text box.**

8. **Enter the amount of the transfer in the Amount text box.**

9. **Click the OK button.**

   Back in the Connect window (refer to Figure 8-6), the instruction to transfer money appears along with the other instructions.

By the way, you can also give the instruction to transfer money online by choosing Electronic Transfer (Xfer) in the Number drop-down list on a Transaction form in an account register. (Refer to Figure 8-1.)

Using Online Bill Payment

Paying bills online with Money 99 is actually cheaper than sending checks through the mail. Besides not having to rummage through desk drawers to find stamps and envelopes when you pay bills online, you save about 13 cents per payment, because sending a bill online costs 20 cents whereas a stamp costs 33 cents (and that cost could rise at any time).

In this section, I give you instructions for recording an online payment and providing the payee information that Money 99 needs in order to send the check to pay your bill. When you send a check with the bill-payment feature, an instruction to send the check goes to the Online Services Corporation. That company actually cuts a check and sends it through the mail (except in some cases, when the company can send electronic funds to large, well-known companies such as phone companies, for example).

Recording an online bill payment

Paying bills with the Money 99 online bill-payment feature is a snap when you get the hang of it. Basically, you just give Money the information that it needs to issue and mail a check. Follow these steps to tell Money 99 to send an online bill payment:

1. **Click the Online button on the Navigation bar or choose <u>Go</u>⇨<u>O</u>nline Finances.**

   You land in the Online Financial Services window.

2. **From the Online drop-down menu in the upper-left corner of the screen, choose the bank from which you will draw the funds for the online payment.**

3. **Click the <u>C</u>onnect button.**

   You see the familiar Connect window (refer to Figure 8-6).

4. **Click the Pa<u>y</u>ment button.**

   You can find the Payment button on the bottom of the window. After you click the button, you see the Edit Transaction dialog box shown in Figure 8-12. Notice that the Number list box reads Epay (for Electronic Payment).

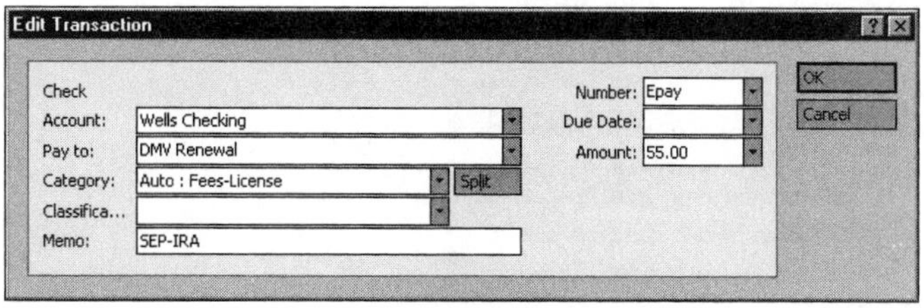

Figure 8-12:
Record an online payment as you would any other payment.

Edit Transaction		? X
Check		OK
Account:	Wells Checking	Number: Epay
Pay to:	DMV Renewal	Due Date:
Category:	Auto : Fees-License Split	Amount: 55.00
Classifica...		Cancel
Memo:	SEP-IRA	

5. **In the Account drop-down list, select the account from which you will draw the money for the payment.**

   A lightning bolt appears next to the names of online accounts. Be sure to choose an online account on the list.

6. **In the Due Date text box, enter the date by which you want the payment to be made.**

   The bank usually requires five days to process and mail a payment, so be sure to pay bills at least five days ahead of their due dates.

7. **In the Pay To box, choose the payee.**

   Filling out the Edit Transaction dialog box is frightfully similar to filling out the form on a transaction register (refer to Figure 8-1).

8. **Enter the amount of the payment in the Amount text box.**

9. **Click OK.**

   You return to the Connect window, where your payment is listed and ready to be sent. You return there, I should say, as long as the payee's address and other particulars are on file with Money 99. If they're not on file, you need to provide information about the payee (which I explain in the next section).

Providing information about the payee

In order to send an online payment, the Online Services Corporation needs some background information. The Online Services Corporation is the company that handles online payments.

When you record an online payment to a company or person for the first time and you click OK in the Edit Transaction dialog box (refer to Figure 8-12), the Online Payee Details dialog box shown in Figure 8-13 appears. Use this dialog box to provide information about the payee. And enter the information correctly. If you don't, the Online Services Corporation can't administer or send the payment.

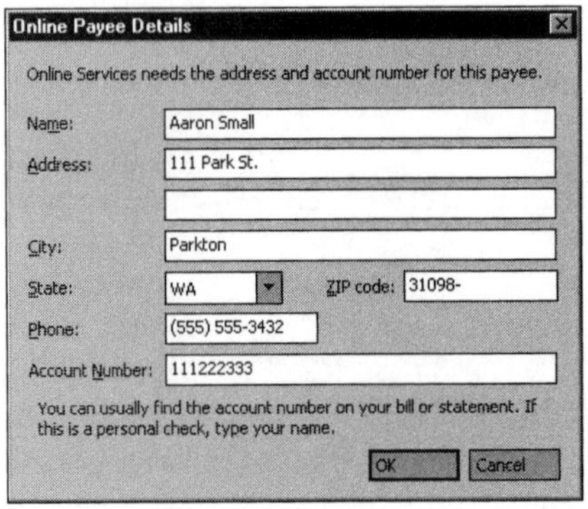

Figure 8-13:
In the Online Payee Details dialog box, you give the particulars about the payee.

Online Payee Details

Online Services needs the address and account number for this payee.

Na_me_:	Aaron Small
_A_ddress:	111 Park St.
C_i_ty:	Parkton
_S_tate:	WA
_Z_IP code:	31098–
_P_hone:	(555) 555-3432
Account _N_umber:	111222333

You can usually find the account number on your bill or statement. If this is a personal check, type your name.

OK   Cancel

Exploring Other Online Features in Money 99

Money offers a small handful of other online amenities besides its online banking and online bill-payment features. Be sure to check out the features of Money 99 that I cover in the following sections. (The Decisions Center and Microsoft Investor are available only to users of the Money 99 Financial Suite.)

Online stocks and mutual funds

You can download stock, bond, and mutual fund prices from the Internet. Money enters the current prices of the stocks, bonds, and mutual funds in your portfolio automatically if you track your securities in Money 99. Click the Investments button on the Navigation bar to see your portfolio. This is a great way to stay up to date with investment prices. And the Investments window offers ways to compare investments and track their value over time.

Decisions Center

From the Decisions Center window, you can read articles about saving and reducing expenses, get advice for buying cars (or go on the Internet to research or even shop for different brands of cars), and use the calculators to go online and investigate such matters as how to reduce taxes and how to figure your retirement expenses.

Microsoft Investor

From the Microsoft Investor Web site, you can research investment opportunities online. The Investor offers business profiles and charts, market statistics, and articles.

To visit the Microsoft Investor Web site, click the Investments button on the Navigation bar, click the Microsoft Investor button (which you see along the left side of the window), and click a hyperlink in the Portfolio window. Figure 8-14 shows the Microsoft Investor Web site.

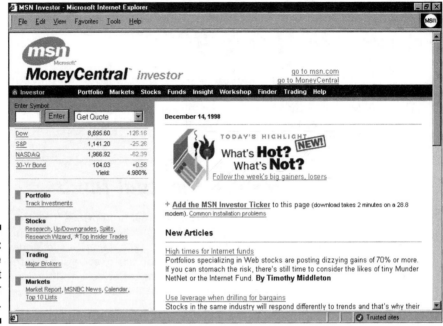

Figure 8-14:
The
Microsoft
Investor
Web site.

Chapter 9

Online Banking with Managing Your Money Software

*M*anaging Your Money (MYM, pronounced *mim*) is one of the big three personal finance manager (PFM) programs available today, along with Quicken and Microsoft Money. Like the other PFM packages, MYM enables you to track and manage every detail of your personal finances. But, unlike Quicken and Money, you can't find MYM on the shelf at your local computer store. You get MYM from your bank when you sign up for the bank's online banking service.

Why Can't I Find Managing Your Money at the Software Store?

If you can't find MYM on the software shelf next to Quicken and Microsoft Money, don't panic. And whatever you do, don't call the store manager. MYM isn't available through normal software outlets. Rather, you get MYM directly through a bank.

Ever notice that everything you receive from your bank has the bank's name on it? No bank can pass up an opportunity to stamp its name on whatever it gives you — and software is no exception. MECA Software, the company that developed MYM, recognizes that fact and incorporated it into the design of MYM. MECA identified the most popular PFM features and built one software product. This is all fine and good, but what sets MYM apart is that MECA intentionally left room for banks to customize the software with their own names and logos.

The approach appears to work quite well. After all, banks can offer all these features to their customers without going through the hassle and expense of building their own software. But the bank still gets to put its name and logo on the software, which is more attractive to the bank than relying on a commercially available product such as Quicken or Money.

If you, as a consumer, want to use MYM, your best bet is to find a bank that offers it. The following are just some of the banks that offer MYM:

- ✔ Bank Of America
- ✔ Citibank
- ✔ Fleet Bank
- ✔ National City Bank
- ✔ NationsBank
- ✔ New England Financial
- ✔ PNC Bank
- ✔ Royal Bank of Canada
- ✔ US Bank

Getting to Know the Managing Your Money Features

Your bank can provide you with the MYM software, along with instructions on how to install the software on your computer. The MYM user's guide is easy to follow, but you barely need to refer to it because MYM gives you a series of dialog boxes with very basic directions to lead you through the installation. After you install MYM according to the instructions (check the beginning of the MYM software user's guide) and run the program, you see the SmartDesk screen, shown in Figure 9-1.

The SmartDesk is, by design, an easy starting point for navigating around the program. The designer of the SmartDesk had some fun in the process. For example, you can click the statue of *The Thinker* on top of the bookshelf for help and click the mouse hole in the wall to exit.

Click here for help

Toolbar

SmartDesk

Menu bar

Click here for online banking options

Click here to exit MYM

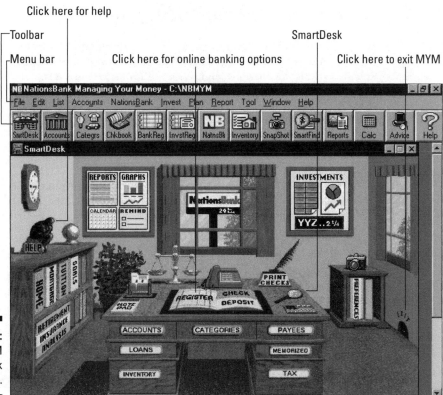

Figure 9-1:
The MYM
SmartDesk
screen.

Reports, Graphs, Remind, and Calendar, all on the bulletin board on the wall, give you access to features in those categories. (See 'em there on the left side of the wall, behind the desk?) You can also track all your investments. If you click the bank sign that you see outside the window, you connect with the bank. (In some versions of MYM, the bank logo appears on a computer screen on the desk.) The fun level's almost up there with Microsoft Bob!

Clicking around on the SmartDesk isn't the only way that you can navigate through MYM. If you're a traditionalist, you can choose commands from the menu bar, just as you can in any other Windows program. For quick, single-click access to the most common program features, click a button on the toolbar (the row of buttons just below the menu bar in Figure 9-1). Notice that the bank's name and logo appear prominently on the menu bar and toolbar as well as in the SmartDesk screen. (By the way, in this chapter I refer to the bank's name in commands and such as *MyBank.*)

Using the Account Register

Like the other PFM programs, MYM records detailed transaction data for each of your accounts in a register. The register appears in the Account Register window (shown in Figure 9-2). It looks just like a register from a paper checkbook, which helps make it familiar and easy to use.

The account register maintains the following information, just like your paper checkbook register:

- **Date of the transaction:** The date on which the transaction occurred.

- **Transaction type or number:** Normally the check number, but occasionally ATM, TRANSFER, or any of several other identifiers that sometimes serve to list the type of transaction.

- **Name or other memo:** Whom you made a payment to or received a deposit from.

- **Category:** An income or expense category that you can assign each transaction to.

- **Payment amount (if applicable):** The amount of the transaction (if it's a payment or other transaction where money comes out of your account).

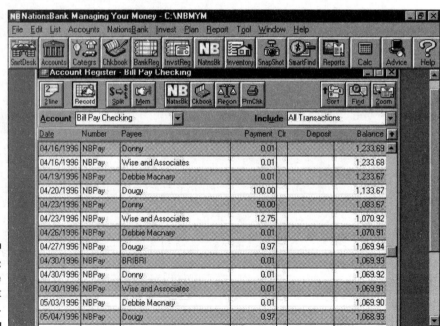

Figure 9-2:
A sample
account
register.

> ✔ **A box to check when items are reconciled:** Checking this box when you reconcile the account can help you keep up-to-date with outstanding transactions.
>
> ✔ **Deposit amount (if applicable):** The amount of the transaction (if it's a deposit or other transaction where money is added to your account).
>
> ✔ **A running balance:** The balance in your register after the transaction has occurred.

Managing categories

Part of the power of a PFM is the ability to categorize transactions; then MYM can use the category assignments to generate reports, graphs, and budget projections with transactions grouped and subtotaled by category. (If you need to, you can refer back to Chapter 2 and review the role of categories in PFM software like MYM.)

When you receive your copy of MYM from your bank, it comes preloaded with a list of categories so that you don't have to fork over the cash for a few accounting courses just to learn how to set that up properly. Choosing Lists⇨Categories opens the Categories window where you can view the entire list of available categories. If necessary, you can add, edit, and delete categories to customize the list to meet your needs.

Setting Up for Online Banking

Because you usually get the MYM software from your bank in response to your request for online banking services, the set-up process for online banking is a little simpler than it is in the other PFM programs. Unlike Quicken and Money, you don't need to download information about your bank or enter a lot of information about your bank accounts in order to use the online banking features of MYM. You do, however, have to enter some personal identification information and tell MYM where to find your modem. If you haven't entered this information before you attempt to connect to the bank for the first time, MYM prompts you to enter the information, but I prefer to get such chores out of the way ahead of time.

To enter the set-up information that MYM requires, follow these steps:

1. **From MYM's menu bar, choose MyBank⇨Change Personal Information.**

   MYM displays the Enter Personal Information dialog box. (Keep in mind that I'm using *MyBank* in places where you see the actual name of your bank.)

2. Enter your customer ID and your name, address, and phone numbers in the text boxes provided.

Your customer ID is usually your social security number, but it may be another number assigned by the bank. You find your ID in the welcome packet information that the bank sent you. The rest of the information is standard stuff, but be sure to enter it carefully.

3. Click OK.

This closes the Enter Personal Information dialog box.

4. Choose File➪Modem Setup➪MyBank from the menu bar.

The Modem Setup Information dialog box appears.

5. Review the settings and edit them if necessary.

The contents of the Modem Setup Information dialog box are already configured with default settings that work in many situations. For example, the software normally arrives with the bank's private data network phone number preset. You may need to change some of the modem settings, however. You can select your modem brand and type from the Modem drop-down list box (although the Default selection usually works pretty well). The settings that you probably need to change are the Comm Port and Baud Rate settings. Select the appropriate values from the drop-down list boxes to match the location and speed of your modem.

6. Click OK.

This closes the Modem Setup Information dialog box and records the settings.

One unusual thing about MYM is that you don't have to create account registers for your online accounts and enable them for online access before connecting to the bank. MYM automatically downloads information about your accounts when you connect to the bank the first time. Then MYM gives you the option to automatically create account registers to correspond to your online banking accounts or link the online accounts to MYM account registers that you created previously.

Connecting to the bank

MYM's PC Banking Center (shown in Figure 9-3) is your master control center for online banking activities in the program. So, naturally, MYM gives you more than one way to reach the PC Banking Center:

- ✔ From the menu bar, choose MyBank➪PC Banking Center.
- ✔ Click the MyBank Center button in the toolbar.
- ✔ Click the MyBank logo in the SmartDesk window.

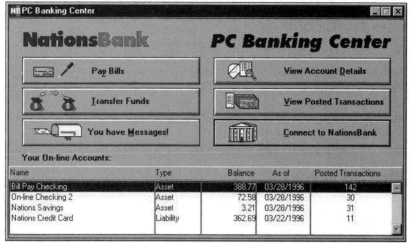

Figure 9-3:
The MYM
PC Banking
Center
window.

MYM displays the PC Banking Center window, no matter which route you take to get there. You can perform many tasks from the PC Banking Center, but the first thing you probably want to do is connect to the bank to update information about your accounts.

To update your account balances, simply follow these steps:

1. Click the Connect To MyBank button in the PC Banking Center.

MYM displays the Connect Instructions dialog box, shown in Figure 9-4, which gives you a chance to review the instructions that you're about to send to the bank (such as Pay Bills, Transfer Funds, and so on). You can enable or disable instructions by clicking on the corresponding check boxes.

Figure 9-4:
The MYM
Connect
Instructions
dialog box.

2. Click Continue.

The Enter PIN dialog box appears.

3. Type your PIN in the Enter Your PIN text box and click Connect.

MYM displays a Session Status message box to keep you informed of its progress as the program uses your modem to call in to the bank over a private data network and exchange information about your accounts with the bank's online banking server.

The software connects with the bank via a private telephone number. During these transactions, your data doesn't travel over the open Internet, which makes it technically more secure than if it did travel over the Internet. If you're really concerned about Internet security, keep in mind that MYM is a good way to take the Internet out of the picture. (See Chapters 11 and 12 for more on security issues.)

When MYM completes the online session with your bank, it automatically disconnects the phone connection and returns to the PC Banking Center.

Viewing account details

After MYM exchanges data with your bank, you can check several pieces of updated information. You can get a quick overview of your account status by clicking the View Account Details button in the PC Banking Center window. The Account Details dialog box (shown in Figure 9-5) appears, showing you account balances that MYM downloaded from your bank. (Refer to Chapter 4 for explanations of ledger balance and available balance.)

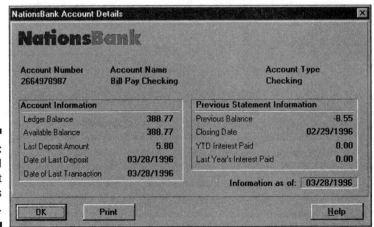

Figure 9-5:
The MYM
Account
Details
dialog box.

Viewing posted transactions

The power of a PFM like MYM really begins to kick in when you use the software to *automatically* update the registers in your PFM without having to enter each transaction manually. After connecting to the bank and downloading updated account information, you can click the View Posted Transactions button in the PC Banking Center. This opens a window where you can view and edit the transactions that MYM downloaded from the bank and transfer them into your MYM account register. Follow these steps:

1. **Click the View Posted Transactions button in the PC Banking Center.**

   The Posted Transactions window, shown in Figure 9-6, appears. The Posted Transactions window displays a list of items that the bank reports as being cleared but not yet transferred to the register in your MYM software. MYM automatically compares the posted transactions to the transactions in your account register and indicates in the Status column whether each transaction is new (New) or matches an existing transaction (Found.)

2. **Pick the account that you want to view by selecting it from the Account drop-down list box.**

   Transactions for the selected account are listed in the Posted Transactions window.

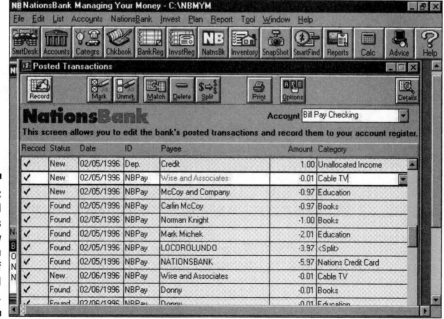

Figure 9-6:
The Posted
Transactions
window
shows you
a register of
your posted
transactions.

3. **Review the list of posted transactions and edit them if necessary.**

   You need to add a category to each transaction, and you may also want to edit the Payee to show something more descriptive than "Check."

4. **Select the transactions that you want to move into your account register by clicking in the Record column to toggle the check mark on or off.**

   A check mark in the Record column means that the checked transaction will be recorded in your account register.

5. **Click the Record button.**

   A message box appears asking you to confirm the action.

6. **Click OK to dispense with the message box.**

   MYM automatically records the selected transactions in your account register. If a posted transaction is marked Found, MYM simply marks the corresponding transaction in your account register as having cleared the bank. If a posted transaction is marked New, MYM enters it in your account register as a new transaction and marks it as cleared.

   After recording all the posted transactions, MYM closes the Posted Transactions window and returns to the PC Banking Center.

Transferring money

Transferring money between your MYM accounts is the definition of easy. All it takes is a few mouse clicks and entering the amount. Just follow these simple steps:

1. **In the PC Banking Center window, select the account from which you want to transfer the money in the Your Online Accounts list.**

   Click an account, such as Online Checking 2, in the Your Online Accounts list at the bottom of the window.

2. **Click Transfer Funds.**

   The Checkbook window for the selected account appears, with the transfer slip displayed in the lower half of the window. (See Figure 9-7.)

3. **Select the account to which you want to transfer the money.**

   Click an account, such as Bill Pay Checking, in the To drop-down list box on the transfer slip.

4. **Add the date of the transaction on the Date line.**

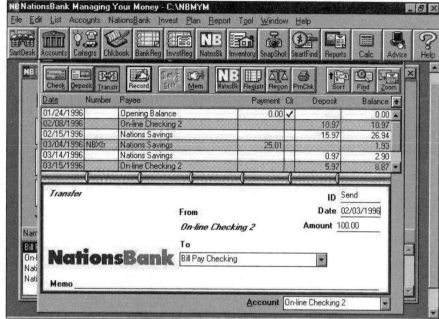

Figure 9-7:
The
Transfer
Funds
window.

5. **Add the amount of the transfer on the Amount line.**

6. **Add a memo to the Memo line to help you remember the purpose of the transfer.**

7. **Click Record.**

    MYM records your transfer in the account register and adds the transfer request to the list of items to be submitted to the bank. Remember, though, that the transfer hasn't been sent to the bank yet, which doesn't happen until the next time you connect to the bank. So, don't forget to connect to the bank for an online banking session before you exit MYM.

Paying bills online

You have two ways to pay bills with MYM: printing a regular check or using the online bill-payment service. Paper checks are passé, and besides, this is a book about online banking. You're ready to move into the next century and make your bill payments online.

Assuming that you've made the appropriate arrangements with your bank to provide online bill-payment service, MYM already detected the capability when you connected to your bank and activated the feature in your MYM software. Actually creating an online bill payment in MYM is easy; you just fill in an on-screen form almost exactly like an old-fashioned paper check.

Follow these steps to set up a payment:

1. **Click the Pay Bills button in the PC Banking Center window.**

    The Checkbook window appears with a graphical representation of a blank check for you to fill in (as shown in Figure 9-8). Notice that Send appears on the Number line of the check to indicate that the payment will be sent to the bank for online processing.

2. **If necessary, select the appropriate account from the Account drop-down list box.**

    Select the account that's enabled for online bill-payment service. (Normally, MYM automatically opens the checkbook for the correct account.)

3. **On the Pay To The Order Of line, type the name of the payee.**

    If you previously defined the payee, you can just select the payee name from the drop-down list box.

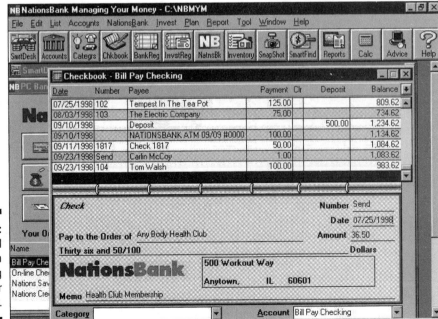

Figure 9-8:
Paying a bill with Managing Your Money.

4. **On the Amount line, enter the amount of the payment.**

5. **On the Date line, enter the pay date (or due date).**

You need to check with your bank to find out whether you should enter the pay date (the date that the payment should be processed) or the due date (the date that you want the payment to arrive at the payee). Some banks need one date; some banks need the other.

6. **On the Memo line, type a notation to help identify the payment.**

The memo is optional, but highly recommended.

7. **Select a category from the Category drop-down list box.**

8. **Click the Record button at the top of the Checkbook window.**

If the payee that you entered for this bill payment is already on your online payee list, you're done with the payment definition. MYM records the payment as a transaction in your account register and adds the payment instruction to the queue of items awaiting transmittal to the bank.

If the payee for this bill payment is new, MYM proceeds to the next step by displaying the Add Online Payee dialog box.

9. **Fill in the name, address, phone number, and account number in the appropriate text boxes in the Add Online Payee dialog box.**

Most of the information requested in this dialog box is self-explanatory. You can probably find all the information that you need on the bill you're paying. The Nickname textbox enables you to define an alternate name for this payee that appears in the Online Payee List and in the drop-down lists in the account register and check form.

Always check and double-check the information that you add to the payee information list, including your account number with the payee. Sure, the account number isn't a big issue with a smaller company, such as a friend or your dentist; they probably know who you are just by looking at the name and address on the check. This issue is much more important when you send payments to larger payees, though, such as large credit card companies and utilities, because they process so many payments (in the millions) a year.

At the top of the dialog box, you see two buttons: Business and Individual. If you are entering a business, like your credit card company, you use the Business option (the default). In that case, the Add Online Payee dialog box has spaces to fill in just the standard address information and such. Clicking the Individual button opens up more options in the Add Online Payee dialog box. Another set of text boxes appears, where you can enter the bank account information of an individual. If you fill in this information, the online bill-payment service can pay the bill by depositing funds directly into the payee's bank account instead of sending a paper check through the mail. That makes this your own personal Electronic Funds Transfer process. Now that's cool! (Complete details for setting this up are included in your guide to MYM, which comes with your software.)

10. **Click OK.**

After you define the payee, MYM records the payee information in your Online Payee List and adds it to the information to be sent to the bank. MYM also records the online payment as a transaction in your account register and adds the payment instruction to the queue of items awaiting transmittal to the bank.

Creating a payment is not the same as sending it! If you want the bank to process your payments, you must send the payment instructions to the bank as part of an online banking connection. Just click Connect To MyBank in the PC Banking Center to initiate the connection, as explained in the "Connecting to the bank" section earlier in this chapter. You don't have to send each payment individually; you can create several payments and transfers and then send them all at once. Just don't forget to send them!

Managing investments

MYM also enables you to track your investments. MYM maintains your investment records in a register, as it does your other accounts. It's a simple and reasonably powerful system that enables MYM to track investments right along with all your other financial information.

Just keeping simple records of investments isn't really enough. You're probably curious about how your investments are doing. Because you have a computer, a modem, and the investment information, getting online quotes and updating your investment balances is pretty convenient. MYM uses the QuoteLink service to update your Investment register with current prices.

The QuoteLink service is offered through the CompuServe network. If you're a CompuServe subscriber, you can get stock quotes as part of your regular service (at no additional cost). If you aren't a regular CompuServe member, you can still get QuoteLink quote information by dialing a 900-number — but it costs $1 per minute. When you're connected via CompuServe, MYM sends the list of securities up to the CompuServe computer, which then sends back the current values for each one; MYM then closes the connection. If you have a dozen or so investments to track, these connections to CompuServe or the 900-number shouldn't take long. If you have hundreds and hundreds of stock quotes to check, you're probably really rich and you can afford it!

Exploring Other MYM Features

In addition to its balances, transfers, payments, and investing services, Managing Your Money offers several other features geared toward helping you complete financial tasks online and helping you manage all your finances from one software package. The following is a brief list of the many useful MYM features:

- ✔ **E-mail:** MYM includes an e-mail feature that you can use to exchange e-mail directly with your bank. The good news about this feature is that you know that the e-mail is secure as it travels over the private data network — rather than over the open Internet. The not-so-good news is that you can check for e-mail messages from your bank only by using MYM e-mail.

- ✔ **Loan management:** Managing loans can be a hassle — and I don't mean keeping up with the payments. For example, a mortgage payment entails just one payment a month, but you may have to account for four or five different categories when you enter the payment into a PFM (namely, principal, interest, homeowner's insurance, other fees, and so on). MYM provides a Loan tool that helps you manage loan transactions and categories.

- ✔ **Budgeting:** Are you spending more than you should spend on utilities? How are you doing with your efforts to save a little extra money for that second honeymoon in Hawaii? With all the transactions that you perform each month, you probably have a hard time answering such questions. MYM offers a tool to help you compare what you think you're going to spend (your budget) with what you actually spend.

- ✔ **Home Inventory:** MYM can also help you keep track of the possessions in your home as a part of your overall financial picture. The Home Inventory feature makes it easy to get organized, take an inventory of your possessions for insurance purposes, or list your possessions as an asset when you apply for a loan or home refinancing. Because the inventory is on the computer, you can easily add and remove items to keep the inventory up-to-date.

- ✔ **Tax estimation:** When you enter deposits into your register, you can track the details of your paycheck, including how much was withheld for taxes. Charitable contributions, medical expenses, and interest all have register categories. And you can use the Investment Register in MYM to keep track of your stock trades, including buy and sell orders. For many families, these factors comprise about 90 percent of the information necessary to complete their taxes. MYM feeds this information into a tax-planning feature that can prove rather helpful as you come to the end of the year and are trying to decide which year-end tax steps are the best for you and your family.

✔ **Planning and reports:** MYM reports can help you review the data that you enter into the program and use it to gain insight into your financial situation. Get a report of your net worth, a summary of your income and expenses, or any one of several other reports. MYM also offers 15 different planning tools to help you plan for the future. The planning tools range from estimating payments for a loan to deciding on the right amount of life insurance. If you have young children, one of the planning tools that you may want to work with is the Tuition Planning tool (shown in Figure 9-9).

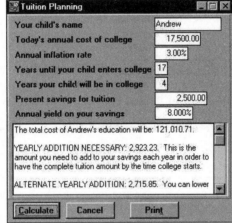

Figure 9-9:
The MYM
Tuition
Planning
tool.

Chapter 10

Online Banking with Business Accounting Software

. . . .

. . . .

*O*nline banking makes managing your personal funds pretty easy. But if you own or operate a business, one question is probably burning in your brain: "Can I use online banking for my business?" Yes, you can. You may also wonder, "Does online banking work the same way for my business as for my personal accounts?" Well, no — not exactly.

This chapter explains the special considerations that you need to think about when you use online banking for your business. This chapter also gives you details about how to use QuickBooks (which is the most popular small- and mid-sized business accounting software program in use today, and the only popular program with online banking and online bill-payment features) and other business accounting software.

Comparing Business Banking and Personal Banking

The bookkeeping and accounting needs of a business, even a small business, are usually somewhat more complex than the needs of an individual or family. Businesses have more rules and regulations to follow and more tax issues to consider, as well as a larger variety and volume of transactions to deal with. As a result, businesses usually need more robust accounting tools than individuals need. Also, banks treat business accounts differently than they treat individual accounts.

All these differences mean that you probably can't use exactly the same software, bank accounts, and online banking features for your business that you use for your personal finances. (Okay, a few of the smallest sole-proprietor type businesses can get by very nicely operating out of a "personal" bank account and managing it with Web-based banking or the online banking features of a PFM such as Quicken or Money; but most businesses need more.)

Banks and large corporations have been working together for years to develop and implement all kinds of services and procedures to save time and expense and increase efficiency. Electronic Funds Transfers (EFTs), direct deposits, lockbox payment processing, and various computerized payment and payroll services are just a few examples. But most of these initiatives have been available only to larger companies with the computer resources and expertise to exchange data with the bank's mainframe computers.

Until recently, small and medium-sized businesses couldn't take advantage of online banking and online bill payment. The consumer-level products and services weren't appropriate for business use, and smaller businesses lacked the clout and the computer resources to play with the big corporations and their mainframe systems. But all that is changing! The latest generation of accounting software for small and mid-sized businesses incorporates online banking and online bill-payment features similar to the features found in the leading personal finance manager software packages, and banks are lining up to support these features with online services for small and mid-sized businesses.

Online banking was a couple of years late in coming to the business segment of the market, but it's catching up fast!

Introducing QuickBooks

QuickBooks 6.0, developed by Intuit (the makers of Quicken), is an accounting software package for small to mid-sized businesses. QuickBooks is the overwhelming leader in the market for commercial accounting packages for these businesses. When you're choosing accounting software, no true size standards exist to help you decide whether your business is a *small* business, a *large* business, or a business that falls in between. If you consider your business to fit into the small to medium portion of the spectrum, give

QuickBooks a try. It's very popular with small, one-person companies as well as with many firms with dozens of employees.

In previous chapters, I refer to Quicken and products of that type as personal financial manager (PFM) software. (See Chapter 2 for a full explanation.) In other words, software like Quicken is designed to manage personal finances; keep track of account registers for bank accounts, loans, and credit cards; handle budgeting and financial planning; and facilitate financial chores, such as paying bills. And of course, the PFMs that I mention in this book all support online banking and online bill payment.

QuickBooks has most of the same characteristics as a PFM. It's personal computer software for managing account registers, handling budgeting, and facilitating paying bills. QuickBooks performs these tasks on a scope and scale that is appropriate for businesses. The latest version of QuickBooks includes the capability to exchange banking and bill-payment information with financial institutions online. You can think of QuickBooks as a PFM that is meant for business rather than personal purposes.

QuickBooks helps you manage many of the financial tasks and issues that go hand in hand with running a business. These tasks include:

✔ Establishing and maintaining a chart of accounts

✔ Managing customers, invoices, and accounts receivable

✔ Managing vendors and accounts payable

✔ Managing an inventory of goods or the time spent delivering services

✔ Creating payroll checks, setting aside employment tax payments, and preparing the necessary tax filing reports

✔ Creating reports to show the status of your business activities

To help you figure out whether QuickBooks is for you, a trial version of both QuickBooks 6.0 and QuickBooks Pro 6.0 is included on the CD inside the back cover of this book.

Navigating throughout QuickBooks 6.0

QuickBooks is a large and robust program with many components and features. However, despite its size, QuickBooks is an easy program to move around in. Like most Windows programs, QuickBooks has a menu bar at the top of its program window that gives you access to all its features. But

QuickBooks also includes the QuickBooks Navigator window (shown in Figure 10-1), which provides a graphical representation of the various program features and enables you to identify and move among the program's many activities.

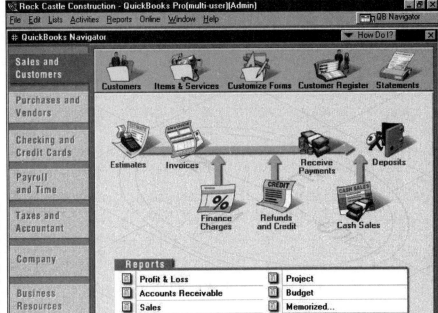

Figure 10-1:
The QuickBooks 6.0 Navigator window.

The tabs on the left side of the QuickBooks Navigator window list the major feature areas of the QuickBooks software. Clicking a tab causes QuickBooks to display icons for related activities arranged in the rest of the Navigator window. The row of icons across the top of the window represent occasional activities. The main activities in the selected feature area are in the central part of the window. Smaller icons at the bottom of the screen lead to reports related to the selected feature area. For example, Figure 10-1 shows the Sales and Customers tab selected, where the main activities are tasks such as preparing estimates and invoices, receiving payments, and making deposits. Occasional activities on this tab include maintaining lists of customers, managing lists of items and services, and generating statements.

You can return to the QuickBooks Navigator instantly from anywhere in the program by clicking the QB Navigator button in the menu bar.

QuickBooks is a very helpful program, going the extra mile to provide lots of instruction and assistance to help you become familiar with (and remember) how to use the program's features. The following list summarizes the main help features:

✔ **The How Do I? button:** Visible just below the menu bar on the right side of most QuickBooks screens, you see the How Do I? button. Clicking this button drops down a list of common areas of interest to QuickBooks users. For example, one of the items on the drop-down list is Get started using QuickBooks. Sliding your mouse over this item causes another screen to pop up and offers more options for finding the information or feature that interests you. This is a very slick feature.

✔ **Qcards:** Qcards are small boxes of information that QuickBooks shows as you move through the program. These boxes offer just a few sentences to explain where you are and what you may want to do next.

✔ **Help:** QuickBooks also comes with a great deal of assistance built into the software to help you with program functions and accounting issues. You can always select Help⇨Help On This Window from the menu bar to get help right away.

It's a good idea to keep nearby the QuickBooks CD that you used to install your software, preferably in your computer's CD-ROM drive. In addition to the program files, the QuickBooks CD offers audio multimedia help and instructions for many parts of the program. To use help, look for the green Show Me button when you're in the help file. Simply click it to hear more about a help topic.

Checking Out the QuickBooks Online Banking Features

QuickBooks 6.0 is a full-featured software program that performs a broad range of helpful financial functions — even more functions than most of the PFM packages that I cover in Chapters 7, 8, and 9. QuickBooks also performs a host of online banking functions that make it a great package for doing business banking online.

QuickBooks offers so many financial features that I can't cover them all in the space of this one chapter. In this chapter, I concentrate on the online banking and bill-payment features of QuickBooks rather than on the everyday financial features. Look for Steve Nelson's *QuickBooks 6 For Dummies* (IDG Books Worldwide, Inc.) to find everything that you need to know about QuickBooks.

QuickBooks offers the following online options to supplement the traditional QuickBooks software financial features:

- ✔ Accessing bank accounts and receiving account balances and detailed transactions information
- ✔ Accessing credit card accounts and receiving credit card account balances and recently posted transactions
- ✔ Transferring funds between accounts
- ✔ Paying bills
- ✔ Paying your payroll and payroll taxes

The following sections help you get started with some of the basic online banking tasks in QuickBooks.

Enabling your accounts for online access to QuickBooks

Before you can use online banking to access your accounts, you must apply for the service from your bank and you must enable your QuickBooks accounts for online access. And you need to configure QuickBooks to use your Internet connection, too. Here are the steps to follow to set up QuickBooks for online banking:

1. **From the QuickBooks menu bar, choose Online⇨Online Banking ⇨ Getting Started.**

   QuickBooks displays the Getting Started with Online Banking dialog box, shown in Figure 10-2.

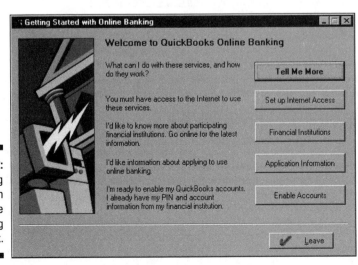

Figure 10-2: The Getting Started with Online Banking dialog box.

2. Click the Set Up Internet Access button.

The Internet Connection Setup dialog box appears. This is the first page of a wizard that walks you through the process of selecting your Internet access options and configuring QuickBooks to use them.

3. Respond to the prompts and questions in the Internet Connection Setup wizard, clicking the Next button to move to each new dialog box in succession. In the final wizard dialog box, click the Finish button.

QuickBooks records your settings and returns to the Getting Started with Online Banking dialog box.

4. Click the Financial Institutions button and then click OK to allow QuickBooks to launch your Web browser and connect to the Internet.

QuickBooks launches your Web browser, connects to the Internet, and loads a page from the Intuit Web site, which provides information about financial institutions that support online banking with QuickBooks. Follow the instructions on the Web site to select your bank and apply for online banking access, credit card account access, and bill-payment services from your bank (assuming that your bank is one of those that supports online banking with QuickBooks).

Don't forget that if your financial institution doesn't offer online banking information, you can still enjoy online bill-payment services. Simply look for the Intuit Online Payment service.

Some banks offer an online application. Others ask you to print a form from your computer, fill it out, and mail it to the bank. Others allow you to apply by phone. To find out exactly what your bank requires, simply click Apply. Then follow those instructions to apply for online banking services.

5. Click Exit in the browser window to return to the Getting Started with Online Banking dialog box.

QuickBooks downloads some information about the financial institutions that you selected on the Web site and then returns to the Getting Started with Online Banking dialog box.

6. Wait for the welcome kit to arrive from your bank.

Your online banking information packet should arrive from the bank in a few days to a couple of weeks. For security reasons, your password or personal identification number (PIN) may arrive in a separate envelope delivered a day or two apart from the rest of the information packet. You need the information contained in the information packet to finish setting up QuickBooks to access your accounts.

When the information packet arrives (both parts of it), you're ready to return to QuickBooks and complete the process of enabling your accounts for online access. Follow these steps:

1. **From the QuickBooks menu bar, choose Online⇨Online Banking⇨Getting Started.**

   The Getting Started with Online Banking dialog box appears.

2. **Click the Enable Accounts button and then click OK to allow QuickBooks to close all windows.**

   The Online Banking Setup Interview dialog box appears. This is a wizard that prompts you for information about which account you want to enable for online banking and bill-payment access.

3. **Respond to the prompts and questions on each page of the wizard and click Next to proceed to the next page. Continue to the last page and then click the Leave button.**

   The Online Banking Setup Interview gets all the information that it needs to identify which accounts you want to enable for online banking and bill payment. The wizard updates your accounts and then exits.

Visiting the Online Banking Center

The QuickBooks Online Banking Center (shown in Figure 10-3) is the hub of all online activity. QuickBooks doesn't connect to your bank separately to process each individual bill payment or statement update as you enter them. Instead, as you perform online banking-related activities in

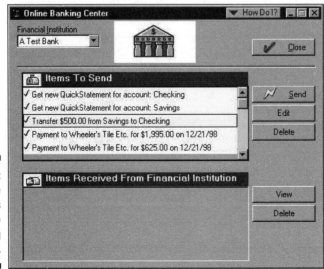

Figure 10-3:
The
QuickBooks
Online
Banking
Center.

QuickBooks, the program creates requests to complete online tasks such as paying bills, transferring funds, and getting updated account information online (features I talk about in the next few sections). Those requests accumulate in the Online Banking Center. Then you can use the Online Banking Center to manage those requests and control the connection to your bank.

When you're ready to send a batch of online banking requests to your bank, execute them from the Online Banking Center using the following steps:

1. **Make sure that you're connected to the Internet before you send any requests from the Online Banking Center.**

   QuickBooks uses the Internet to send and receive messages and data between your computer and your bank. If you are connected to the Internet before you send your requests, the process will go much smoother because you won't have to wait while the software connects with your ISP.

   QuickBooks software uses the strongest security measures possible to protect data as it passes over the Internet. For complete details about online banking security, check out Chapters 11 and 12.

2. **Go to the QuickBooks Online Banking Center**.

   If it isn't already running, start the QuickBooks software. Then open the Online Banking Center dialog box by doing one of the following:

   • From the menu bar, choose Online⇨Online Banking⇨Online Banking Center.

   • From the QuickBooks Navigator screen, click the Checking and Credit Cards tab and then click the Online Banking icon (the dollar bill with a lightning bolt in the middle).

   QuickBooks displays the Online Banking Center dialog box. (Refer to Figure 10-3.)

3. **Select your bank from the Financial Institution drop-down list box.**

   QuickBooks updates the contents of the Online Banking Center dialog box to show the queue of requests pending for the selected bank.

4. **Review your outgoing transactions and edit them if necessary.**

   It's a good idea to review the transactions that you're about to send, especially when you send bill payments. To review the details associated with each transaction, highlight the entry by clicking it in the Items to Send list and then clicking the Edit button. QuickBooks takes you to the form displaying that transaction so that you can edit it. For example, Figure 10-4 shows a pending bill payment open for editing. Click OK to return to the Online Banking Center.

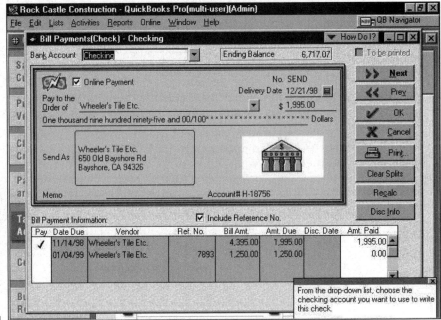

Figure 10-4:
Editing a transaction in the Online Banking Center queue.

I discuss entering bill payments in the "Paying Bills Online with QuickBooks" section later in this chapter.

5. **Select which pending items to send to the bank.**

   A check mark beside an item in the Items to Send list indicates that QuickBooks will send it to the bank for processing during the next online banking session. Clicking an item in the list toggles the check mark on or off.

6. **Click the Send button to send the transactions to your bank.**

   The Send button is the one with the yellow lightning bolt. Quicken displays a dialog box asking for your Online Banking PIN.

7. **Enter your PIN and click Send.**

   After receiving the correct PIN from you, QuickBooks executes the pending transactions in the Online Banking Center queue. The program displays a series of messages to keep you informed of the status of the connection to your bank.

8. After it completes its assigned tasks, QuickBooks disconnects from the bank and displays a summary of transactions that just occurred.

The Online Transmission Summary dialog box appears, as shown in Figure 10-5. In addition to the transactions that you initiated from the Online Banking Center, the summary lists any other transactions that have occurred since your last connection (such as automated transactions to pay the monthly fee for the bill-payment service).

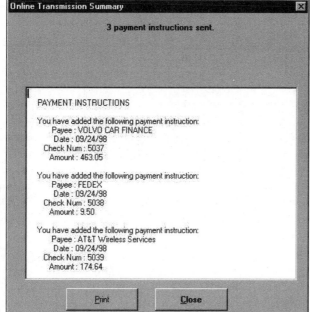

Figure 10-5:
Online
Banking
Center
queue
confirmation
report.

9. Click Close to dismiss the Online Transmission Summary dialog box.

When QuickBooks completes its update process, it returns to the Online Banking Center. At this point, if QuickBooks downloaded updated account information, you have the opportunity to review it before posting it into your QuickBooks registers. In addition to making sure that the transactions are correct, this is your opportunity to attach category information to the transactions downloaded from your bank.

Online banking users often wonder, "Were the instructions that I sent via the Online Banking Center processed?" The way QuickBooks manages the online banking process leaves little doubt. If something goes wrong, QuickBooks lets you know about it. For example, the warning shown in Figure 10-6 appeared after I lost the connection to my Internet service provider while I was in the middle of sending a few online payment instructions. This warning clears up any questions that you may have when you're disconnected or are otherwise wondering whether your transaction was completed. If your transaction wasn't completed, you receive a warning box, and you simply resubmit the transaction. If you don't receive the warning, you can assume that your transaction was fine. The QuickBooks procedures are very thorough when handling any online trouble.

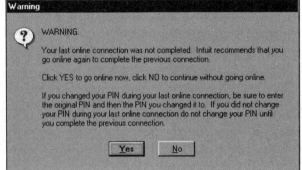

Figure 10-6:
Lost
connection
warning
dialog box.

Many online banking software users develop a routine that they follow when exchanging online information with their banks. For example, my routine is as follows:

- Connect with my bank and receive updated online statement information and balances before I do anything else

- Create my bill payment and funds transfer requests

- Reconnect with my bank and upload my requests

Using QuickStatements for balance inquiries

QuickBooks maintains a running balance in each of the account registers that it maintains. For example, each checking, savings, credit card, and money market account maintains a balance in the QuickBooks software based on the transactions that are posted to each account.

By going online, you can update your statement detail with QuickStatements, which updates your register balances. When you go online, you also retrieve the available balance according to your bank's computers. The difference between your register balance and online balance for a given account is the sum of the transactions that have not yet posted to your account, unless a mix-up occurred at the bank.

A QuickStatement lists the transactions that have occurred and posted to your accounts since your last download. A request for QuickStatements from each of your online accounts automatically appears in the Online Banking Center's Items to Send list.

When you go online, the software grabs any account information detail that has been posted to your account since your last download. When the information comes back to the Online Banking Center, you can click and view entries in QuickStatements in the Items Received from Financial Institution screen. This screen provides you with an opportunity to review the information before it's posted to your registers.

Transferring funds

You say that you want to transfer funds from one online account to another? Yep, QuickBooks can do that. All you have to do is fill in a simple Transfer Funds form, like so:

1. **From the menu bar, choose Activities⟳Transfer Money. Or click the Checking and Credit Cards tab in the QuickBooks Navigator and then click Transfer Money.**

   QuickBooks displays the Transfer Funds between Accounts window, shown in Figure 10-7.

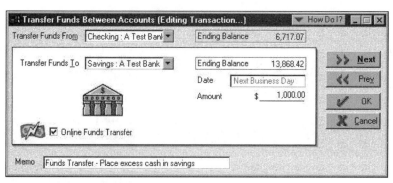

Figure 10-7:
The
Transfer
Funds
between
Accounts
window.

2. **Select the account from which you want to transfer funds in the Transfer Funds from drop-down list box.**

3. **Select the destination account in the Transfer Funds to drop-down list box.**

No, you can't move money between personal and business accounts

Uncle Sam and his tax code aren't very open to mixing personal and business funds. So transfers between personal and business accounts generally are not allowed by the bank. *Sole proprietorships* (businesses that are solely owned by a single individual and are not incorporated) are usually the only business form that can transfer between business and personal accounts, because all the funds are shared by the same person. Some banks prohibit such transfers even for sole proprietorships, so you may want to clarify this policy with your bank.

4. **Enter the effective date of the transfer in the Date box.**

5. **Enter the amount of the transfer on the Amount line.**

6. **Click the Online Funds Transfer check box.**

   Make sure that a check mark appears in this check box if you want your transaction to be an online transaction. (If you don't check that box, you need to transfer the money in some other way, such as using an ATM or — dare I say it? — actually visiting the bank branch.)

7. **Enter a note in the Memo text box if desired.**

8. **Click OK.**

   QuickBooks records the transaction in the appropriate account registers and adds the transfer request to the queue of pending items in the Online Banking Center.

Completing the Transfer Funds between Accounts form doesn't actually transfer the money between accounts. That doesn't happen until you transmit the request to the bank for processing. QuickBooks adds the transfer request to the queue in the Online Banking Center, but you have to remember to go to the Online Banking Center and send the request to the bank.

Paying Bills Online with QuickBooks

For me, paying bills online is one of the coolest things to come along in a long time. I *hate* writing paper checks and digging through my desk for stamps.

Using QuickBooks, paying bills is very easy. Just tell the software who, how much, and when to pay. Like funds transfer, the process of paying bills online is almost identical to entering handwritten checks (or having QuickBooks print checks for you). The following sections give you all the details about how to pay your bills online.

Paying bills online is like issuing any other payment. If you decide to use online bill payment for your business, use the same accounting procedures and safeguards that you use for issuing checks. Just keep in mind that transmitting a bill-payment instruction is the same as signing a check in terms of the way your bank looks at the process.

Entering bills

For many companies, paying bills is a part of the accounts payable process, and that procedure begins with entering your bills into QuickBooks. Entering bills into QuickBooks isn't really an integral part of the online bill-payment process, but entering bills and then paying them with online bill payments just seems so natural that I think of the two features together.

To begin entering bills into QuickBooks, choose Activities⇨Enter Bills from the menu bar or click the Purchases and Vendors tab in the QuickBooks Navigator window and then click the Enter Bills icon. Either method opens the Enter Bills window, as shown in Figure 10-8. Just fill in the on-screen form with information from the bill you received and then click OK. QuickBooks records the bill in its accounts payable area. Then you can use the QuickBooks Pay Bills feature to create online bill payments.

Figure 10-8: The Enter Bills window.

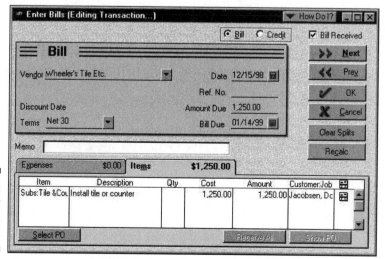

Paying your bills from the Pay Bills window

After you enter your bills into QuickBooks, you can use the Pay Bills function to pay them. It's a fast and convenient way to pay several bills at one time. And you can pay those bills with online bill payments in addition to paying them with paper checks or credit cards. Here are the steps:

1. **From the QuickBooks menu bar, choose Activities⇨Pay Bills, or click the Purchases and Vendors tab in the QuickBooks Navigator and then click the Pay Bills icon.**

   The Pay Bills dialog box appears, as shown in Figure 10-9.

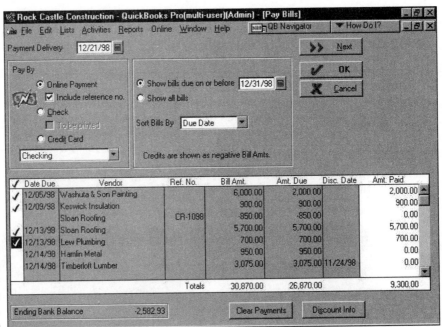

Figure 10-9: The Pay Bills window.

2. **In the Pay by area, click the Online Payment option and select the account (that you want to use to pay the bills) by selecting it from the drop-down list box.**

   Make sure that you choose the bank account that you enabled for online bill payment.

3. **Enter the due date in the Payment Delivery text box.**

   This is the date when the payment should reach the payee, not the date when you want the bank to begin processing the payment.

QuickBooks defaults to the earliest possible date (usually four days after the current date). You can change the date to any later date.

4. Select bills for payment by clicking in the check mark column.

You can select one or several bills for payment.

5. Click OK (and then click OK again to confirm, if necessary).

QuickBooks creates online bill payments to pay each of the bills you selected. The program enters transactions in the appropriate account registers and places bill-payment requests in the Items to Send queue in the Online Banking Center; those requests will be ready for you the next time you go online.

6. Go to the Online Banking Center and send your payment.

You can postpone this step until later — after you define other payments and transfer requests — but don't forget about it. Refer back to "Visiting the Online Banking Center" section for instructions.

Making online payments by using the Write Checks feature

If you don't want to go through the two-step process of entering bills and then paying bills, you can also use the QuickBooks Write Checks feature to create online bill payments. If you've ever filled out a paper check, you only need to take one look at the on-screen form in the Write Checks window (shown in Figure 10-10) to know how to use this feature. Follow these steps:

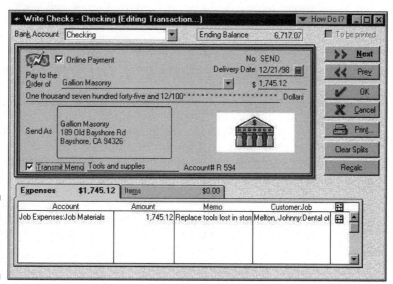

Figure 10-10:
The Write
Checks
window.

1. **From the menu bar, choose Activities➪Write Checks, or click the Checking and Credit Cards tab in the QuickBooks Navigator and then click the Write Checks icon.**

   The Write Checks window appears. (Refer to Figure 10-10.)

2. **Select the bank account that you want to use from the Bank Account drop-down list box.**

   Make sure that you choose the bank account that you enabled for online bill payment.

3. **Click to place a check mark in the Online Payment check box.**

   The Online Payment check box tells QuickBooks that you want to make this an online payment instead of a printed check.

4. **Fill in the check.**

   You've probably done this before and remember the drill. Type the payee's name on the Pay to the Order of line or click the drop-down arrow and select the payee from the drop-down list box. Enter the amount of the payment on the $ line and the due date on the Delivery Date line. If you want to add a memo, check the Transmit Memo box and type the memo. Notice that the check number is SEND, which confirms that this is an online payment.

5. **Enter expense categories on the Expenses tab below the check.**

6. **Click OK (and click OK again to confirm, if necessary).**

   QuickBooks adds the payment to the Items to Send queue in the Online Banking Center and adds transactions to the appropriate account registers.

7. **Don't forget to go to the Online Banking Center and send the payment request to the bank for processing.**

Entering payee (vendor) information

When you pay a bill online, you need to ensure that QuickBooks has all the important information about the person or business to whom you're sending a payment. QuickBooks draws the information that it needs from your regular Vendor List. However, if you attempt to create an online bill payment to a payee that doesn't have complete information available in the Vendor List, QuickBooks prompts you to enter the missing data before it completes the online payment.

For example, if you attempt to make an online payment to Kershaw Computer Services and QuickBooks determines that it doesn't have an address and account number on file, the program displays the Edit Vendor dialog box with the Address Info tab selected, as shown in Figure 10-11. You need to fill in the missing address there and enter the account number on the Additional Info tab (shown in Figure 10-12) as well.

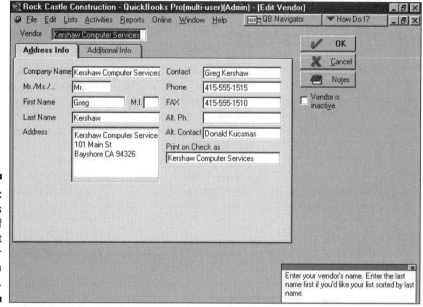

Figure 10-11:
The Address Info tab of the Edit Vendor information window.

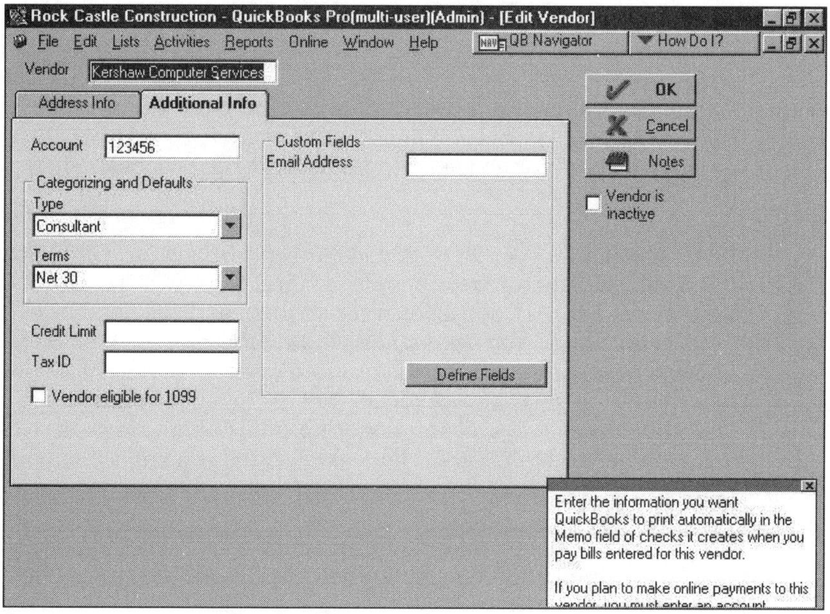

Figure 10-12:
The Additional Info tab of the Edit Vendor information window.

After supplying the missing information, click OK to close the Edit Vendor dialog box. QuickBooks updates the payee's information in the Vendor List and uses that information to complete the online bill-payment request.

Using the QuickBooks Online Payroll Functions

In several of its previous versions and in version 6.0, QuickBooks offers small businesses the ability to manage the process of creating payroll checks, while setting aside and paying payroll-tax liabilities. QuickBooks also enables users to download the latest tax tables (those charts that you use to calculate how much of an employee's paycheck should be withheld and how much should go to the employee).

With QuickBooks 6.0, you still have the opportunity to update your payroll information online, and you can also submit your payroll for online processing and payment, much like the online bill-payment feature.

Processing a payroll with QuickBooks

QuickBooks provides a very robust payroll system. You can pay full-time staff members and part-time hourly employees with the QuickBooks payroll service. QuickBooks also offers a great feature for inputting the hourly activity of all employees and attaching that information to specific jobs and projects. If you have employees who earn both fixed and hourly fees, this feature is very helpful.

All the payroll functions are available through the QuickBooks Navigator on the Payroll and Time tab. When you set up QuickBooks, create an Employee database record for each employee. Repeat the process each time you hire a new employee.

If you recall from the last time you started working for a company, you filled out a federal (and for most people, a state) form W-4. This form asked for your name, address, social security number, and the number of tax withholding accounts. You need all this information for each employee when you create a new employee record. You also need to know whether the employee is an hourly or salaried worker, as well as the employee's pay rate. QuickBooks can track all sorts of other information, such as sick days, vacation days, commissions, and so on. After you enter your employees, you can start paying them.

You can create payroll checks by selecting the Create Paychecks option from the Payroll and Time tab in the QuickBooks Navigator. The process to create paychecks is very similar to the process for paying traditional bills; after all, payroll checks are essentially just payments.

Trying the QuickBooks tax table service

The QuickBooks tax table service is a tool that you can use to keep the most current payroll-withholding information in your version of QuickBooks. It's *very* important to stay current with your company's tax withholding obligations; even the most minor infractions can lead to penalties and interest on incorrect amounts of taxes that you pay late.

When you purchase QuickBooks, you get a few free tax updates, after which you have to pay a charge. The tax table service includes federal and state taxes. If you have a company with employees in more than one state, having an online way to update this information is very convenient and well worth the nominal cost.

Submitting your payroll tax information online

One of the QuickBooks announcements that coincided with the release of QuickBooks 6.0 is the availability of a new service to submit payroll information online to a third party, who does the following:

- Performs direct withdrawal of payroll money from your company account
- Places direct deposit payroll checks into your employee accounts
- Collects, forwards, and files the paperwork and the tax money that you send to the federal and state governments
- Prepares end-of-year documents reporting income to the government and sends form W2 to each of your employees
- Updates your QuickBooks registers for each transaction

This service is very high-powered stuff for your average small business! The payroll submission service was in beta testing as I put the finishing touches on this book, and Intuit is already taking names of companies that want to go online to use the service.

Financial considerations: When does the money come out of your account?

All online payroll submission services have one big drawback: They take all the money out of your account two days before payroll is due. For example, if you pay your employees on the 10th and 25th of the month, all your payroll money will go out of your accounts on the 8th and 23rd. This includes the net pay that you have to pay your employees on payday *plus* the taxes. Normally, you don't have to turn in those taxes until a few weeks after the pay day.

The frequency with which you have to pay your payroll tax withholding money depends in large part on how much you pay. My company turns in payroll withholding money once a month on the 15th day of the month after the payment is made. In other words, if I pay the taxes myself, I get to hold half the tax money for a month and the other half for two weeks before it has to be paid. During that time, that money is earning interest in one of my accounts. If I use an online payroll submission service (such as the company that does this task for QuickBooks), that service gets to hold the money until it is due — in addition to the amounts that it charges for this service. Your company has to make a choice between the loss of interest on the payroll money and the convenience of using the online payroll service.

Selecting the Right Version of QuickBooks

There are two versions of QuickBooks 6.0: the regular edition and the Pro edition. The Pro edition includes all the features of the regular edition plus more elaborate job costing, estimates and bids, time tracking, and the capability for multiple users to work with the software simultaneously. While you're thinking about selecting accounting software, you might want to consider Quicken Home and Business, which has the same features as the Quicken Deluxe PFM package but also includes simple invoicing and accounts receivable capabilities, accounts payable functions, and an assortment of reports and graphs that are appropriate for small business use. Quicken Home and Business isn't as powerful as QuickBooks, but it may be all you need if you run a very small business or you're a self-employed independent contractor.

Exploring Other Business Accounting Software

QuickBooks is the best selling product in the small to mid-sized business accounting market, but it isn't the only product available for that market. Several other accounting programs are available that may be a better match for your accounting and bookkeeping needs. As this book goes to press, the latest versions of QuickBooks (and its smaller sibling Quicken Home and Business) are the only small-business accounting programs offering full support for online banking and online bill payment. However, look for that situation to change as other software developers add more online features to upcoming versions of their products.

If you're looking for an accounting program, check out the following:

- **Quicken Home and Business:** Essentially, this program is the Quicken Deluxe personal finance manager software with the addition of simple invoicing and accounts receivable and accounts payable features. It supports online banking and online bill payment, but not online payroll.

- **Peachtree Complete Accounting:** Peachtree makes several small business accounting programs, ranging from Peachtree First Accounting to Peachtree Windows Accounting to Peachtree Complete Accounting. The programs are very roughly comparable to QuickBooks in general scope. The current versions have limited online bill-payment features, support for online payroll services, and an interesting feature that links the accounting software to easy Web-site design and creation.

- **One-Write Plus:** This software is a computerized version of the manual bookkeeping system of the same name that has been a favorite of small businesses for many years. No online banking features are in the current version, but it does support links to Web-page creation (like its Peachtree brethren).

- **MYOB:** MYOB stands for Mind Your Own Business, an interesting name for a small-business accounting package from Best Ware. MYOB is a nice, easy-to-use accounting program, but the current version (8.0) doesn't support online banking or bill payment.

Part IV
Addressing
Security Issues

The 5th Wave   By Rich Tennant

"Rags has learned a new trick — he who buries the file password to the online banking account rules the house."

In this part . . .

Let's face it. A lot of people are concerned about the security of their money and personal information as they consider online banking. I don't want to give away too much of the plot of this part in the first few pages, but I provide enough evidence to help you feel comfortable with the security of online banking. I also show you many precautions and security measures that you can employ to further guarantee the security of your transactions. Now I've said too much!

Chapter 11

Examining Online Banking Security

I am convinced that online banking is much safer than some of the more conventional methods used by consumers to access banking information. I also believe that online banking is more secure than most other forms of electronic commerce. But my convictions are beside the point. The important point is that you're probably not going to feel confident about using online banking until you share my belief that it's safe — and right now, you probably have some concerns about that.

So where do people's concerns with the safety of online banking come from? Most of the concern is simply fear of the unknown. Combine that fear with some widely publicized stories of hijacked credit card numbers and invasions of privacy, and it's only natural that you would be concerned about the privacy and security of personal information as sensitive as the details of your bank account balances and financial transactions.

Most people use the Internet without really understanding how it works. You can take the steps to get online, type in a Web address or two, and view a newspaper from 3,000 miles away. With a few more keystrokes, you can look at the local grade-school lunch menus. You don't need to know the technical details that explain how the information made its way to you in order to accept the fact that the Internet is doing its job; you can see the result you asked for on the screen.

As long as you're viewing only news and general information on the Web, reliability isn't a big issue. If you try to access a popular Web site and the connection doesn't work, you can easily accept that the problem is caused by excess traffic or a minor glitch somewhere between here and there. You don't give the failure a second thought. But if it's your personal financial transactions you're trying to view, then any system blip, no matter how minor, can cause fear that something is really wrong. You may start to wonder whether the bank has lost your account records, or whether some malicious hacker has tapped into your communication with the bank and diverted the information for some sinister purpose.

The reality is that online banking is safe. I hope that this chapter puts your fears to rest by familiarizing you with some of the security precautions that a bank takes to ensure the safety of your money.

Misperceptions about Threats to Your Money from Online Banking

When I discuss security with potential and current online banking consumers, I ask about their specific concerns. Most frequently, consumers fear that making their regular bank accounts accessible for online banking increases an unauthorized person's ability to gain access to their money, and to information about their financial history and habits. The following list presents these concerns and gives evidence showing why they are unfounded:

- ✔ **Customers believe that someone can move money out of an account without the account holder or anyone else knowing about it.** For the following three ironclad reasons, people can't move money out of your account without you or the bank knowing about it:

  - • **All transactions are logged.** Online banking is just an extension of traditional banking. The only difference is that instead of going to an ATM or a branch to transfer funds between accounts or to pay a bill through the mail, you make the request from your computer. All transactions — including all online transactions — are logged as they occur and appear on your statement like anything else that happens with your bank account.

    If you ever have any question about a transaction, simply notify the bank within a reasonable amount of time after you discover an error on your statement, and they will take the appropriate steps to rectify the problem. By using online banking, you have the ability to check your account balance frequently and see a list of transaction details, which actually means that you have a better chance of discovering a problem early and getting it corrected quickly.

- **Transfers are limited to your accounts.** If someone did gain access to your online banking ID and password and wanted to transfer money, that person would be able to transfer money only into another one of your accounts that has been enabled for online banking. This transfer may be a hassle, but your money could not leave your accounts via funds transfer. And, of course, these transactions would be logged for easy review.

- **All bill payments create a paper trail.** Online banking bill payments require much more information than a regular check. So if someone stole your ID and password and wrote out a check, that person would have to enter *a lot* of information. In addition to the name of the person to whom the check would be payable, the thief would have to provide a valid address to which the post office could deliver the check. All this information would be readily available to provide clues about what happened with the transaction. As a result, thieves would have much more difficulty getting away with making fraudulent online payments than they would by forging checks using lost or stolen paper checks.

✔ **Customers think that someone can learn about their financial position and habits by accessing their online banking information.** Fortunately, banks take precautions to ensure that it is practically impossible for an unauthorized person to gain access to your account information at the bank. And banks use the same strict security to ensure that online banking systems do nothing to compromise the protection of your accounts. Furthermore, if someone managed to intercept your encrypted online banking data as it traveled between the bank and your computer, that data would be indecipherable and, therefore, useless. But perhaps the most important reason that activating online banking won't compromise the security of your financial information is that most of your financial information is already available to interested individuals and companies from other sources, which happen to be easier to access.

Most people are shocked to find that their financial information is so readily available by means easier than computer piracy. For better or worse, much of your financial information is available from legitimate sources. People with good or bad intentions don't need to hack into your online banking account or the bank's computer, because they can uncover your personal financial data and habits (such as whether you have a mortgage or how many months are left on your car loan) in much easier ways.

The junk mail that you almost certainly receive provides ample proof that important information about you is widely available. Many companies solicit people for home equity lines of credit, new car loans, low-interest credit cards, and a host of nonfinancial products. Much of the information that the soliciting companies need is a matter of public record (such as real estate and property tax records), and they can obtain other information from credit reporting agencies, magazine publishers, and mortgage companies.

It's not just the mortgage lenders and credit card companies that have access to your credit information. With the popularity of on-the-spot financing and fast credit approvals, many merchants — from car dealers to appliance stores — have the ability to retrieve credit reports with software loaded on a PC. All that is necessary for your credit information to be compromised is a momentary lapse in the merchant's control over access to that machine.

If this fact disturbs you, you are not alone — but this situation really isn't an online banking issue. The bottom line is that your use of online banking has no impact on the amount of information available about you and your finances.

How the Pyramid of Protection Keeps Your Money Safe

Online banking security isn't something that a bank does at its main office. It's more than just the security precautions at the bank's computer center and the security features of the software on your computer. It's all of this and more. Online banking security is built one layer on top of the next, in a pattern that I like to call the *pyramid of protection* (shown in Figure 11-1).

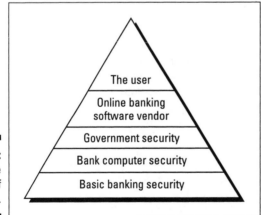

Figure 11-1:
The
pyramid of
protection.

The pyramid of protection is an illustration device that I use to explain the layers of security protecting online banking. The pyramid consists of five levels, with the bank's basic security at the base of the pyramid. The other security levels are the bank's computer security, government banking security, online banking software security, and your own personal security measures (at the pinnacle of the pyramid). The following sections explain each security level in the pyramid.

Bank security: The backbone of banking culture

The bank's physical security includes the locks on the doors, the guards in the lobbies, the vaults, and the surveillance cameras. All of these are visible evidence of the bank's efforts to ensure that your deposits are secure. But the bank's security efforts extend far beyond these obvious trappings.

A major part of a bank's culture is to be safe and secure. From the way buildings are designed to the way they hire people, banks add security into just about everything they do. For example, when I visit banks for meetings and to work on projects, the security is very rigid. It's not uncommon for my laptop computer and briefcase to be searched when I go in and out of a bank office or computer center. The use of keycards, locked doors, and video surveillance is common in bank computer centers. Often, bank security policies dictate that I can't go past the guard in the lobby until the person I'm visiting comes down to the guard desk and signs me in to the building and escorts me to the meeting. All these security measures combine to prevent unauthorized access to your money or to any information (such as passwords and account numbers) that could be used to steal your money.

When I visit with my nonbank clients, the security culture is distinctly different. Yes, receptionists are in the main lobby, and I must usually sign a log and get a visitor badge before entering. But I am rarely required to have an escort while in the building. This is not to say that nonbanks do not have security policies. Banks just make stricter security an integral part of their culture.

Security of the bank's computerized systems and transactions

Banks spend a lot of time and money to secure their computer systems. Most banks have a very detailed security policy to manage their computer systems and network security needs. The security policy outlines the different ways that the bank will and will not connect its networks to the outside world and, once connected to outside networks such as the Internet, to what degree access will be allowed. One of the tools used to implement a computer security policy is a firewall.

A *firewall* is a computer that protects the computers and data inside a company-wide network from access by any outside resource or network such as the Internet. The firewall sits at the point where the network connects to the outside world and acts like a guard at the gate, checking each delivery attempting to pass through against a list of what's acceptable and what's banned. Anything that doesn't meet the strict specifications of the security policy doesn't make it past the firewall. Firewalls allow networks to be connected to the Internet, while maintaining the security of the network by protecting it from unauthorized access from the outside.

Why banks need a firewall between their systems and the Internet

The network that eventually became the Internet was originally designed to be used inside highly secure government-owned installations back in the 1960s. These locations included military sites and research facilities. The thinking at that time was that there was no need for security features in the network itself because only government employees and contractors were allowed access to the network from within highly classified locations.

The tools and software that ran the early Internet were copied by the academic community to interconnect universities, nonclassified research sites, and other data sources, linking them into a network where they could share files and collaborate on projects. Again, use was limited to a select group of academic researchers and the like, so security issues were not a priority.

The Internet sort of took root and grew until it was hooked to almost every college and university in the country and began to spread to businesses as well. The tools and policies for sharing data over the early Internet became the accepted standard as the network grew and expanded into the worldwide network that we refer to as the Internet.

The only problem is, there wasn't an opportunity to add security features back into the Internet. This lack of security means that anyone with a network with sensitive information on it — most companies and every bank — must install some sort of security device to protect their network from the Internet. Firewalls were designed to fill this need.

The best way to illustrate the functionality of a firewall is to draw a comparison with the security guard at the local furniture warehouse where my wife and I just purchased a new chair for our TV room.

When we went to the warehouse to pick up the chair, we weren't able to drive on the lot, grab a forklift, and run through the warehouse looking for our chair. We had to start with the security guard at the warehouse's front gate. I drove up, presented my receipt from the showroom to show that I truly had furniture to pick up, and presented my driver's license so that the guard could verify who I was.

I then proceeded into the lot, where we parked and went to the will-call desk. I presented my receipt and driver's license again, and the clerk made a call into the warehouse authorizing one of the forklift drivers to get our chair and bring it to the loading dock. The clerk stamped our paperwork, and we waited by the car. We had no idea how large the warehouse was or how the furniture was organized, but that had no bearing on our chair so we didn't care. A few minutes later, the forklift rolled through the door and placed the chair on the dock. With a little help, we loaded the chair into the back of our car and were on our way out. We made one last stop at the gate, where the guard checked our paperwork and our trunk, logging our visit into his journal as we headed home.

A firewall works the same way. For example, suppose that you want to use online banking to check the current balance in your checking account. After logging on to your bank's Web site by entering your ID and password, you make a request for your balance and press the Enter key. The request goes to the bank, where a firewall just outside the bank's network verifies who you are by using your password; then the firewall sends a message to a computer inside the bank to get your specific balance information (and nothing else). The information returns to the firewall, where the firewall checks to make sure that the specific kind of information is permitted to leave the premises, and then forwards your balance back to the party that requested it (you). In seconds, the information that you requested shows up on your screen.

At no time in the process did you ever have direct access to any computer on the inside of the bank. The technical term for this security setup is a *proxy-based firewall;* the firewall serves as a go-between (or *proxy*) between you and the bank.

As you decide which online banking method is best for you, look for a mention of security and firewalls in the sales and informational literature at your bank. Many of these details are covered at the bank's Web site. If you still have a question about your bank's security, call or e-mail the bank's customer service group and ask to talk to someone from the team dedicated to online banking issues.

Government security regulations

The government provides the next level in the pyramid of protection. The government regulates and oversees banks to make sure that they are sound and functioning in a safe manner. All banks operate under the watchful eye of bank examiners who audit the bank's operations and ensure that the bank follows government regulations and meets strict standards. Nowadays, computer and online banking security issues are a growing part of a bank examiner's audit, contributing to the examiner's opinion of the overall soundness of the bank. Two important examples of these government security measures are FDIC insurance and Regulation E.

FDIC insurance

The federal government does more than protect bank customers indirectly by enforcing standards on the banking industry. The government also protects customers by insuring bank deposits against loss or failure of the bank. Whether you bank online with your PC, use an ATM machine, or conduct transactions only during a personal visit to the bank lobby, FDIC insurance guarantees that your money is safe. The Federal Deposit Insurance Corporation protects the money that you deposit into your bank account up to $100,000. Online banking doesn't compromise your rights to this protection.

Regulation E

The federal government, with the help of Congress, has enacted a series of laws and regulations outlining every aspect of the banking industry. One of the most important regulations — known as Regulation E — for anyone planning to use online banking has to do with consumer protection related to the use of Electronic Funds Transfers.

You may already be familiar with the protections Regulation E affords, but you're probably not familiar with the name. Regulation E is the law stating that if you notify your bank within two days of learning of an unauthorized use of your credit card, your liability is limited to $50. (See, you have heard of it before, haven't you?)

What you may not know is that Regulation E also covers online banking transactions. So if someone gains unauthorized access to your accounts through online banking — despite all the security measures — and makes an unauthorized transaction, your liability is no more than $50. You do need to report this unauthorized access to your bank within 48 hours of the time that you become aware of a fraudulent transaction.

In other words, the same government regulation that protects you when you use a credit card (or any Electronic Funds Transfer as described in the U.S. code for Regulation E) protects you when you make online banking transactions.

It's nice to know that you're protected by Regulation E, but what's even better is knowing that you'll probably never need it. Online banking customers very rarely have problems that require resolution under the terms of Regulation E.

Thanks to the power of the Internet, you can visit the National Archives and Records Administration Web site and read the entire text of Regulation E. It's more than a federal regulation; it's a powerful sleep aid. You can find it at:

```
www.access.gpo.gov/nara/cfr
```

At the bottom of their Web page, you can enter search words. To find information on Regulation E, enter 12CFR205 and from the search response look for the file with the following description:

```
12CFR205-- PART 205--ELECTRONIC FUND TRANSFERS
(REGULATION E)--Table of Contents
```

Security at the online banking software level

The next layer of the pyramid of protection is the security features that are part of the online banking software and its implementation. Online banking software (and its supporting components) protects your data as it moves between the bank and your computer. The diagram in Figure 11-2 shows the main components of the online banking transaction process. Read on to find out about the security features along the way.

Figure 11-2:
The three
main
components
of an online
banking
system.

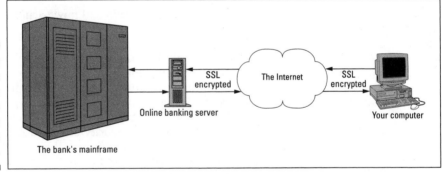

Securing the bank's computer system

When a bank offers an online banking service, it's not really granting you direct access to its mainframe computer systems. In most cases, the bank installs a group of separate computers that stand between the mainframe computer and the network that will deliver the data to your computer. (Those computers are represented by the online banking server illustrated in Figure 11-2.) The online banking server is the device used to assemble and prepare the data for online banking. The online banking server may also serve as a firewall, or it may work in conjunction with a separate firewall computer. (See the "Security of the bank's computerized systems and transactions" section, earlier in this chapter, for an explanation of how firewalls work.) Like firewalls, online banking servers obtain information from the bank's computers on your behalf, protecting the bank's mainframe computer from direct outside access by you or anyone else.

Protecting data that passes between you and the bank's computer

The online banking server not only protects the bank's mainframe computer system as it processes online banking transactions and requests, but it also plays a role in protecting your data as it travels between the bank and your computer. Usually, software capable of supporting the *Secure Socket Layer (SSL) protocol* is loaded on the online banking server.

SSL is a method for encrypting (or scrambling) data as it passes over unsecured networks such as the Internet. Your data is encrypted by the SSL software on the online banking server and decrypted (unscrambled) by the SSL software in your Web browser. SSL encryption guarantees that your data will be unintelligible to anyone that may come into contact with it as it passes over the Internet.

See Chapter 12 for the details of SSL encryption and how to make sure that your Web browser supports it.

SSL encryption is used for almost all Web-based online banking and is incorporated into some personal finance manager (PFM) software as well. Some PFM software and bank-branded software use RSA encryption (which is similar to SSL but not exactly the same) or some other encryption system. A few online banking programs (usually the older packages) do not employ encryption, but rely instead on the relative security of data traveling on a private data network. Personally, I'm more confident in the security of encrypted data on an open network such as the Internet than I am of unencrypted data on a private network.

In Chapter 3, I explain the computer and software requirements for online banking, and I mention that you need a Web browser that is compatible with your bank. The compatibility issue with a Web browser is whether it supports the level of SSL encryption required by the bank when using that bank's online banking service.

When you access a bank Web site (or a portion of the bank's Web site) that is running on a secure server running SSL, you should see a little security icon on your Web browser. Figure 11-3 shows an online banking Web site in a Netscape Navigator Web browser window. The small lock in the lower-left corner indicates that SSL is active.

Figure 11-4 shows the Microsoft Internet Explorer Web browser displaying a page from a secure server connection. The small lock symbol indicating that SSL is active is located in the center of the status bar at the bottom of the window.

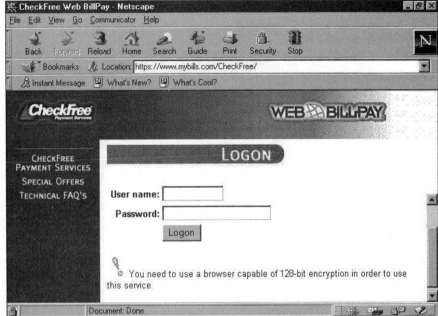

Figure 11-3:
An SSL-protected banking Web site viewed with Netscape Navigator with SSL encryption active.

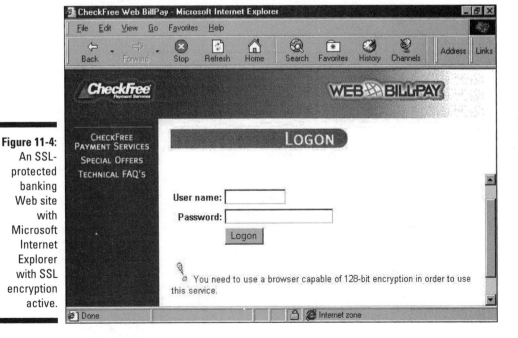

Figure 11-4:
An SSL-protected banking Web site with Microsoft Internet Explorer with SSL encryption active.

If you have the latest version of Netscape Navigator or Microsoft Internet Explorer, your Web browser is almost certainly compatible with the encryption and security of most online banking sites. Banks have been very good about keeping customers informed about which browser they need, usually within the first few pages of their Web sites. Most banks also include a link that you can click to get the latest browser if you need an updated version.

Security that the user enforces

The last component of online banking security and the pyramid of protection is the user — that's right, you and I. The preceding section explains that if the bank uses SSL to secure data transmissions, the data will be safe as it passes from the bank to your computer. The final step in the online banking process takes place in your computer. So you need to consider security issues relating to your own PC.

Unless you work for a large company or government agency, the issue of desktop security may not be a frequent topic of discussion. In fact, many computer users never consider the concept of security at their desktop.

Unfortunately, the weakest link in the online banking process is at personal computers. Granted, the risk of an unauthorized person using your home computer isn't likely to be huge. After all, only your family will have access to it. The biggest threats to a home computer are things like spilled soft drinks and kids who delete your files to make room to install the latest game. On the other hand, you may want to consider locking up the computer if you host a large party or have other people in the house without direct supervision.

One step that you can take is to activate the start-up log-on feature that is available on most computers. It requires you to enter a password in order to start the computer. It's not a strong protection, but it will often deter casual attempts to access your system.

A bigger security risk exists because people can access their online banking functions from more and more places. Imagine that you have Internet access at work and you have just logged on to your bank's site to do some online banking. The phone rings, and you're called away to an urgent meeting. If you don't stop and take a moment to log off and close your Web browser, your computer and account information will be accessible to anyone that walks by. If you use a PFM program, you don't even need to be logged on to the bank's Web site to expose your financial information. If you leave your computer unattended, someone could simply start the PFM and use it to browse through your account registers. Laptop computers are even more vulnerable.

I hope that you get the point that it's very important to secure the computers where you will be accessing your online banking information. The first and most important step is to be aware of the risk. Then security is mostly just a matter of taking a few common sense precautions.

Chapter 12

Employing Security Tools and Other Security Measures

*W*ould you feel comfortable getting your bank statement delivered on a postcard with your balance printed where it is clearly visible to anyone handling the postcard? Of course not! You expect private information to be delivered in a sealed envelope.

Sending a message over the Internet is like mailing a postcard. Just as a note on a postcard is visible to postal workers and others who handle the postcard, the content of a typical Internet message is visible to anyone who can read the address (which includes system administrators and other authorized, and perhaps unauthorized, people who come in contact with the message as it bounces from computer to computer during its journey across the network). No Internet envelopes hide the contents from view.

So software developers have had to come up with other ways to keep private information traveling on the Internet safe from prying eyes. This chapter is about the technology that most banks use to protect the privacy of online banking transactions.

Encrypting for Your Security

The lack of basic privacy safeguards for Internet messages (and that includes e-mail messages and Web-page content alike) may seem like a serious flaw. However, the lack of privacy really isn't a result of the Internet structure.

The Internet is simply the delivery mechanism for all sorts of messages. Just as the postal system delivers both postcards and letters (in sealed envelopes), the Internet can deliver plain-text messages (that are openly readable) and also messages that are encrypted to make them unreadable. *Encryption* (scrambling the contents of a message with a secret code) is a separate add-on feature and not an inherent part of the Internet structure itself, but it works nonetheless.

Most people are surprised to learn that, unlike the postal system, the Internet carries mostly plain-text messages (postcards) and relatively few encrypted messages (letters in sealed envelopes). In theory, this lack of security seems like a big problem, but in practice, it isn't so bad.

The truth of the matter is that intercepting nonsecure data on the Internet is definitely not a trivial task. One of the benefits of the Internet data transmission protocol is that individual *packets* (chunks of data) from the same transmission may take entirely different routes to the destination, and then those packets get reassembled on arrival. So even though it's theoretically possible to intercept data using a device called a packet sniffer, in practical terms it's not likely that an Internet snoop would get anything but disjointed fragments of messages. Intercepting raw data isn't so difficult — but locating and assembling anything useful is extremely difficult.

Still, as the business world started using the Internet, the need for security based on something more than the inconvenience of gaining unauthorized access to messages became an issue. As a result, several methods of encrypting data have been developed. *Encryption* protects data by scrambling it into a secret code that can only be *decrypted* (unscrambled) by the intended recipient. If an encrypted message gets intercepted by an unauthorized party, the message appears to be a meaningless jumble of gibberish.

Digging into the Secure Socket Layer

The majority of today's online businesses (including banks, credit unions, and savings and loans) protect sensitive data with encryption technology called *Secure Socket Layer (SSL)*. SSL is built into special, secure Web servers and into Web browser software. When your Web browser establishes contact with a secure Web server, SSL encrypts your data before sending it out over the Internet, and SSL then unscrambles the encrypted data at the other end.

Although SSL is primarily used to secure communications on the Web, the same (or very similar) technology is available for incorporating encryption capabilities into PFMs and other software. Even though I use SSL- and Web-based banking in the examples in this chapter, remember that you can get the same SSL protection when you use properly equipped PFM software and bank-branded software. But be sure to ask whether your online banking software uses encryption.

Technically speaking, SSL is a *protocol* (a fancy word for *method*) that manages the relationship between a *client* (the Web browser software that you run on your computer) and a *server* application (the software that manages online banking back at the bank). SSL enables secure commerce on the Internet by providing a standard method for managing the encryption process, taking what would normally be nonsecure information and making it secure for safe passage across the Internet.

How does SSL work?

SSL encrypts messages between you and your bank (or any other online merchant) by starting a session between the client (your computer) and the server (the bank's computer) to securely exchange secret numbers known as *keys*. The keys are then used in the mathematical operations that encrypt the messages going back and forth between you and the bank.

When you visit your bank's Web site and enter the online banking area, you have to identify yourself by logging on (which usually involves entering a user ID and password). When you connect to the online banking portion of your bank's Web site, the online banking server uses SSL to negotiate with your computer the details for encrypting and decrypting your private data during this session. The encrypting and decrypting uses numerical *keys*, generated by the software at the bank, which *lock up* (or *scramble*) the data before it leaves the bank and then unlock that data upon arrival at your computer. And, of course, the keys serve the same purpose when the process is reversed as you send information to your bank.

Encryption scrambles information numerically, based on the value of a key. This scrambling is possible because computers store and manipulate data (text and numbers alike) as numbers. SSL uses the key as a factor to conduct mathematical operations on the information, turning the information into an unrecognizable, encrypted message. SSL in your browser uses a complementary key to reverse the encryption process and decrypt the data into its original form. Without the key, no one can decipher that encrypted data. Using larger and more complex keys creates stronger security.

If someone other than you intercepts the information as it travels between you and the bank, the information appears as gibberish unless the interceptor can guess the number to use as the key to unlock the information. Hackers can't read your private information because the key numbers are so large that they are practically impossible to guess, even if the hacker uses a fast computer and special software programs for breaking codes. Breaking SSL encryption quickly enough to identify and then disrupt the current online banking session certainly isn't possible.

SSL uses one complex key for all encryption and decryption procedures during a single online banking session that you establish. When you log on to the bank's Web site later for another online banking session, SSL uses a totally different, random number as the key. So, if hackers managed to figure out one set of encryption keys from one online banking session, they couldn't use them to decrypt other messages in the future.

How strong is SSL?

Encryption and decryption techniques have been around for a long time. People who study such things have come up with ways to guess the key numbers used to decrypt a message by using computers to test different numbers until they find the correct key number. When encryption software uses a small number for a key, today's computers can break the encryption in relatively short order. Conversely, when encryption software uses a larger number as the key, more complicated calculations are required to break the code and more time and computer power are necessary to perform those calculations. As a result, encryption strength is measured by the size of the numbers used as the keys.

You can see the power of SSL in the large numbers that it uses to encrypt and decrypt numbers. SSL is available in several different key lengths, and those keys are measured by how many computer bits are needed to represent the key number. Early versions of SSL used keys that were 40-bit or 56-bit numbers, which would certainly qualify as very large numbers. But the news gets better for you (and worse for the hackers). The most common key length today — the one that your browser and your bank's software probably use — is a 128-bit number (which is absolutely *huge*). When a bank advertises its online banking with the phrase, "Our bank uses 128-bit encryption," this concept is what they're talking about.

Encryption keys that use 128-bit numbers are extremely hard to crack. Experts consider 128-bit keys to be the safest method for securing information passed over the Internet. To get a grip on just how large and complex 128-bit numbers are, think about the following examples:

✔ Suppose that you have a briefcase (like the one I got as a college graduation gift) that's secured by a three-wheel combination lock. Each wheel on the lock has 10 possible numbers. If you lose the combination to the lock, you would need to try each one of the 1,000 possible combinations to crack it open. If you could try one combination every second without stopping, you could try all the possible combinations in 16 to 17 minutes. (Hmm, I could have broken into that briefcase before the commencement address was over.)

If you could get a briefcase with a lock that had the same number of possible combinations as the SSL key that encrypts your online banking data, the lock would have 32 wheels with 16 digits each (or 39 wheels, most of them with 10 digits and some with fewer digits). If you could try one combination every second without stopping, you would need years (actually, millions of millennia) to go through all possible combinations. If you need to break into a briefcase with this type of lock, I recommend using a big screwdriver instead.

✔ Pretend that you have a penny — not a dollar, but a penny — for all the possible numbers that could make up your 128-bit key number. If you add up your pennies, you have enough money to buy every share of Microsoft stock, currently valued at about $250 billion, 54 trillion times. And you still have some money left over to pick up the entire IBM company a couple times over.

✔ If all the talk of trillions is just too hard to grasp, try this analogy: If each possible number in a 128-bit encryption key was a grain of sand, you would have a very big sandpile to play in — more than just enough for some elaborate sand castles. That much sand would make a whole beach or perhaps even a desert. It's not an infinite quantity, but it's one whopping big number.

Because of the sheer size of the numbers involved, cracking the encryption of data secured with a 128-bit SSL key mechanism is practically impossible. As a result, when you use SSL, your data is safe and secure even though it travels on the highly public network of the Internet.

The math behind SSL encryption

To understand the math behind the encryption process, remember that, in their day-to-day lives, people work with a decimal-based numbering system using the numbers 0 through 9. (The prefix *deci* stands for *ten*.) Almost all the devices that you interact with are based on the numbers 0 through 9. From the cash register at the local frozen custard stand to the altimeter in a jumbo-jet airplane, machines use the numbers 0 through 9. Just look at your car's odometer. After the far-right number reaches 9, it next turns to 0 and the number to its left increases by 1. Each number in the odometer can count 10 positions (0 to 9) before it has to roll over and start again.

The computers that you use on your desktops don't use the 0 through 9 decimal system. Instead, computers use the binary system of numbers. Computers reduce information to its smallest elements and place those tiny elements into *bits*. According to the binary system, every bit has a value of 1 or 0. So, if you use 128 bits to define an encryption key, you can have 2^{128} possible combinations. (That's 2 raised to the 128 power.) The number of possible combinations comes out to a staggering 340,282,366,920,938,000,000,000, 000,000,000,000,000. Most people don't even try to give names to numbers that big; they just call these numbers *astronomical*.

How far have the hackers come in cracking SSL?

Nothing gets a group of hackers more excited than a good, old-fashioned challenge to break a code. And Netscape challenged a group of hackers in order to prove the viability of the encryption method in SSL. In 1998, a group of computer scientists based in Europe answered the challenge and were able to decipher a message encoded with a 40-bit version of SSL. Well, kind of.

To crack the single message offered in the challenge, the group utilized 120 computer workstations and two supercomputers for eight days and nights before deciphering one SSL-encrypted message. They did not randomly go out, find a session on the Internet, assemble all the pieces of a message, and decipher anything while it was in progress. They were working on a sample message that was posted in its entirety on the Netscape Web site. This effort was driven by the computing power equivalent to using one computer capable of calculating one million instructions per second for 100 years.

Another group of computer scientists has recently made news by cracking a challenge message that was encrypted using a 56-bit key. They designed and built a special supercomputer (that cost a quarter of a million dollars) to do the job. Still, the effort took over 56 hours of continuous computer processing to crack a single short message.

Do you think that anyone would go to that much expense and effort to get a glimpse of your bank statement? Nah . . . I didn't think so.

To date, no one has cracked a message encrypted with a 128-bit key. In fact, encryption with 128-bit keys is so powerful that the U.S. government restricts the export of this level of encryption outside the United States and Canada because such strong encryption is classified as munitions — crazy, but true.

Implementing Security in Your Browser

So how do you know if you have all the software necessary to take advantage of 128-bit SSL security? The easiest way to find out is to visit your bank's Web site and see if it lets you in. Figure 12-1 shows you what happened when I tried to access a Web site that requires 128-bit encryption when the version of the browser software was only capable of supporting 40-bit encryption.

Figure 12-1:
A 128-bit secured Web site stopping a 40-bit Web browser from accessing the site.

The Web site offers several links to locations around the Internet where you can get a free copy of a Web browser that will support 128-bit encryption.

Get the latest Web browser software

If you don't have the latest browsers with 128-bit SSL encryption, you have a couple of options for getting them. Your best option is to pull out the CD-ROM from the back of this book and install the browsers that you find there. I included both Netscape Communicator with Navigator version 4.0 and Microsoft Internet Explorer version 4.0 on the book's CD. These packages include the latest 128-bit software that you need. See the Appendix for instructions on loading the software.

If your dog has been using the CD as a chew toy, you can use your current Web browser to locate and download the software online:

✔ If you want to get Netscape Navigator, go to the Netscape Web site and be sure to check the option for the stronger U.S./Canada Only versions. (SSL with 128-bit encryption can't be legally exported out of the United States.) The Netscape download page is located at the following address:

```
www.netscape.com/download/client_download.html
```

✔ The Microsoft download page for Internet Explorer 128-bit software is located at the following address:

```
www.microsoft.com/ie/download/128bit.htm
```

✔ If you're an AOL subscriber and you haven't upgraded to its latest software, go to keyword 128browser and follow the instructions.

Investigate the details of an SSL session in your Web browser

After you have a Web browser that supports the right version of SSL, you can connect to the secure portion of your bank's Web site. When you do, a padlock icon will appear in the status bar at the bottom of your Web browser window to indicate that a secure SSL session is in progress. (See Chapter 11 for more information.) But that padlock icon is just the beginning. Your Web browser can tell you a lot more about your session with the SSL server.

When you double-click the padlock icon, your Web browser opens a dialog box to display information about the owner of the SSL server you're connected to. For example, Figure 12-2 shows the results of clicking the padlock icon during an SSL session in Internet Explorer. Figure 12-3 shows the corresponding dialog box in Netscape Navigator.

Figure 12-2:
The
Properties
dialog box
for
Microsoft
Internet
Explorer
shows you
security
certificate
information.

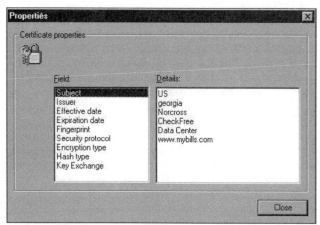

Figure 12-3:
The
Netscape
security
information
dialog box.

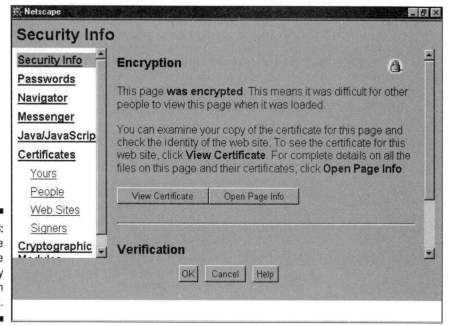

Although the two dialog boxes are cosmetically different, they operate much the same way. You select an information category by clicking an item in the list on the left and view detailed information on the right. You may need to click a button to get more details.

As you look at the information about your SSL connection, you will see references to Certificates. *Certificates* are registered public keys that a company uses in establishing an SSL connection. Certificates are assigned to companies when they set up secure online transaction systems. For example, when your bank sets up the security portion of its online banking system, it pays a fee and registers that server with a Certificate Authority. A *Certificate Authority* is a company that assigns and keeps track of unique public keys and serves as a directory where people can look up who registered a public key.

A *public key* is a special encryption code key that can be used to encrypt messages so that they can be decrypted only with a corresponding (secret) *private key.* A message encrypted with the bank's public key can be decrypted only by the bank using its private key. Conversely, a message encrypted with the bank's private key can be decrypted only with the complementary public key, which effectively validates its origin as being from the bank. SSL uses a combination of public and private keys to achieve its security.

The most important information displayed in the dialog box (that appears when you double-click the padlock icon) is information on the owner of the certificate you are currently engaging with to create a secure transaction environment. For more information, click any of the other fields. Another notable field (in the Internet Explorer dialog box) is the Fingerprint field. This field will display the public key for this Web site, which by the way, is 32 characters long with either a number from 0 to 9 or a letter from A to F.

Why would you want this information? On a day-to-day basis, you really don't need to worry about it. However, if there is ever a doubt about who you are dealing with, or you need to confirm some information during a customer service call about your Internet connection with the bank, these are the screens you will need to turn to.

Checking Out the Security Features of PFM Software

The other sections of this chapter focus on SSL and encryption as they are used on the Web and the Internet for Web-based online banking. However, encryption technology isn't confined to Web-based banking alone. The leading personal finance manager (PFM) software programs also incorporate encryption to protect the security of your online banking data as it travels between your computer and the bank.

For example, when you install Quicken 99 or Money 99, the set-up programs for both products offer to install a copy of a Web browser equipped for 128-bit SSL encryption for use with the programs. The programs' own data communications with the bank are protected with the same SSL encryption (or something equally effective). Most earlier versions of Quicken and Money that included online banking also included some form of data encryption, although it may not have been the same 128-bit SSL system that is commonly used in the current versions of the software.

It's difficult to make any meaningful general statements about the security features of the proprietary online banking software that you may receive from individual banks, except to say that you can be sure that the bank has included data security considerations in the design of its banking software. Most of the bank-branded software is designed to use a private data network instead of the public Internet, so the potential exposure is much lower than on the Internet. Some banks rely on the security of these private data networks to protect your data; others use SSL or other encryption systems operating over the Internet, and you may find a few that use encryption even on a private data network. The only way to be sure whether your bank-branded online banking software uses encryption is to ask the technical support staff at the bank.

Finding Security Information Online

If the other sections of this chapter have piqued your interest in the world of security, you can take a look at the following Web sites for more information:

- ✔ **IETF:** The Internet Engineering Task Force is the group assigned to set and enforce standards on the Internet. Security is one of the areas that falls under the group's responsibility and its Web site includes an overview of the IETF, current RFCs (requests for comment), and the activities of several working groups including one that discusses security. The Web site is at www.ietf.org.

- ✔ **RSA:** The three founders of RSA — Rivest, Shamir, and Adleman — have built a company that is a major player in the Web security business. They have created several products and services to help companies and individuals manage their security needs including SSL. The Web site is at www.rsa.com.

✔ **Univeristy of British Columbia Links Page:** This site has a very helpful list of cryptography links and definitions. You can find plenty of information on the finer points of security and encryption. The Web site is at `axion.physics.ubc.ca/crypt.html`.

The Banking Online
For Dummies
Internet Directory

The 5th Wave   By Rich Tennant

"If it works, it works. I've just never seen
Citicorp and the National Bank of England
connected with Chinese handcuffs before."

In this directory . . .

You may think that online banking is just in its infancy, but this directory filled with hundreds of financial institutions that offer online banking will change your mind. You have many well-established online banking institutions to choose from — and the list is growing quickly. The majority of the listings in this directory are for banks and credit unions, but Web links are also included for useful software companies and government sites. Using the listings in this directory, you can find out just about anything that you'll ever want to know about online banking.

Banking Online For Dummies Internet Directory

•••

*T*he Internet is flourishing with valuable information — and growing more every day, both in content and popularity. You see advertisements or business cards with e-mail addresses or Web addresses almost daily. The most remote parts of the world and the smallest home businesses have an electronic presence on the Web, right along with the rest of the world.

The banking industry is also experiencing tremendous growth, due in no small part to the success of the Internet. More bank and financial services information goes online every day. This directory helps you find Web resources for financial institutions and other financial information quickly and easily.

Given the rate of change on the Internet — not to mention all the mergers in the financial services industry — compiling a comprehensive list of banks that offer online services is impossible. (I tried, mind you.) If you are interested in a particular institution that you don't see here, enter its name into an Internet search engine, such as Yahoo (www.yahoo.com) or Excite (www.excite.com), to see what sort of online services the institution offers.

To help you quickly determine certain facts about the banks that I describe here (such as whether the bank offers Web-based bill payment), I include special miniature icons. These icons indicate important attributes of the Web site entries that they accompany:

ATM   ATM/branch locator

BBS   Online banking software that's built or customized to the bank's specifications

BNOW   The BankNOW service on America Online

MSM   Online banking functions of Microsoft Money

D-4

MYM	Online banking functions of Managing Your Money
Q	Online banking functions of Quicken
QB	Online banking functions of QuickBooks software
TB	Telephone-based banking and inquiry system
WBNK	Web-based banking functions
WBP	Online bill payment
WINS	Web-based insurance products and services
WINV	Online investing
WL	Online loan or credit applications

Banks

This section lists banks that offer online transactions, such as checking balances, paying bills, and so on. It doesn't include banks that post Web sites just to advertise the bank's conventional services.

1st Choice Bank

www.1stchoicebank.com

WBNK WINV

Use the site from 1st Choice Bank, located in Greeley, Colorado, for various banking needs: Check stock quotes, access your account, and direct your kids to the Young Investors section.

1st Source

1stsource.com

MSM Q WBNK WBP

The Web site for 1st Source Bank (located in South Bend, Indiana) enables you to obtain account balances, find out which checks and withdrawals have cleared, transfer funds, obtain your monthly statement online, and export account information to the financial software package of your choice. Need more? Bill paying is also available.

Alliance Bank

www.alliancebnk.com

WBNK

Find out about the many Alliance Bank (of Orlando, Florida) products and services, check out the useful links page, and access your accounts from your home or office.

Amarillo National Bank

www.anb.com

WBNK WBP WINV

Click. See your account balances and transfer funds. Point. Click. Pay your bills. Point. Click again. Now you've checked stock quotes. The Amarillo (Texas) National Bank Web site lets you accomplish all these banking tasks while you're waiting for your breakfast!

American National Bank

www.accessanb.com

ATM MSM Q WBNK WBP

With AccessANB Internet Banking (provided by American National Bank of Muncie, Indiana), you can see every check, deposit, ATM transaction, automatic payment, and CheckCard transaction. You can transfer funds between accounts and make loan payments. You can also balance your checkbook with a few mouse clicks, as well as download account information to other financial management programs such as Microsoft Money and Quicken.

American National Bank and Trust Company of Chicago

www.anbchicago.com/

BBS MSM Q QB

American National Bank and Trust Company of Chicago is a wholly owned subsidiary of First Chicago NBD Corporation. ANB leads the Chicago area businesses market, primarily serving banks with $5 million to $150 million in annual revenues. You may know of them as "The Bank for Business."

AmSouth Bancorporation

www.amsouth.com

ATM BBS MSM WBP WL

AmSouth Bancorporation is based in Birmingham, Alabama. If you need a splash of color in your day, wander through this site. Internet banking is coming soon to this site, but you can currently use a direct-connect bill-payment service. You can also apply for accounts and loans online.

Associated Bank

www.assocbank.com

WINV

View your portfolio holdings and transactions with Associated Trust Online, provided by Associated Bank of Green Bay, Wisconsin. And you thought Green Bay had only a football team to brag about!

Bank Atlantic

www.bankatlantic.com

BNOW MSM Q

In addition to a full range of banking products and services, including cash management and small business services, Bank Atlantic is very involved in the south Florida communities. (Bank Atlantic is based in Fort Lauderdale, Florida.) Some of the bank's efforts include providing for the housing needs of low-to-moderate income families, helping schools improve students' learning skills, and developing many of the cultural opportunities that the diversity of Florida offers.

Bank Of America

www.bankamerica.com

ATM BBS BNOW MSM MYM Q WBNK WBP WINS WINV

Bank Of America (based in San Francisco, California) offers many online banking options. You can access accounts via the Internet, America Online, or Managing Your Money direct-access software. Download your account information into Quicken or Microsoft Money, and, for a small fee, you can pay your bills online. If you have a BankAmericard credit card, you can also check your balances, view up to seven months of your account history, and gain direct access to customer service. Also available: online banking for small businesses.

BankBoston

www.bkb.com

ATM BBS MSM Q WBNK WBP

You can access BankBoston's Homelink by using a Web browser or through direct-connect software. Homelink is compatible with Microsoft Money and Quicken, and now features balance forecasting. Bill paying is available free with some accounts. A similar service for small businesses, called Officelink, is also available. And whether you're thinking about home ownership or you just need help balancing your checkbook, check out this site's online calculators.

Bank of Cleveland

www.bankofcleveland.com

WBP

With Bank of Cleveland (based in Cleveland, Tennessee), you can access your accounts and pay bills online, all for free.

You can also order checks, check interest rates, and get investment information at this site. And use the financial calculators to plan your budget and savings.

Bank of Edwardsville

www.4thebank.com

WBNK WBP

The Bank of Edwardsville is the largest locally owned and independent bank in southwestern Illinois, and it gives you the convenience of online banking and bill paying. Test-drive the Magic Online Bill Paying and then use this site to sign up.

Bank of Elk River

www.the-bank-er.com

WBNK

The family-owned Bank of Elk River (based in Elk River, Minnesota) offers World-Wide Banker, an online banking service that allows you to access accounts, view balances and transactions, and transfer funds from, well, you know, anywhere in the world.

Bank of Hawaii

www.boh.com

MSM Q WBNK WBP WINV

Aloha, e-bankoh! E-bankoh is the name given to this site's Web-based account access. And, since Bank of Hawaii is a Pacific Century Company, Pacific Century clients may review their investment information at this site. Check out the demos for both the online banking and online investment services. Bill paying is available for an extra fee.

Bank of New York

www.bankofny.com

BBS WBP

Bank of New York is the oldest bank in the United States, founded by Alexander Hamilton. The Bank of New York Direct 24 PC Banking offers account information and bill payment through a direct connection to the bank.

Bank of Stockton

www.bankstockton.com

MSM Q

The Bank of Stockton, based in Stockton, California, packages its online banking offerings very aggressively. One account offers free online banking and bill payment for a year.

Bank of Versailles

www.bankov.com

MSM WBNK WBP

The Bank of Versailles, based in Versailles, Missouri, features an online application for Certificates of Deposits, available for as little as $500. It boasts low rates of overhead and one of the lowest loan loss rates in Missouri.

Bank One

www.bankone.com

ATM BBS WBNK WBP WINS WINS

Bank One (of Columbus, Ohio) offers free account inquiries and transfers, and charges a fee for the bill-payment option. Try out online banking before you sign up! Bank One's site offers a demo of its online banking service. If you decide to use it, you can access accounts and pay bills on the Internet or through direct-connect software. You also can use tools such as financial calculators and online insurance estimates to investigate insurance and investment options.

Bank United

www.bankunited.com

ATM   BBS   WBP

Bank United offers direct-connect software for PC banking and bill payment. (Bank United is based in Houston, Texas.) Visit the Web site to find out about free checking until the year 2000 and use the online loan calculators to estimate monthly payments.

Bayshore National Bank

www.bankbnb.com

WBNK

The Bayshore National Bank (of Laporte, Texas) site is simple and to-the-point: Click left for online banking, click right for a demo of online banking. More options and information coming soon!

BB&T Corporation

www.bbandt.com

ATM   BBS   WBP

BB&T Online is a direct-connect service that offers basic banking services and bill payment. (BB&T Corporation is based in Winston-Salem, North Carolina.) The Web site features BB&T's News Retriever, which scrolls the latest BB&T news.

Cabarrus Bank

www.cabarrusbank.com

WBNK   WBP   WL

At the Web site for Cabarrus Bank (of Concord, North Carolina), you can apply for a loan, browse some hot links, check out products and services, and head your kids in the right direction with the Looney Tunes Savings Club. Then access your accounts to transfer funds or view balances. And do it all, anytime.

California Federal

www.calfed.com

BBS   WBP

California Federal Bank (of San Francisco) offers Cal Fed Connection, a direct-connect software package that gives you basic banking functions and bill payment. Catch the huge wave on California Federal's home page as you surf the net, and apply for a loan (maybe for a real California surfing vacation?). *Note:* You need Adobe Acrobat Reader to download the loan application.

CCB Financial

www.ccbonline.com

ATM   BBS   WBP

Download a demo of CCB Financial's Computer Banking software and try it out. This direct-connect software includes bill paying. You also can use online calculators and get information on various products and services. (CCB Financial is based in Durham, North Carolina.)

Central National Bank & Trust

www.cnb-ok.com

WBNK WL

Home banking? Yep. An online loan application? That, too. How about loan calculators, current rates, and other information about products and services? You can find it all at this site offered by Central National Bank & Trust (of Enid, Oklahoma).

Centura Banks

www.centura.com

ATM BNOW MSM Q QB

At the Centura Banks (of Rocky Mount, North Carolina) Web site, you can use Quicken and Microsoft Money to access your Centura accounts day or night, seven days a week. You also can use the small-business software QuickBooks (by Intuit) to manage your small business accounts with the same ease of your personal accounts. And — yes, there's more! — AOL subscribers can use BankNOW (also by Intuit) to access personal accounts using a Web browser. These options include bill payment as well.

Charter One Bank

www.charterone.com

BBS WBP

The Web site for Charter One Bank, based in Cleveland, Ohio, offers bill-payment services through NOW Banking, a direct-connect service. Use the Financial Advisor link to access investment options, a move-planning kit, and mort-gage calculators.

Chase Manhattan

www.chase.com

ATM BBS MSM Q WBNK WBP WINS

Chase Manhattan (of New York City) emphasizes security through a direct connection to the Chase banking network and offers a top ten reasons list for banking online. The software and service is free if you use the bank's software. You pay a monthly fee to use Microsoft Money or Quicken. The monthly fees also include bill paying and up to 12 connections per month. Not sure what to do? Try out the demos for the online software or for Microsoft Money or Quicken.

Citibank (Citicorp)

www.citibank.com

ATM BBS MYM Q WBNK WBP WINV

Citibank (of New York City) offers online banking through both the Internet and a private network. Citibank claims that its Direct Access is the most complete online banking service. Pay bills, transfer funds, get stock quotes, and more for no monthly fee. For as little as $19.95, you can even trade stocks. This site also offers extensive college and financial aid information, including a financial aid application that you can download.

Colonial Bancgroup

www.colonialbank.com

ATM BBS WBP

Colonial Bancgroup, based in Montgomery, Alabama, enables you to transfer money, check balances, review account histories, and pay bills with direct-connect software called *Colonial Connection PC Banking*. Also, check out service and product information at this site.

Comerica

www.comerica.com

ATM MSM Q WBNK WBP WINV

Comerica, based in Auburn Hills, Michigan, offers Internet banking and bill payment with Home ATM. Check out the banking services available in California, Florida, and Texas; trade securities online; or browse online publications.

Commerce Bank

www.commercebank.com

MSM Q WBNK WBP

The Web site for Commerce Bancshares, based in Kansas City, Missouri, lets you apply for a credit card online at its Web site. Commerce Bancshares also displays its current stock price (*note:* fifteen-minute delay). And here's a super idea: Take a class in student banking via the Money:101 link.

Commercial Federal

www.comfedbank.com

MSM Q WBP

Commercial Federal Bank, based in Omaha, Nebraska, maintains a Web site where you can apply online to access and review your Commercial Federal accounts and check balances, reconcile accounts instantly, transfer funds between accounts, pay bills online, track your investments, create budgets, create reports and graphs, and prepare for tax time via direct-connect software. The current charge for 20 online bill payments and 8 account access sessions per month is $7.50.

Compass Bank

www.compassweb.com

BNOW MSM WINV

In addition to offering BankNOW online banking, Compass Bank (based in Birmingham, Alabama) offers a thorough Web-based online investment service.

Crestar Financial

www.crestar.com

ATM BNOW MSM Q WBNK WBP WINS WINV

Crestar Financial, Virginia's largest consumer bank, is merging with SunTrust (of Atlanta). Personal and business banking, investment banking, and mortgage loan banking are accessible online through Crestar. The site also offers information on a variety of insurance products.

Deposit Guaranty Corp.

www.dgb.com

ATM BBS MSM WBP

The Deposit Guaranty Corp. Web site enables you to use either GuarantyConnect PC Banking for basic banking, or Microsoft Money for banking, bill paying, and more. If you're interested, you can download a demo of the basic banking software. (Deposit Guaranty Corp. is based in Nashville, Tennessee.)

Dime Savings Bank

www.dime.com

ATM WL

Go to the Web site for Dime Savings Bank (of New York City) to get information about current rates, investment services, and insurance so that you can invest your ten cents wisely. Also use this site to apply online for credit and to find the Dime Savings ATM nearest you.

Eastern Bank

www.easternbank.com

MSM Q QB WBNK WBP

Eastern Bank of Lynn, Massachusetts, founded in 1818, offers a wealth of online banking options. In addition to furnishing a full-featured banking Web site, the bank offers consumer tips and helpful information aplenty. Take a look at the Information Overpass for links to some great financial Web sites.

European American Bank (EAB)

www.eab.com

ATM BBS MSM Q WBP

The drop-down menus and toolbars at the European American Bank (of New York City) Web site allow for easy navigation. View a demonstration of the bank's PC banking product, apply for a preapproved mortgage, or calculate college expenses.

Fifth Third Bank

www.53.com

WBNK

The Fifth Third Bank (of Cincinnati, Ohio) offers account inquiry and online trading services through the Internet at its Web site. It promises that transfer capabilities are coming soon. Join Club 53 to keep up with the highlights of financial services and seminars that Fifth Third offers.

First American

www.first-american.com

ATM BBS MSM WBNK WBP

The online service for First American Bank (based in Decatur, Alabama) is called BankSmart Electronic Home Banking. The site features information about the Dinosavers Club, a savings account for children. Check the calendar icon for monthly specials as well.

First Chicago NBD

www.fcnbd.com

ATM MSM Q WBNK WBP WINS WINV WL

First Chicago's online services extend beyond financial services and into the retail marketplace. Buy books, compact discs, or flowers; plan trips; or order in from a favorite restaurant through links provided at this home page. You may never have to leave home again.

First Citizens Bank

www.firstcitizens.com

ATM BBS WBP WINS

The Online Banking Association has recognized the First Citizens Bank (of Raleigh, North Carolina) Web site as one of the "Best Business Web Sites." You can use direct-connect banking software to access accounts and view investment accounts online.

First Hawaiian Bank

www.fhb.com

BBS BNOW MSM Q QB

The Web site of First Hawaiian Bank offers a wide variety of online banking options. If you visit the site, be sure to look at the museum and check out the implosion of First Hawaiian's old bank building. (I bet Butch and Sundance are sighing happily in their graves.) First Hawaiian Bank just merged with Banc West of California.

First National Bank of Durango

www.fnbdurango.com

WBNK WBP

Through the First National Bank of Durango (Colorado) Web site, you can access any accounts that you set up with the bank. Online Banker allows you to view current activity on your accounts (as well as previous statements), transfer funds between accounts, view check images, make loan payments, keep an eye on interest rates, and pay all your bills around the clock.

First National Bank of Grady County

www.fnbgrady.com

WBNK

The pointing arrow on the home page of First National Bank of Grady County (based in Cairo, Georgia) tells you where to go, whether you want a demonstration on Web-based account access or you're ready to get down to the business of banking online. Also check current loan rates and get other product information at this site.

First National of Omaha

www.fnbomaha.com

ATM WL

First National of Omaha will bring 24-hour Banker to its Web site very soon. While you wait, apply for a credit card online and use the ATM locator to find the nearest source of Nebraska cash.

First Security

www.firstsecuritybank.com

ATM WINS WINV WL

First Security (of Salt Lake City, Utah) features online brokerage services at its Web site. The site also contains information on mutual funds, insurance, and other financial products and services. Apply for loans online as well.

First Tennessee Bank

www.ftb.com

MSM WBNK WBP WINS

First Tennessee Bank's FTB Online is one of the first true Java-based online banking sites in the country. Choose Web access or direct-connect software, both with the option of bill payment. At this time, Web-based FTB Online supports only Internet Explorer 4.0 with 128-bit encryption on Windows 95 and Windows NT. In addition to online banking, FTB Online provides a robust Web-based financial planning tool.

First Union

www.firstunion.com

ATM BNOW MSM Q WBNK WBP WINS WINV WL

First Union of Charlotte, North Carolina, has created a Web site that lets you apply for accounts and loans online. Use Cyberbanking for Internet access to personal accounts, including credit card, time deposit, and term loan accounts. Access is also available from Quicken and Microsoft Money, and from BankNOW (offered by America Online). Online business banking is available as well.

First Virginia Banks

www.onlinebank.com/firstvirginia/
online.htm

ATM   MSM   WBNK   WBP

The First Virginia Banks Web site offers a Web banking demonstration, a listing of contacts for investment services, a branch locator, and more. Web banking with bill payment is available at First Virginia Banks.

Firstar

www.firstar.com

ATM   BBS   MSM   WBNK   WBP

Firstar Bank of Milwaukee offers a Web site where you can access accounts via the Web or a direct connection. The direct-connect service includes bill-payment options, but the Web-based service does not. Review the Financial News Resources online.

Fleet Financial

www.fleet.com

MSM   MYM   Q   WBNK   WBP   WINV

Use Managing Your Money software to connect directly to the Fleet Financial Web site.(Fleet Financial is based in Providence, Rhode Island.) Consolidate banking, budgeting, and financial planning. Web-based banking functions are on the way. Until then, the site has pages of financial planning information you can peruse. Also, be sure to check out the highly useful tool for income and expense planning — a form you can download for use to your own section of the site.

Harlingen National Bank

www.hnb-bank.com

WBNK   WBP

From deep in the heart (Harlingen, to be exact) of Texas comes a virtual place to bank. Go to this site for convenient online account access. Also use the hand loan calculator to figure payments and get information about products and services.

Harris Bank

www.harrisbank.com

WBNK

Harris Bank of Chicago offers a Web site with its own cartoon character. The tail-wagging cartoon, Hubert the Financial Lion, offers simple, straight answers to a variety of questions. You also can get basic Internet banking services through the Harris Bank Web site.

Hibernia Bank

www.hiberniabank.com

BBS

Hibernia Bank (of New Orleans) has set up a Web site with a TABBSnet feature, which allows direct-access basic banking for small businesses. Need to try it out first? No problem. Try the online Shockwave demo or download a demo to your PC.

Home Savings of America

www.homesavings.com

MSM   Q   WBNK   WBP

Home Savings of America Bank (based in Irwindale, California) has merged with Washington Mutual. The Web site lets you

D-14 Banks

review your account history, check balances, transfer funds, and pay your bills — or do it all through Microsoft Money or Quicken.

HSBC

www.hsbcgroup.com

BBS WBP

HSBC (of Buffalo, New York) offers Hexagon, an electronic system that allows individual and corporate subscribers to conduct their banking business on their PCs, and adds bill payment for business customers. Access to international trade business is available as well.

Hudson Savings Bank

www.hudsonsb.com

ATM WBNK WBP

Hudson Savings Bank is a community bank serving central Massachusetts. The Web site offers Internet banking and bill payment. Check out other product and service information as well. And use the online calculators to predict loan payments and to help evaluate the difference between renting and buying.

Huntington Bancshares

www.huntington.com

ATM MSM Q WBNK WBP WINS

Huntington Bancshares (based in Columbus, Ohio) recently added online credit services and support for Microsoft Money and Quicken access. Customers at the Huntington Bancshares Web site also can access account information, transfer funds, and pay bills online through the Web.

Kansas State Bank

www.kansasstatebank.com

WBNK WBP WL

Showing a business sense that another town named Manhattan is known for, Kansas State Bank (of Manhattan, Kansas) presents a very professional home page for its Web site. Click the cup of coffee for home banking, or check out the demo. You can also check rates and apply for a loan online.

KeyCorp

www.keybank.com

BBS MSM Q QB WBNK WBP WINS

KeyCorp (of Cleveland, Ohio) offers "Key2Your$," a suite of financial services online. Pull-down menus include interactive products such as loan calculators. Internet banking is available, as is banking with Quicken, Microsoft Money, or even QuickBooks for small businesses. Not sure which option to choose? Demos are available to help you make up your mind.

Laredo National Bank

www.lnb-online.com

Q QB

Visit the Web site of Laredo National Bank (of Texas) and you can read about the bank in either English or Spanish. Look for Quicken support for your personal online banking needs and QuickBooks support for your business banking needs.

LaSalle Banks

www.lasallebanks.com

BBS MSM Q QB TB WBNK WBP

The LaSalle Banks (of Chicago) are subsidiaries of ABN AMRO Bank N.V., the 14th largest bank in the world. Enjoy this site's list of Top Ten Reasons to bank online with LaSalle PCLink. You can use this software for your home or your business to access accounts and pay bills, and it is compatible with Quicken or Microsoft Money. Other points of interest on this site include an online newsletter and a page of LaSalle links.

Lincoln Bank of NC

www.lincolnbanknc.com

WBNK WBP WL

It's 4 p.m. on a Saturday and your family is bored? Use the Web site of Lincoln Bank (of Lincolnton, North Carolina) to find some fun links, check out products and services, and get your kids headed in the right direction with the Looney Tunes Savings Club. Then access your accounts to transfer funds, view balances, or apply for a loan.

Mascoma Savings Bank

www.mascomabank.com

WBNK WBP

If you're not sure whether you'll like the bank@mascoma feature at Mascoma Savings Bank (of Lebanon, New Hampshire), try the online demo first. You can use this site to sign up for online banking and then access accounts, transfer funds, and check account histories. You can also check rates and find out more about products and services here.

Marshall & Ilsley

www.mibank.com

ATM BBS WBNK WBP

You can easily find what you need on the Marshall & Ilsley Web site. Choose Internet banking and bill payment, or opt for a direct connection. As an added incentive, Marshall & Ilsley (based in Milwaukee) gives customers free personal Web sites. Still not convinced? Try the online banking demo!

M & T Bank

www.mandtbank.com

ATM BBS BNOW MSM Q QB WBP

"All the bank you'll ever need" is the slogan from this bank. M & T Bank (of Buffalo, New York) offers many changing financial specials through its Web site; visit the bank's Web site often to keep up.

MBNA Corporation

www.mbnainternational.com/index.htm

WL

MBNA (of Wilmington, Delaware) is the largest independent credit card lender in the world. You can use this site to apply for a credit card online and to find information about consumer financing options and insurance products.

Mellon Bank

www.mellon.com

ATM BNOW MSM Q WBNK WBP WINS

Visit Mellon's "Summertime Fun" site for tips and information for travel, recreation, health, weather, and kid stuff.

D-16 Banks

Mellon Bank, based in Pittsburgh, offers Bank-by-Web and online trading. Access through Quicken, Microsoft Money, and BankNOW (with America Online) is also available.

Mercantile Bankshares Corp.

www.mercantile.net

WINV

Mercantile Bankshares Corporation (of Baltimore) is a family of community banks, each with its own name and management. Go to this site to access the site of any member bank. Also, you don't need an account number or a special PIN to get a stock quote from NASDAQ at this site.

Merchants Bank of California

www.merchantsbankca.com

WBNK   WL

Merchants Bank of California provides financial services to businesses and the professional market. The bank recently expanded to provide specific services for real estate mortgages, a full range of services for check cashing stores, and wire transfers to Romania. The site provides Internet banking and an online mortgage application.

Metro Bank

www.metrobanker.com

WBNK

Follow the yellow brick links to home banking and more at the Metro Bank (of Farmington Hills, Michigan) Web site. Access accounts, transfer funds, and view account histories from home. You can also get information about loans and use the loan calculator to figure payments.

Michigan National

www.michigannational.com

ATM   MSM   Q

Michigan National Bank's Web site lets you access accounts and pay bills through Microsoft Money or Quicken. Web banking is currently under development. Need more incentive? Michigan National likes to offer prizes, such as a sweepstakes for the chance to win free Internet access for a year.

Morris State Bank

www.morrisstate.com

ATM   WBNK

If you're looking for the history of Dublin, Georgia, you've found the right site. But if you need to get to the business of banking . . . this is still the right site! Also featured: an ATM locator and kid links.

National City Bank

www.national-city.com

ATM   BBS   WBNK   WBP

National City Bank, based in Cleveland, Ohio, offers online banking through its Web site, direct-connect software, or both. Pricing is based on using one service or both services. Also check out the Invest It!, Own It!, and Afford It! links for advice and information about investments, home buying, and loans, respectively.

National Penn Bank

www.natpennbank.com

MSM   Q   QB

National Penn Bank of Boyertown, Pennsylvania, really puts its money where its mouth is when it asserts that it will not be bought. If you opened a certain type of account before December 31, 1998, and National Penn Bank is sold and changes its name before January 1, 2004, you are guaranteed a $1,000 bonus! And, yes, fine print abounds.

NationsBank

www.nationsbank.com

**ATM BBS MYM WBNK WBP
WINV WL**

NationsBank (based in Charlotte, North Carolina) allows customers to access accounts via the Internet and promises Internet-based bill payment in the near future. Already available, you can also use Managing Your Money for bill payment. Small business solutions and online trading are also available, along with online credit applications.

Northern Trust

www.ntrs.com

ATM BBS WBP

The online banking service at Northern Trust (of Chicago) is called Private Passport and is a direct connection to the bank. Keep up with market information at the Research desk.

Norwest

www.norwest.com

BBS MSM Q WBP

Norwest Bank (of Minneapolis) is merging with Wells Fargo. The Norwest Web site updates visitors on the merger even as it continues to help users bank from home. Use direct-connect software to check balances, pay bills, and get continuous updates on stock and mutual fund prices. Use the mortgage and home equity calculators to calculate payments. And there's more — pay a visit and check it out.

Old Kent Bank

www.oldkent.com

ATM WINS WINV

You can use the Old Kent online investment service to get real-time quotes, account information, investment information, and enter trades. Old Kent (of Grand Rapids, Michigan) currently doesn't offer online banking at this site.

Oxford Bank

www.oxfordbank.com

WBNK WBP

At the Web site for Oxford Bank (of Oxford, Mississippi), you can inquire on your accounts, transfer funds from account to account, make loan payments, and even add some extra money to your Christmas Club — all from your personal computer. Currently, the charge is $4.00 per month, with bill paying available for another $4.00 a month.

Pavilion State Bank

www.pavilionbank.com

WBNK WBP

A quick history lesson: Before the first branch was established in 1914, Pavilion State Bank (of Pavilion, New York), a family-owned independent bank, was a traveling branch. A loan officer would travel to Pavilion and work out of the old general store to lend money to people in need. Now Pavilion reaches out in a different way: You, too, can go online to access accounts and pay bills.

Pennview Savings Bank

www.pennview.com

WBNK WL

All you need is a PC with a modem and access to the Internet to use the Anytime Banking Online features at the Web site for Pennview Savings Bank (of Souderton, Pennsylvania). Similar to the security of an ATM, the only way that you can access your account is by using your PIN. Check out the demo if you need help making up your mind. You can also apply for a loan at this site.

People's Bank

www.peoples.com

ATM BBS WBP WINV

Check out the latest news, sports, and weather; check TV or movie listings; or view upcoming events from the People's Bank Web site. People's Bank, based in Bridgeport, Connecticut, features Internet trading and direct-connect banking functions, including bill payment.

PNC Bank

www.pncbank.com

ATM BNOW MSM MYM Q WBNK WBP WL

PNC Bank (of Pittsburgh) has created a Web site where you can access accounts and pay bills via the Web, or through direct-connect software such as Managing Your Money or Quicken. Try it at no charge for a month. College-bound individuals (or consumers whose money is going toward some special child's school bills) can check out the Learning Link for information about financial aid and colleges. You can also apply for a loan online.

Premier Bank

www.premierbnk.com

WBNK WBP

Click the word *Virtual* to become a Virtual Banker on the Premier Bank (of Tallahassee, Florida) Web site. Virtual Bankers have access to Premier Bank's mainframe computer and can conduct any deposit transaction, review loan relationships, and handle any investment needs. Need help navigating the rest of the site? Just pass your cursor over the navigation bar and a link description appears by magic (well, really by Java). Enjoy!

Provident Bank

www.provident-bank.com

WBNK

At the Provident Bank (of Cincinnati, Ohio) Web site, you can use the latest version of Internet Explorer, Netscape Navigator, or America Online to access your accounts from the Web. This site provides all that you need, including a demo version, an online signup, and the links to download the appropriate browser.

RCB Bank

www.bankrcb.com

WBNK WBP

RCB Bank (of Claremore, Oklahoma) created this site with a space theme. Click the rocket ship and try out the online banking demo. After you try it, you can use Net Teller to access accounts or pay bills. Or send your kids to the Just for Fun page and let them surf away.

Regions Financial

www.regionsbank.com

ATM BBS MSM Q WBNK WBP

The Regions Financial (of Birmingham, Alabama) Web site offers Internet banking, direct connection through financial software (Quicken, Microsoft Money), and a Web page that provides links to its interactive partners.

Republic National Bank of New York

www.rnb.com

ATM BNOW MSM Q

The Republic National Bank of New York Web site has a PC Touch Banking feature, through which customers can choose between Quicken or Microsoft Money for online banking services with bill payment. Software is offered free to customers upon enrollment. The site also offers a list of bank-owned properties for sale.

Sanwa Bank California

www.sanwa-bank-ca.com

ATM BBS BNOW MSM Q QB WBP

Sanwa Bank California (of Los Angeles) bills itself as "the bank that goes where you go." Use Sanwa's own direct-connect software or BankNOW, Microsoft Money, or Quicken to pay bills. Need a financial system for your small business? Sanwa also supports QuickBooks interactivity.

SouthTrust Bank

www.southtrust.com

ATM BBS MSM WBP WINS

SouthTrust Bank of Birmingham, Alabama, offers online service through a direct-connect program called, fittingly, SouthTrust Online. Loan calculators are

available for financial planning. Thinking about changing insurance carriers? You can request online insurance quotes at this Web site. Also, check out the Mortgage Center link to get information about closing costs and the loan process; you can apply online if you decide you want a loan from SouthTrust.

Sovereign Bank

www.sovereignbank.com

WL

With the acquisition of 93 CoreStates branches, Sovereign Bank (of Wyomissing, Pennsylvania) has branches in Pennsylvania, New Jersey, and Delaware . . . and a loan center on the World Wide Web. Apply online for loans and credit cards at this site. You can then gather the family around and check out the KidsBank.Com link; the Java version introduces cartoon characters that teach kids about money, banking, and the principles of saving.

Star Bank

www.starbank.com

ATM BBS WBNK WBP

Star Bank of Cincinnati is merging with Firstar Bank, and Star Bank's Web site has both PC and Internet banking. View the bank's latest stock price on the ticker tape. Also, be sure to check out the audio message from the bank's chairman in RealAudio.

State Central Bank

www.statecentralbank.com

WBNK WBP

Take care of all your banking needs at the Web site for State Central Bank (of Keokuk, Iowa). Check out the online banking demo, sign up online, and, of course, access your accounts online after you sign up. Check out loan rates and product information. Then surf from the links page, which includes community links, links to information about purchasing an auto, and kids' links.

State Street Boston

www.statestreet.com

WBNK

State Street Boston serves institutional investors. This bank proves that Web-based banking is not just for individuals and small business. Global Link is a Web-based tool for treasury professionals. MMOMS (Money Market Order Management System) is a real-time interactive order system using the Internet for automated transaction processing. The State Street Prime-Meridian product platform provides a linked set of cash management services.

Summit Bank

www.summitbank.com

ATM   BBS   WBP   WINV

Summit Bank (of Princeton, New Jersey) offers the Summit Direct service, with two online banking services: Summit PC Banking with basic banking services and PC Banking Plus with added bill-payment capability. Peruse bank-owned properties or look into aircraft financing. (Aircraft financing? Why not?)

Suntrust Bank

www.suntrust.com

ATM   BNOW   MSM   Q   QB   WBP   WL

Need help with your sunny disposition? Try Suntrust Bank of Atlanta. Save time and effort by using online banking and bill payment through personal financial management software, such as Quicken, Microsoft Money, and QuickBooks. Need a loan to finance that yacht? Apply for a loan online. Decide to get a remote-control toy yacht instead? Apply for a credit card online.

UMB Bank

www.umb.com

ATM   BBS   MSM   WBP

At the Web site for UMB Bank (of Kansas City, Missouri), you can use Home ATM (the bank's software) or Microsoft Money to access accounts and pay bills. Art lovers: Choose the Information link on the home page to go to the UMB online gallery. Useful and fun!

Union Bank of California

www.uboc.com

ATM   BNOW   MSM   Q   WINV

Union Bank of California (San Francisco) features online investing and direct-connect banking and plans to add Web-based banking in the near future. Find out about Union Bank's 401(k) and mutual fund resources on this site as well.

Union National Bank

www.univest-corp.com/union.cfm

WBNK   WL

If the home page of the Union National Bank Web site looks amazingly similar to the home page of Pennview Savings Bank, don't be surprised. Both banks are subsidiaries of Univest. (Union National is based in Souderton, Pennsylvania.) This site offers online banking and online loan applications. Check it out!

U.S. Bank

www.usbank.com

ATM BBS BNOW MSM MYM Q WBNK WINV WL

U.S. Bank (based in Minneapolis) provides free Internet access to accounts through this Web site. It also offers bill-payment services through Managing Your Money, Quicken, Microsoft Money, and AOL's BankNOW. Not sure if you want to start managing your investments online? Try out the online investing demo. If you decide to sign up for the service, it's free to all U.S. Bancorp Investment customers.

Wachovia

www.wachovia.com

TB WBNK WBP WINV WL

Wachovia, based in Winston-Salem, North Carolina, is one of the first banks to offer both online banking and online investing through the Internet. The Wachovia Bank Web site's PCAccess feature offers both Online Banking and Online Investing through one convenient location at the Web site. You also can apply for credit and even for employment, all online.

Washington Mutual

www.wamu.com

ATM WBNK WBP

Washington Mutual (of Seattle) offers a creative Web site. If you love Webby gizmos, move your cursor over near the buttons on the home page and check out the menus that appear, as if by magic. Neato! Washington Mutual has merged with Home Savings. The bank promises the availability of online banking (including bill payment) to arrive very soon. For now, you can fill out the online survey and tell the bank which online services you would use. You can also find ATM and branch locations online.

Webster Bank

www.websterbank.com

ATM BBS WBP

Webster Bank of Waterbury, Connecticut, says of its Web site, "If you've ever used an ATM, then you already know how to use our new PC Banking service. That's because Webster Bank's Home ATM looks and works like an ATM machine." Not a bad pitch. You have to call or e-mail to get the direct-connect software. You can also look up banking terms here in the online Webster's Dictionary.

Wells Fargo

www.wellsfargo.com

ATM MSM Q WBNK WBP WINV WL

Don't let the stagecoach fool you: Wells Fargo (of San Francisco) is one bank that's not stuck in the wrong century. An online banking pioneer, Wells Fargo features a variety of personal banking and investment services via the Internet. Bill paying is free if you keep a combined monthly balance of $5,000 in your personal accounts. Also, Wells Fargo is currently piloting a system that allows electronic cash purchases over the Internet.

World Savings

www.worldloan.com

WL

If you're thinking of buying a home, visit the World Savings (of Oakland, California) Web site. World Savings concentrates almost exclusively on real estate finance. Apply online for a home loan, have a customized loan analysis e-mailed to you, and check out the list of real estate agents in your area.

Wyoming County Bank

www.wycobank.com

WBNK

Check out the home page of Wyoming County Bank (based in Warsaw, New York), which doubles as the *Wyoming County Bank Times*. As with a normal bank newsletter, you can find out local community news and current rates. Unlike a normal newsletter, this site allows you online access to your accounts, 24 hours a day.

Zions Bank

www.zionsbank.com

ATM BBS MSM Q WBNK WBP WL

Zions Bank (of Salt Lake City, Utah) offers free access to stock quotes and investment news and access to investment accounts via its Web site. Zions offers direct-connect software with bill-payment functions and basic banking services through the Web. Haven't done enough banking for one day? You can also use this site to apply for a loan online.

Credit Unions

The number of credit unions offering online banking services is growing as quickly as the number of traditional banks. This section includes only the credit unions that offer transactions online (and excludes credit unions that use Web sites for advertising purposes only).

66 Federal Credit Union

www.66fcu.org

TB WBNK WBP

The 66 Federal Credit Union Web site enables you to transfer money among accounts, view your account history, and check balances online for free. Making loan payments is also free, but paying bills (the Bill Payer feature) costs $5 per month for unlimited transactions. Also available: 24-hour telephone banking.

102 Federal Credit Union

www.102fcu.org

TB WL

At the 102 Federal Credit Union Web site, you can use the 24-hour telephone service, Access 24, to check account balances, make transfers and check withdrawals, make loan payments, request tax information, and more. Use the Downloads link to get Acrobat-based membership and loan applications.

1st United Services Credit Union

www.1stuscu.org

MSM WBNK WBP WL

Apply for a loan or a bank Visa card online at the 1st United Services Credit Union Web site. Use the online wizards to calculate loan payments, retirement financial status, and mortgages. You can also manage all your bank accounts. Go to the Online Banking Center last, though, because you cannot back up to other parts of the site after you link to the account number/password page.

Abbott Laboratories Employees Credit Union

www.alecu.org

WL

Use the Abbott Laboratories Employees Credit Union Web site to get rate and product information and to apply for a loan 24 hours a day.

ABCO Public Employees Federal Credit Union

www.abcopefcu.org

WL

You must have a user name and a password to apply for a loan at the ABCO Public Employees Federal Credit Union Web site. New applicants can fill in the text fields provided with a new user name and password; previous applicants must choose new information if they forget their password.

Affinity Federal Credit Union

www.affinityfcu.org

MSM TB WBNK WBP WL

Affinity Federal Credit Union's Web site enables you to access your accounts, pay your bills, and fill out the online enrollment form. Other features include financial wizards for comparing loans, calculating mortgages, and figuring retirement. Also check out AutoVantage for online car-buying services.

Air Academy Federal Credit Union

www.aafcu.org

WBNK WBP WL

The Air Academy Federal Credit Union Web site is a virtual bank that does everything except give you cash. You can pay your bills, transfer funds, check your loan status, reorder checks, look at your statements, stop payments, and more.

Alaska USA Federal Credit Union

www.alaskausa.org

MSM Q TB WBNK WL

The Alaska USA Federal Credit Union Web site lets you do all your general banking online, including transferring funds, arranging automatic loan payments, and requesting direct deposit. You can also download transactions directly to Microsoft Money or Quicken.

Alcoa Employees Community Credit Union

www.aeccu.org

MSM TB WBNK WL

In addition to the usual online banking services and account access, the Alcoa Employees Credit Union Web site has tons of wizards and calculators — for mortgages, loans, and retirement, but also for figuring out the cost of a college education, college financial aid estimates, budgets, and savings account interest earned. Useful!

American River Healthpro Credit Union

www.arhcu.org

TB WBNK WBP

The American River Healthpro Credit Union Web site is still expanding. However, basic banking functions are available through the Internet or by phone, and a bill-paying function is expected soon. The site also offers information about the credit union's products, services, and even employment opportunities.

America's First Federal Credit Union

www.amfirst.org

WBNK WL

The America's First Federal Credit Union Web site lets you apply for loans and credit cards, perform routine transactions among your bank accounts, and authorize direct deposit. You also can order checks, look at check styles, check stock quotes — all on the most patriotic-looking credit union site on the Web.

Anheuser-Busch Employees' Credit Union

www.abecu.org

WBNK WL

When you take the tour of the Anheuser-Busch brewery, you get free samples at the end of the tour. Too bad they don't do that at the credit union! At the Anheuser-Busch Employees' Credit Union Web site, you can do your basic banking and apply for a loan, as well as use the financial calculators to figure loan payments and the like. And you thought that beer and financial planning didn't mix!

APL Federal Credit Union

www.aplfcu.org

MSM WBNK WBP WL

In addition to the typical online banking services, use the APL Federal Credit Union Web site to look at cars and homes for sale on the Virtual Vehicles and Real Estate Center pages. You can also pay some bills online and download membership, credit card, and loan applications.

APPLE Community Credit Union Ltd.

www.air.on.ca/users/applecu

WL

The APPLE Community Credit Union Web site provides good, basic information on how a credit union (as opposed to a regular bank) works. It also provides a detailed online loan/mortgage application. Other useful benefits of using this credit union include direct deposit and direct debits.

Arkansas Federal Credit Union

www.afcu.org

MSM TB WBNK WBP

Try the Arkansas Federal Credit Union Web site's online banking demo first to get a taste of everything this site has to offer in the way of Internet services. You can manage your bank accounts, transfer funds, pay bills, and more.

Army Aviation Center Federal Credit Union

www.aacfcu.com

MSM WBNK WBP

You may access your accounts, sign up to pay bills, and download a credit application at the Army Aviation Center Federal Credit Union Web site. You have to use Adobe Acrobat to view the application, and then print out and either fax or mail it back to the credit union. You can also check out the current loan rates and get a short history lesson about the credit union.

Arsenal Credit Union

www.arsenalcu.org/frames/index.shtml

MSM WBNK WBP WL

Along with basic online banking and online loan application, the friendly Arsenal Credit Union Web site features the most popular financial wizards: You can crunch numbers concerning your retirement, your mortgage, and your loan financing amount and payment options. Current loan and investment rates are also available.

AT&T Family Federal Credit Union

www.attffcu.org

TB WBNK WBP WL

Does the AT&T Family Federal Credit Union Web site offer online banking? Yes. Paying bills? Yes. Financial wizards and online calculators? Yes. Loan and service applications? Yes. Free cash? No.

Atlantic Fleet Federal Credit Union

www.affcu.com

WL

Attention on deck! At the Atlantic Fleet Federal Credit Union Web site, you can compare loan rates, calculate payment options, apply for a loan online, and — not yet, but coming soon — order checks online as well. (Currently, you can browse check styles.)

Austin Area Teachers Federal Credit Union

www.aatfcu.org/home.shtml

MSM Q WBNK WINV WL

The Austin Area Teachers Federal Credit Union Web site offers basic online banking and much more! Download

information to your Quicken or Microsoft Money software, receive current stock quotes and investment information, and track the daily high, low, and last-quoted stock price (with a 15-minute delay) for up to 20 stocks. These don't have to be stocks of which you own shares. However, if you do own shares, you can input the number of shares purchased, amount per share, and commission paid to calculate your current profit or loss for each stock. Also check out the online loan application and auto links.

Barksdale Federal Credit Union

www.bfcu.org

WL

The Barksdale Federal Credit Union Web site offers a selection of repossessed vehicles, an opportunity to fill out a home banking survey, and the *Home and Family Finance Online* e-zine. You can also fill out an online application and check loan rates.

Beaumont Area Educators Federal Credit Union

www.baefcu.org

MSM Q WBNK WL

Access your account online and download the information into Quicken or Microsoft Money at the Beaumont Area Educators Federal Credit Union Web site. You may also apply for membership, loans, and credit online, or use the loan calculator and other financial wizards to budget.

BESTSOURCE Credit Union

www.bestsourcecu.org

MSM WBNK WL

The BESTSOURCE Credit Union Web site's features include home banking; online applications for membership; loans and

D-26 Credit Unions

credit cards; financial wizards such as Loan Calculator, Loan Amortization, and Retirement Planning; current rates; and check ordering.

Black Hills Federal Credit Union

www.blackhillsfcu.org

WBNK WL

At the Black Hills Federal Credit Union Web site, you can become a credit union member, do basic banking, apply for a loan or credit, and plan for retirement from the comfort of your own home. This site offers financial wizards for loan comparison and loan amortization as well.

Boston Post Office Credit Union

www.bpoecu.org

WBNK WL

Check out current rates and apply online for loans at the Boston Post Office Credit Union Web site. This site offers online access to your accounts, too. Tell Cliff we'll meet him at Cheers for a drink.

Boulder Municipal Employees Federal Credit Union

www.bmecu.org

TB WBNK WBP WINV

Looking for something to do? The Boulder Municipal Employees Federal Credit Union Web site offers account access, bill paying, and financial wizards for loan payment calculation. You can view this credit union's products and services, track your stock portfolio, or purchase a savings bond online.

Burlington Credit Union

www.bcune.org

WBNK

The Burlington Credit Union Web site provides online banking, information about products and services, and loan and savings rates. As is standard for most of these sites, if your browser supports encryption, you can choose to link to the secure site.

Campus Federal Credit Union

www.campusfederal.org

MSM WBNK WBP WINV

Try the following options on for size at the Campus Federal Credit Union Web site: online banking with a demo for first-time users, Web-based bill payment, and 15-minute delayed stock quotes. The site allows you to receive up to 20 stock prices, and it allows you to enter custom-ized portfolio information, such as number of shares purchased and amount paid per share, while the system updates your current portfolio value.

Capital Area School Employees Credit Union

www.casecu.org

MSM WBNK WBP WL

At the Capital Area School Employees Credit Union Web site, you can access your account to transfer funds and do other basic banking functions. You can apply for loans, calculate loan payments, and check current rates. You may have to run out for coffee before you pay your bills from home, though — at this writing, the credit union was still testing the software.

Capital City Savings

www.capcity.ab.ca

WBNK

Capital City Savings in Edmonton, Alberta, recently introduced Net Banking. Now you can pay bills, transfer funds, check account balances, and view comprehensive transaction histories from your PC. This credit union's policy is to issue passwords in person.

Central Bergen Federal Credit Union

www.centralbergen.org

TB WBP

The Central Bergen Federal Credit Union Web site offers home-banking and bill-paying options, along with 24-hour account access by phone, direct deposit, and payroll deduction. Direct debit is also available.

Chevron Federal Credit Union

www.chevronfcu.org

WBNK WBP

The Chevron Federal Credit Union Web site allows you to use PC Access to review account histories and balances and to transfer funds. You can also pay bills from this feature. At this writing, this site's online banking system did not interact with Quicken or Microsoft Money, but that capability is coming soon.

City Employees Credit Union

www.cityemployeescu.org

MSM WBNK WBP

The space-themed Web site for City Employees Credit Union offers online banking and bill payment. Though you can sign up for the account access online, you must mail in a sign-up form to pay bills on the Web. The home banking is free, but currently you pay a charge for the bill-payment feature: a one-time enrollment fee of $3.95, followed by a charge of $5.95 per month for the first 20 transactions and $.30 for each additional bill thereafter.

CommonWealth Central Credit Union

www.commonwealthcu.org

MSM WBNK WL

The CommonWealth Central Credit Union Web site offers four online applications: for membership, for a savings or checking account, for a loan, or for a credit card. Talk about never leaving your easy chair! As you make your way to couch-potato status, you can calculate how much you need to save for your retirement or calculate loan payments and amortization. Finish up by looking at savings and loan rates and ordering checks.

Commonwealth Credit Union

www.commonwealthcu.com

WBNK WL

From the comfort of your desktop, you can look into membership, apply for a loan, find current rates, and order checks at the Commonwealth Credit Union Web site. The home page contains a link to *Everybody's Money,* which contains more financial tips and advice. Oh yeah, and you can click the home banking button for online access to your account, too.

CommonWealth One Federal Credit Union

www.cofcu.org

TB WBNK WL

At the CommonWealth One Federal Credit Union Web site, click the "online branch" for account access. As with some other online banking sites, you can return to the other pages from this page only by going to the bottom Home button (the browser's Back button doesn't work). You also can use AutoVantage, a car-buying service, through this site, and you can browse through the e-zine, *Home and Family Finance Online,* for various finance tips. The site also offers online loan applications, current rates, and the usual financial wizards for calculating loans, mortgages, and retirement.

Community Credit Union

www.communitycu.org

MSM WBNK WL

At the Community Credit Union, Ltd. Web site, you can access your account at any time and you can also check current rates, order checks, or use the financial wizards to calculate loan payments or to plan retirement. You can also access an auto-buying service and use Secure Tax, an online tax preparation service.

Community Credit Union, Ltd.

www.makingthingshappen.com

ATM MSM WBNK

The Community Credit Union, Ltd. Web site, which operates under the makingthingshappen.com moniker, provides information about the credit union's products and services as well as online access to your accounts.

Constellation Federal Credit Union

www.constellationfcu.org

MSM WBNK WL

Let the Shockwave flash-enhanced home page at the Constellation Federal Credit Union Web site knock your socks off before you get down to the business of banking. You can apply for membership, accounts, loans, or a checkcard. Then you may access your account, order checks online, and use the financial wizards to calculate loans, mortgages, and retirement.

Corning Credit Union

www.corningcu.org

MSM WBNK

At the Corning Credit Union Web site, while you're online to do basic banking, you can also use AutoVantage to help you find a car to purchase. Then you can check loan rates; if you're interested, you may request that the credit union mail you a loan application (to arrive in two to four days). The site also offers financial calculators for loans, mortgages, and retirement planning.

Corporate America Family Credit Union

www.cafcu.org/home.shtml

MSM WBNK

The Corporate America Family Credit Union Web site allows you to perform basic banking functions online, such as transferring funds and pulling up account histories. You can also research the credit union's products and services. Another feature is the Focus on Family button, which links you to financial tips specifically for parents, college-bound teenagers, and seniors, as well as fun Internet activities for kids.

DCU Federal Credit Union

www.dcu.com

MSM WBNK WINV WL

Offering basic banking from your desktop, the DCU Federal Credit Union Web site also links to Member Investment Access (offered by the financial services division of American Express). Other features include online calculators and loan applications.

Decibel Credit Union

www.decibelcu.com

WBNK

Visit the Decibel Credit Union Web site to do online banking and to review the products and services that this credit union offers. You also can check out the online newsletter, *Decibel Sounds*.

Department of Commerce Federal Credit Union

www.docfcu.org

WBNK WL

Pop open a soda, view your account balances and transfer funds, and check loan rates while you're at the Department of Commerce Federal Credit Union Web site. Also check out the What's New button, which calls up tips on loan rates and allows you to apply for a loan online when you click it.

ESL Federal Credit Union

www.esl.org

MSM WBNK WL

At the ESL Federal Credit Union Web site, sign up to receive e-mail when this credit union is offering specials on products and services, or fill out the online request to have product information mailed to you.

Other features are the financial calculators, the online check ordering, the AutoVantage car-buying service, and the Swap Sheet: a place where members can place ads to sell used cars, boats, and other vehicles.

Eastman Credit Union

www.eastmancu.org

MSM WBNK WL

The Eastman Credit Union Web site features online banking, the most popular financial wizards (for loans, mortgages, and retirement planning), and current loan rates. You can also apply for membership and loans online — expect to hear back in two to four days.

Educators and Employees Credit Union

www.eduempcu.org

WBNK WL

Access your accounts, check loan rates, and apply for membership or a loan on the secure Educators and Employees Credit Union Web site. Along with the loan, mortgage, and retirement calculators, this site also features a savings calculator. Kids may want to check out the Kids Connection, which teaches the importance of starting to save and plan at a young age.

Empire Federal Credit Union

www.empirecu.org

MSM WBNK

Online account creation at the Empire Federal Credit Union Web site lets you open a new account from the comfort of your own home. Are you running out of checks? Use the online check-ordering service to order new checks. Click PC Teller to view account balances, loan balances, and account history, as well as to transfer funds between Empire accounts.

FAA Western Federal Credit Union

www.faawestern.org

WL

Features at the FAA Western Federal Credit Union Web site include applications for membership and loans online. Current rates and product information are also available.

Farmers Insurance Group Federal Credit Union

www.figfederal.com

WBNK

You can use the Farmers Insurance Group Federal Credit Union Web site to bank from home. Access accounts, transfer funds, view histories and balances, and more!

FDIC Employees Federal Credit Union

www.fdicefcu.org/home.shtml

WBNK WBP WL

Need a loan? Apply online. Need to pay bills and access your account? Do it on this site. How about ordering checks and budgeting for loans, mortgages, and retirement? The bright and cheerful FDIC Employees Federal Credit Union Web site has it, as well as the AutoVantage car-pricing service and a collection of useful financial and tax-related links.

Federal Express Credit Union

www.fecca.com

WL

For speedy delivery of loan rates, information, and approval, check out the Federal Express Credit Union Web site.

Internet banking is also available, but you must contact the credit union to get the software and pay the one-time set-up fee. I wonder who delivers the software to its members?

Federal-Metals Central Credit Union

www.fmccu.org

WBNK WL

At the Federal-Metals Central Credit Union Web site, you can access current accounts and open additional accounts as needed. Apply for a loan, and then check out the loan calculator to predict your payments. Wondering about possible special promotions for the products you want? Check out the What's Happening page to find out.

Financial 21 Community Credit Union

www.financial21.com

WBNK WL

You can do basic banking and more at Financial 21 Community Credit Union's 21st-century-themed Web site. Apply for membership, loans, and a credit card; order checks; use the loan and other calculators to budget and plan; and check out the consumer-interest links.

First Community Credit Union

www.fccu.org

MSM WBNK WBP WL

You can apply for a loan, check out current rates, and even learn about employment opportunities at the First Community Credit Union Web site. You find an online membership application for eligible members, an online request for more product and service information, and financial wizards for retirement and loan payment calculation. And, note that you can do basic banking and pay your bills at this site as well.

First South Credit Union

www.firstsouth.org

WBNK WBP WINV WL

The First South Credit Union Web site is neatly organized into five main areas: online banking, business services, an auto-buying center, a home-buying center, and investment services. You can choose the Shockwave flash-enhanced home page for fun, and don't even think about skipping the online banking demo. If you decide to set up account access from the Web, you can pay bills, check your stock portfolio, apply for loans, use car-buying services, prequalify for a mortgage, and use the retirement calculator and other planning tools and tips.

First Technology Credit Union

www.1sttech.com

MSM WBNK WBP WINV

At the First Technology Credit Union Web site, you can invest with American Express, do online banking with or without the bill-paying service, check rates, and apply for a loan.

Fort Bragg Federal Credit Union

www.fortbraggfcu.org

MSM WBNK

At the Fort Bragg Federal Credit Union Web site, you can do basic banking online among images of World War II fighter planes. You can also e-mail requests for information or applications, and you can calculate loan and mortgage payments with the online calculators.

Fort Sill Federal Credit Union

www.fsfcu.com

MSM WBNK WL

Fort Sill Federal Credit Union invites you to order checks, open additional accounts, and apply for loans online at its Web site. The credit union also offers some popular financial wizards for payment calculation, and you can bank online via the Remote Access Manager.

Fort Worth Federal Credit Union

www.fwfcu.org

MSM WBNK WBP WL

Not only can you bank online, pay bills, apply for loans, and use loan calculators, but the Fort Worth Federal Credit Union Web site also offers a Kids Club. For instance, the Student Advantage Club account is designed for students 13 to 18 years of age. Teens can check out the skills of saving money while earning dividends. Each student account holder receives a *Teens Guide To Money* book and a Student Advantage Membership Card good for discounts provided by local merchants such as Putt-Putt Golf, McDonald's, and Barnes & Noble Booksellers, not to mention other gifts.

Gold Coast Federal Credit Union

www.gcfcu.org

WBNK WL

Get information about current rates, fees, insurance services, and more at the Gold Coast Federal Credit Union Web site. You can apply for membership, loans, accounts, or credit cards; do online banking; and use the loan, savings, and retirement calculators for budgeting and planning.

Government Agencies Federal Credit Union

www.gafcu.org

WBNK WL

Bank online, browse products and services, review rates, apply for a loan, or find out whether you qualify for membership at the Government Agencies Federal Credit Union Web site. Along with popular financial wizards, this site offers a page called Our Community, where members can display their ideas and talents, trade everything from recipes and advice to used vehicles, and link to other useful Web sites.

Great American Credit Union

www.greatamerican.org/home.shtml

WBNK WL

Got some time? Browse the links page at the Great American Credit Union Web site to find such resources as the Financial Aid Information Page for college students and the Credit Union Online Library. Or, if you're in a hurry to manage your money, go right to the home-banking link. You can also use AutoVantage, a car-buying service, and apply for membership or loans online.

Group Health Credit Union

www.ghcu.org

WL

The Group Health Credit Union Web site features an online loan calculator and application, current rates, and information about purchasing autos and homes.

Guardian Credit Union

www.guardiancu.org

WBNK WBP WL

Check out the CU Fleet Department at the Guardian Credit Union Web site for auto-buying advice or even buying a car online. Available financial wizards include Loan Wizard, Loan Comparison Wizard, Mortgage Wizard, and Retirement Wizard, and the site also offers Internet banking with bill paying, applications for membership and loans, check ordering, and current rates.

Gulf Coast Educators Federal Credit Union

www.gcefcu.org

WBNK WBP WL

You can order checks at the Gulf Coast Educators Federal Credit Union Web site, or you can use the bill-paying utility to cut down on your check use altogether. This credit union charges a flat fee of $7.50 a month to do so, which gives you access to a database with current merchants, the ability to add your own merchant, the ability to view several months of payment history, and the ability to schedule recurring payments. You may also apply for membership and loans, check rates, or use the loan and retirement calculators.

Hanscom Federal Credit Union

www.hfcu.org

MSM WL

Hanscom Federal Credit Union has a pleasant surprise in store for you: an entertaining Web site, as banking sites go, due to the Shockwave flash animation, images of Colonial Minutemen, and the easy-to-use pull-down menus. Request information or common forms, apply for loans, membership, employment, or scholarships. You can also use the online calculators to figure out loans, mortgages, retirement, savings, and even kids' savings.

HAPO Community Credit Union

www.hapo.org

WBNK   WBP   WL

The online teller and online bill payer get the banking ball rolling at the HAPO Community Credit Union Web site. You can also use financial wizards; check rates, products, and services; and apply for loans. Also check out the kids' club if you want to guide your young ones through an early education in money management.

HAR-CO Maryland Federal Credit Union

www.harcocu.org

MSM   WBNK   WL

At the HAR-CO Maryland Federal Credit Union Web site, you can apply for a loan, see current rates, or reorder checks. Use financial wizards to help you estimate everything from mortgage payments to budgeting for retirement. If your browser supports encryption, you can view your personal account balances or submit an online application.

Harvard University Employees Credit Union

www.huecu.org

WBNK   WL

Now you've seen it all — this Web site acts like a cash machine. Fill out the Web withdrawal form at the Harvard University

Employees Credit Union Web site, submit it by 3 p.m., and the check goes out in the mail that same business day. You can also check rates and apply for a loan online.

Heartland Credit Union

www.heartlandcu.org

WBNK   WL

Pass your cursor over the icons on the home page at the Heartland Credit Union Web site to see a description of what's available. Why not try the home banking demo before you decide to set up online account access? You can also use the Auto Expo link for its car-buying services, the American Dream link to prequalify for a mortgage and for other house-buying help, and the Country Life link for farming-related information, including weather reports. You can apply for business and personal loans online, order checks, and use the online calculators to help you plan and budget.

Hiway Federal Credit Union

www.hiway.org

MSM   WBNK   WL

Follow the yellow brick buttons to home banking; loan and credit applications; and loan, mortgage, and retirement calculators at the Hiway Federal Credit Union Web site. You can also order checks and use the auto-buying service.

Hoosier Hills Credit Union

www.hoosierhillscu.org

WBNK   WL MSM

On the Hoosier Hills Credit Union Web site, you can do all kinds of online banking: You can transfer funds, pull up balances, or review your account histories. You can also apply for loans, check current rates, and use the loan calculators to budget.

Horizon Credit Union

www.hzcu.org

MSM WBNK WL

Access your account and apply for loans, membership, or even employment. Use loan calculators to estimate the amount of payments, order checks, and more — all online. The Horizon Credit Union Web site also offers discounted Internet service through its Internet service provider.

HP Rocky Mountain Federal Credit Union

www.hpcu.com

WBNK

From the HP Rocky Mountain Federal Credit Union Web site you can download the software you need to dial directly into the Rocky Remote system. You need a PIN already in place before you can use the system.

Hudson Valley Federal Credit Union

access.hvfcu.org

MSM WBNK WINS

Along with basic online banking, the Hudson Valley Federal Credit Union Web site offers insurance information from Travelers, information on how to phone in an application for a loan in 10 minutes, and access to a pop-up reference library.

IBM Mid America Employees Federal Credit Union

www.ibmcu.com

WBNK

At the IBM Mid America Employees Federal Credit Union Web site, you can access account balances and make loan payments online for a fee.

IBM Rocky Mountain Federal Credit Union

www.ibmfcu.org

MSM WBNK WL

The IBM Rocky Mountain Federal Credit Union Web site offers prizes along with its banking services. Visitors can win free movie passes and trips to places such as Cancun, Mexico. While you're sunning yourself, be sure to use your laptop to do your online banking, check rates, use the financial calculators, and apply for loans or credit. *Bon voyage!*

International Harvester Employee Credit Union

www.ihecu.com

TB WINV

Click the Fast Quote button at the International Harvester Employee Credit Union Web site, and enter the ticker symbol to get stock and mutual fund quotes online. Also available: loan rates, 24-hour phone access, and an online newsletter.

Island Federal Credit Union

www.islandfcu.org

MSM WBNK WBP

At the Island Federal Credit Union Web site, you can access your account and pay your bills among images of seashells. You can request that the credit union mail you loan applications and membership information. You also can use the financial wizards to calculate loan payments and other budgeting.

John Deere Community Credit Union

www.jdccu.org

MSM WBNK WL

Grab your laptop, hop on your favorite John Deere, and bank away into the sunset (don't run your vehicle into the ditch, though). Besides basic banking, the John Deere Community Credit Union Web site offers loan applications — perhaps for that new tractor or backhoe that caught your eye. You can also use loan calculators and the site's Swap Sheet.

Kaiser Permanente Federal Credit Union

www.kpfcu.org

TB WBNK

Use Easy Online to access your account anytime, day or night, at the Kaiser Permanente Federal Credit Union Web site; same goes for the Easy Teller phone line. And fill out the Easy Request online form to request information about many products and services. Easy. Easy. Easy!

Kearney Mesa Federal Credit Union

www.kmfcu.org

MSM TB WBNK

You can do your banking via the Web or your telephone; the Kearney Mesa Federal Credit Union Web site walks you through it either way. You can also research current rates and products and services.

Knight-Ridder Miami Herald Credit Union

www.krmh.com

WL

The Knight-Ridder Miami Herald Credit Union Web site features an online loan application with a loan calculator to help you figure monthly payments; you can receive one-hour turnaround on your loan application during banking hours. Also, link to KRMH's Auto-by-Tel site to price and purchase a new or used car online.

Knoxville Teachers Federal Credit Union

www.ktfcu.org

WBNK WBP

Play with some wizards (financial wizards, that is), fill out an online survey, and do your banking online at the Knoxville Teachers Federal Credit Union Web site. Check loan rates and follow the Equifax link to view your own credit report — it's often smart to take this step *before* you apply for a loan. In the future, you'll be able to pay your bills online as well — stay tuned!

Library of Congress Federal Credit Union

lcfcu.org

WL

Apply for membership or loans online, order checks, and check out the online calculators for savings, loans, mortgages, and retirement at the Library of Congress Federal Credit Union Web site. And don't forget . . . Shhhhhh! No talking!

L&N Federal Credit Union

www.lnfcu.org

MSM WBNK WL

At the L&N Federal Credit Union Web site, you can bank if you want to. You can also authorize payroll deductions and fill out other forms online, or apply for loans, membership, or a credit card. You can use the popular online calculators, too.

Lockheed Federal Credit Union

www.lockheedfcu.org

TB WBNK

At the Lockheed Federal Credit Union Web site, you can access your account online for all those basic banking functions, or do many of them over the phone. You can also apply for a loan by phone for just about any purpose, even buying one of those good old L-1011 Tristar Jumbo Jets. And, last time I checked, it cost about $9,000 an hour to fly one of them, so don't forget to ask for a larger line of credit!

Long Beach City Employees Federal Credit Union

www.lbcefcu.org

WBNK WL

Can you check rates? Oh yes. That and all the other standard features are offered at the Long Beach City Employees Federal Credit Union Web site: financial calculators, applications for loans, and that great convenience, online account access. You can also fill out the site's questionnaire to rate the credit union's services, and you can read about the Web site's security and protection of your information. Informative!

Los Alamos Credit Union

www.lacu.org

MSM WBNK WL

The Los Alamos Credit Union Web site, with its subtle Southwestern flare, makes you hungry for anything with chili peppers. Eat up, and then sit down and access your account, apply for a loan, and budget your loan payments and retirement planning with the online calculators. Yum!

Marriott Employees Federal Credit Union

www.marriottefcu.org

WL

Go to online loan calculators and online loan applications from the Marriott Employees Federal Credit Union Web site's home page. Also look into other member services and available jobs. And don't forget to tip the bellhop!

McGraw-Hill Employees Federal Credit Union

www.mcgrawhillefcu.org

MSM WBNK WL

The McGraw-Hill Employees Federal Credit Union Web site is the site that looks like an ATM . . . without the cash withdrawal slot. Use these buttons to transfer funds, view account balances, apply for a loan, and order checks. And how many ATMs do you see that can help you calculate loan or mortgage payments?

Merrimack Valley Federal Credit Union

www.merrimack-valley-fcu.org

WBNK WL

The Merrimack Valley Federal Credit Union, located in the heart of New England, lets you bank from home, check savings and loan rates, apply for a loan or membership, and keep abreast of credit union issues — all that and more, at its site on the Web.

Mid-Atlantic Federal Credit Union

www.mafcu.org

MSM WBNK WL

Need a one-hour loan? The Mid-Atlantic Federal Credit Union Web site is the right place to go. Also available: Internet account access, financial calculators, an auto resource center, and the latest rates.

MobilOil Federal Credit Union

www.mofcu.org

MSM WBNK WBP WL

MobilOil Federal Credit Union's homey site from the heart of oil country offers banking, bill payment, and loan applications. You can also access Secure Tax through this site for tax information and online tax form preparation.

Mountain America Credit Union

www.mtnamerica.org

MSM Q WBNK WBP WINV WL

Let your computer go to the mountains to do your banking, 24 hours a day, at the Mountain America Credit Union Web site. Download account information into Quicken or Microsoft Money software, track your stocks, and pay bills. Need a new vehicle so that you can take a trip to the mountains yourself? Use AutoVantage and the online loan applications; both are available on this site.

Mutual Credit Union

www.mutualcu.org

MSM WBNK WINV WL

All aboard! The Mutual Credit Union Web site has a steamboat theme and offers account access, stock quotes, and applications for loans, membership, and employment. Use the financial calculators to figure loan payments and amortization.

NASA Federal Credit Union

www.nfcu.org

WBNK WBP WINV WL

Houston, the Eagle has landed! You can do your basic banking, including ordering checks and requesting stop payments, and apply for a loan at the NASA Federal Credit Union Web site. Some members are currently testing the bill-paying feature, so that's coming soon. You can also figure loan payments and the like with financial calculators. And that's not all — the site also includes the ability to enter a stock portfolio and track it!

NIH Federal Credit Union

www.nihfcu.org

MSM Q WBNK WBP WINV WL

The NIH Federal Credit Union Web site offers more-than-basic banking functions by allowing you to download account information to Quicken and Microsoft Money, check stock quotes, and automatically pay on loans and credit cards owned by the credit union. You can apply for loans and check rates. And the links page takes you to car-buying and home-buying services and connects you to the most popular online calculators.

NJDOT Credit Union

www.njdotcu.org

WBNK WL

Don't neglect to check out the 3-D futuristic background graphic at the NJDOT Credit Union Web site before you get down to business. You can access your account, check rates, apply for a loan or membership, and order checks. Or use the AutoVantage car-buying service. And don't forget to indicate which exit you live at.

National Semiconductor Federal Credit Union

www.nsfcu.org

MSM WBNK WL

With visions of lightning dancing in your head, you can do your online banking, check rates, and use the financial calculators to help plan loan and retirement payments at the National Semiconductor Federal Credit Union Web site. Order checks and apply for loans online as well.

Network Federal Credit Union

www.networkcu.com

WBNK WL

At the Network Federal Credit Union Web site, you can get information about savings, loans, insurance, and investments. But wait, there's more. You can access your account online to transfer funds and pay bills. But wait, I'm not done yet. Get stock quotes, use loan calculators, apply for a loan online, and more.

New Mexico Educators Federal Credit Union

www.nmefcu.org

WBNK WL

If you feel like you need more help every time you use those financial calculators or other budgeting tools, you found the right place. The New Mexico Educators Federal Credit Union Web site offers personal finance tutorials to help you establish priorities in your budgeting and money management. After you gain the know-how, use the account access and other features (check ordering and online loan applications) to put it into practice. And check out the online financial newsletter to keep your knowledge current.

Northern Massachusetts Telephone Workers' Credit Union

www.nmtwcu.org

MSM WBNK WL

Check out the phone-in-space graphic on the home page of the Northern Massachusetts Telephone Workers' Credit Union Web site; then access your account online. Or apply for a loan. Or check rates. Or get credit union information, including facts about products and services offered. You have almost as many choices as Northern Massachusetts has telephone numbers.

Notre Dame Federal Credit Union

www.ndfcu.org

MSM WBNK WBP WL

Although the opening graphic may fool you into thinking you're at a bank, sit back and enjoy a candy bar to remind yourself that you're accessing your account from home! You can do all the normal online banking at the Notre Dame Federal Credit Union Web site: access your account, pay bills, and apply for a loan. You can then have another candy bar and do your taxes online as well: This site offers this tax feature after January 15. Pretty painless!

Operating Engineers #3 Federal Credit Union

www.oefcu.org

WBNK WL

In addition to a link to the *MoneyWise* newsletter, the Operating Engineers #3 Federal Credit Union Web site offers account access and the most popular financial wizards. You can apply for a loan online, but of course, you must be a member to do so.

Orange County Federal Credit Union

www.ocfcu.org

MSM WBNK WINS WL

Watch for the image of the growing orange on the first page of the Orange County Federal Credit Union Web site, and then do your basic banking and get information about services and products. You can also apply for a loan, use the loan calculators, and — get this — compare auto insurance rates online.

Orlando Federal Credit Union

www.orlandofcu.org

MSM TB WBNK WL

After Joe Member waves you into the home page at the Orlando Federal Credit Union Web site, you can check out a page of his tips (which includes special

promotions), as well as loan rates and product information. Access your account for basic online banking, or apply for membership. You can apply online for loans here, too.

PACE Credit Union

www.pacecu.org

MSM Q TB WBNK WBP WL

At CyberPACE, the PACE Credit Union Web site, you can transfer funds, make loan payments, view account balances and history, download information into Quicken and Microsoft Money, and update your stocks. Also use this site to calculate loans, mortgages, and retirement funds, and to apply for loans. Last but not least, you can order checks and pay your bills here. Now that's CyberNICE.

Pacific NW Federal Credit Union

www.pnwfcu.org

WBNK WBP WL

You can come to the Pacific NW Federal Credit Union Web site for the features, such as the online banking, bill paying, and financial calculators. You can order checks, apply for credit, or add a new account. Or you can check out the Used Cars for Sale page and meet the Frey Guy. It's all up to you.

People's Alliance Federal Credit Union

www.pafcu.org

WBNK WL

In order to give customers what they want, the People's Alliance Federal Credit Union Web site offers home banking, check ordering, and those handy online financial calculators. It also offers a link to *Home and Family Finance* online magazine, where visitors can get consumer interest information and financial tips. You can apply for membership or loans online as well.

Philadelphia Federal Credit Union

www.pfcu.com

WBNK WL

Ring the Liberty Bell! You are free to manage your accounts online and apply for a loan at the Philadelphia Federal Credit Union Web site.

Point Breeze Credit Union

www.pbcu.org

MSM WBNK WL

The good-looking, very World-Wide-Webby site (see the home page graphic) for the Point Breeze Credit Union offers more than a pretty face; you can click the PC Banking link for online account access or to check current rates at any time. Don't forget to check out the financial calculators, and you may want to consider applying for a loan online.

Postal Credit Union of Los Angeles

www.pcula.org

MSM WBNK WL

Apply for a one-hour loan, or use online account access to transfer funds and review account histories and balances at the Postal Credit Union of Los Angeles Web site. You can also compare rates and get information about various products and services.

Powerco Federal Credit Union

www.powerco.org

WBNK WL

Get energized by the opening graphic at the Powerco Federal Credit Union Web site; then use those powerful fingertips to access your account, check rates, apply for a loan, and figure loan and mortgage payments. You can also use AutoVantage to help research the purchase of a car.

PT&T Federal Credit Union

www.pttfcu.org

MSM WBNK WBP WINV WL

The biggest attraction at the PT&T Federal Credit Union Web site may be the prizes that you can register to win — a free PC, for instance. But after you get to the site, you can access your account, pay your bills, buy U.S. Savings Bonds, and use AutoVantage, a car-buying service. And that's all on top of features like online financial calculators and loan applications.

Public Service Credit Union

www.pscu.org

WBNK

On your way to access your accounts at the Public Service Credit Union Web site, you may want to check out the Kids Safari Club, the Golden Flame Club (for seniors), and the financial planning calculators, as well as other credit union information. You can find all these features at this site.

Red Rocks Federal Credit Union

www.redrocks.org

WBNK

It doesn't matter where you are — if you can sneak in a laptop, you can transfer money, check balances, and balance your checkbook at the Red Rocks Federal Credit Union Web site.

Resource One Federal Credit Union

www.r1fcu.org

MSM TB WBNK WL

The graphics at the Resource One Federal Credit Union Web site are riveting, and there's enough content to hold your interest, too. Do online banking; apply for loans, a credit card, or direct deposit; and use those handy financial calculators to help plan your monthly budget.

Reynolds Carolina Federal Credit Union

www.reynoldsfcu.org

MSM TB WBNK

Check out information about loans and other products and services at the Reynolds Carolina Federal Credit Union Web site. Access your account all day and all night, either through the Internet or by telephone. Also, check out the financial calculators and more.

Riverside Campus Federal Credit Union

www.rcfcu.org

MSM WBNK WINV

What can you do from the Riverside Campus Federal Credit Union Web site? Get account balances and histories, transfer money between accounts, make loan payments, and take line-of-credit advances. You can also order U.S. Savings Bonds, check up to 20 stocks, shop for a car online, receive a monthly online newsletter or a financial tip of the week, receive information about products and services . . . and more.

Safeway Northwest Central Credit Union

www.safewaynw.org

WBNK WL

You can compare loan and savings rates; start a primary or family membership; apply for a loan; review the features and benefits of accounts; access accounts through the link called Day and Night services; choose a financial product like payroll direct deposit, a car-buying service, or insurance protection; and obtain information through the site directory at the Safeway Northwest Central Credit Union Web site. Whew!

Salt River Project Federal Credit Union

www.srpfcuaz.org

MSM WBNK WL

If you have time to browse, you can check out the page of consumer-interest links at the Salt River Project Federal Credit Union Web site. Otherwise, get down to business and manage your money: Access your account, use the financial calculators, apply for credit or a loan, or check out products and services that you may need.

San Diego County Federal Credit Union

www.sdccu.org

BBS MSM Q WBNK WINV WL

At the San Diego County Federal Credit Union Web site, you can view your account balances for savings, checking, and loan accounts. You can also view your transaction history for savings, checking, and loan accounts, or transfer money among your accounts. This site allows you to create your own personalized stock portfolio records, receive updates on stock prices, and import account history into personal financial management programs such as Quicken, Microsoft Money, or SDCCU's Bill Payer Plus. And yes, you can check rates, apply for loans online, and order checks, too.

San Diego Teachers' Credit Union

www.sdtcu.org

MSM Q WBNK WBP WINV WL

If you've been waiting to use Quicken or Microsoft Money, the San Diego Teachers' Credit Union Web site makes it easy by allowing your account information to download into either of these programs. You also can apply for loans and credit at this site. The Consumer Connection page on this site can link you to information about travel, movie ticket discounts, entertainment, insurance services, and tax services.

Sara Lee Credit Union

www.slcu.org

WBP

After your checking account is set up in the Bill PayIt system at the Sara Lee Credit Union Web site, you can, for a charge, set your bills to be paid every month on a certain date. You can also check loan rates and car prices, and print out a loan application.

Schools Credit Union

www.schoolscu.org

MSM WBNK

Stroll into the colorful "lobby" at the Schools Credit Union Web site without ever leaving home. Basic online banking functions are available, as well as rates, online calculators, and product and service information.

Shell Employees Federal Credit Union

www2.sefcu.org

MSM TB WBNK WL

The Shell Employees Federal Credit Union Web site's entry page offers two options: one for members and one for visitors. Visitors can access the many online calculators. They include calculators for new and used auto loans, recreational vehicle loans, home improvement or home equity loans, and ready cash and credit card loans. Loan applications and 24-hour online account access are also available at this large site.

Southwest Airlines Credit Union

www.swacuflash.org

WBNK WL

The theme of the Southwest Airlines Credit Union Web site is transportation, and its pages are filled with animated graphics of rockets, trains, and other vehicles. Swerve around a bit and you'll find online banking, applications for loans, financial wizards (no, they're not the ones driving), and plenty of product and service information. And don't forget to keep your trays and seatbacks in their upright and locked position.

Spokane Railway Credit Union

www.srcu.com

WBNK WL

"We know there are other places you'd rather be . . ." the online service page at the Spokane Railway Credit Union Web site reads, featuring a picture of a smiling woman enjoying the fresh air and the mountains. In order to fulfill this wish, the site offers online access to your account, online loan and membership applications, and online check ordering. Use the retirement calculator (one of six financial wizards) to figure out how much you need before you can retire to "them thar hills."

St. Helens Community Federal Credit Union

www.shcfcu.org

MSM WBNK WL

Check out the exploding volcano at the St. Helens Community Federal Credit Union Web site before you get into your online banking, your online loan application, or begin ordering your checks. The site doesn't provide a calculator for figuring out when Mount St. Helens may erupt again, but plenty of online wizards can help you do your financial planning and budgeting.

Star One Federal Credit Union

www.starone.org

MSM WBNK WL

Click the middle star on the home page at the Star One Federal Credit Union Web site for direct deposit information, or go

right to funds transfer or your account history with the Online Banking link. Also available: online calculators and loan applications.

Suffolk Federal Credit Union

www.suffolkfcu.org

MSM WBNK WL

Need a job? Fill out an employment application at the Suffolk Federal Credit Union Web site. Need cash? Fill out a loan and membership application. After you earn some money, manage it via the online banking features at the site, and start planning for retirement and home ownership with the online calculators.

Technology Groups Federal Credit Union

www.tgfcu.org

WL

You can apply for loans, order checks, open new accounts, and request a stop payment on draft at the Technology Groups Federal Credit Union Web site.

Texas Bay Area Credit Union

www.tbacu.org

MSM WBNK WBP WL

Regardless of whether you're deep in the heart of Texas, you can pay your bills, transfer funds, and check account balances at the Texas Bay Area Credit Union Web site. Also available: financial wizards and online loan applications.

Texas Instruments Federal Credit Union

tifcu.org

WL

Use the AutoVantage auto-buying service to find that new car you want — with less hassle. You can also use the Texas Instruments Federal Credit Union Web site to apply for membership, a loan, or a credit card. You should hear back from the credit union in two to four days.

Three Rivers Federal Credit Union

www.3riversfcu.org

MSM   WBNK   WBP   WL

The online account access at the Three Rivers Federal Credit Union Web site allows you to check your balances, pull account history, see which checks have cleared, transfer money between your accounts, and download your account information to money management software programs such as Quicken and Microsoft Money. Bill paying is also available, as are current rates, loan applications, and, of course, those handy financial calculators.

Treasury Department Federal Credit Union

www.tdfcu.org

MSM   WBNK

Nice brick o' gold! If you have the equivalent of a few of these in your accounts, you can manage those funds from home using the features at the Treasury Department Federal Credit Union Web site. You can also check out products and services, and you can use resources on the Useful Links page.

Triangle Credit Union

www.trianglecu.org

MSM   WBNK   WBP   WL

From the comfort of your desktop, you can apply for a loan; inquire about current loan rates, savings rates, and certificate rates; and even complete an online membership application for eligible members at the Triangle Credit Union Web site. And yes, you can do your basic banking and bill paying from home.

TRW Systems Federal Credit Union

www.trwsfcu.org

WBNK

Review your account histories for up to six months, transfer funds between your own accounts, request that a check be sent to a specified address, and soon, pay bills online. The TRW Systems Federal Credit Union Web site is also full of consumer-interest information, so check it out.

USA Federal Credit Union

www.usafedcu.org/home.shtml

WBNK   WL

You can still access your accounts at the USA Federal Credit Union Web site, even if you don't happen to live near one of the credit union's branches (in California, Nevada, Japan, Korea, and Guam). Basic online banking, current rates, and loan and credit applications are all available at this site. You can also order checks and use AutoVantage for help in purchasing a car.

U.S. Federal Credit Union

www.usfed.org

MSM WBNK WL

At the U.S. Federal Credit Union Web site, you can do your basic banking: check rates; calculate your loan, mortgage, and retirement plan payments; and apply for credit and loans — no matter where you are or what the time. It's enough to make you want to wave an American flag.

U.S. Postal Service Federal Credit Union

www.uspsfcu.org

WL

If it's 3:00 a.m. and you need to know whether you can get a loan, click the one-hour loan button at the U.S. Postal Service Federal Credit Union Web site to apply and hear back right away. Use the financial calculator to figure your monthly payments, and you can still sneak in a couple hours of beauty rest before sunrise.

United Nations Federal Credit Union

www.unfcu.org

WBNK WL

For worldwide convenience, the United Nations Federal Credit Union Web site is *the* site. Basic banking, loan applications, online calculators. Oh, and you can order "cheques," too.

United States Senate Federal Credit Union

ussfcu.org

WBNK WL

Contact the credit union by phone or in person first to set up your online account. After that, you can do basic banking from home through the United States Senate Federal Credit Union Web site. Or, fill out the online form to apply for a loan or credit card. Also, check out the many consumer-interest articles listed on the home page, including money-managing tips from financial guru Ric Edelman.

United Teletech Federal Credit Union

www.teletechfcu.org

MSM WBNK WL

The United Teletech Federal Credit Union Web site has online banking, online loan applications, and the AutoVantage car-buying service. Current rates and financial wizards? Yep — this site has those features, too.

University and State Employees Credit Union

www.usecu.org

MSM WBNK WBP WL

Apply for loans or credit, do basic banking, and pay your bills at the University and State Employees Credit Union Web site. Order checks and look at check styles (always a nice diversion). After you finish, you may want to fill out the questionnaire (found on the pull-down menu on the home page) to tell the credit union which services you found helpful.

University Federal Credit Union

www.ufcu.org

WBNK WL

Get smart! You can access your account online at the University Federal Credit Union Web site, check rates, use loan calculators to figure monthly payments and amortization, and apply for loans online. Also check out some money tips from the online magazine, *Home and Family Finance.*

University of Iowa Community Credit Union

www.iowacity.com/uiccu/

WBNK   WBP

From the University of Iowa Community Credit Union Web site, you can download the software you need to access your account from home and, for a small charge, pay your bills online as well.

University of Utah Credit Union

www.ucreditu.com

MSM   Q   WBNK

Go west, young man! At the University of Utah Credit Union Web site, you can download Home Teller, the software you need to access accounts online, order checks, change your PIN, and download account information into either Quicken or Microsoft Money.

University of Wisconsin Credit Union

www.uwcu.org

WBNK   WL

The University of Wisconsin Credit Union Web site gives you the option to access your account from the Web or to download the software that allows you to dial in directly and securely. You can also apply for a loan online after you check current rates and other product information.

Ventura County Federal Credit Union

www.vcfcu.org

MSM   WBNK   WL

If the sunny mission scene on the home page of the Ventura County Federal Credit Union Web site doesn't make you smile, maybe you should try the Fun in the Sun page: It offers clubs for kids, seniors and young adults. At this writing, home banking was in the final stages of testing for this site, but online applications for loans, membership, and payroll deductions were available.

Virginia Credit Union

www.vacu.org

WL

The Virginia Credit Union Web site features an online loan application, current rates, and information about purchasing autos and homes.

Vista Federal Credit Union

www.vistafcu.org

WL

Vista Federal Credit Union serves the employees of the Walt Disney Corporation, so as you can imagine, the site features a few whimsical images! If you're in the mood for something more substantial, however, you may check rates and apply for a loan at this site.

Water and Power Credit Union

www.wpcu.org

WBNK   WBP

If you use a PC, you need to first download the PC Express software from the Water and Power Credit Union Web site. (Mac users don't need to do so.) Now you've got the power to view your account history, get loan information, make loan payment transfers, and transfer money among accounts. You can also view payroll deposits and current loan and share rates, see your tax information, and download transaction histories to use with other programs. This site is expecting Bill Payer Service soon as well.

Western Federal Credit Union

www.western.org

MSM WBNK WINS WINV WL

To Do: Get insurance quotes from Liberty Mutual, transfer funds, check account balance, review account history, shop for a car from AutoLand, order checks, calculate retirement, and apply for investment services. Does this sound like your "To Do" list? If so, your next stop is the Western Federal Credit Union Web site. *Note:* You need Adobe Acrobat Reader to view and print the applications for membership and for investment and checking services.

XCEL Federal Credit Union

www.xcelfcu.org

MSM WBNK WL

X marks the spot for banking from home and online loan applications at the XCEL Federal Credit Union Web site. Also available: financial calculators and product and service information.

Your Campus Federal Credit Union

www.campuscu.com

WBNK

At the Your Campus Federal Credit Union Web site, you can see up-to-the-minute account information, request stop payments, transfer funds, and more. You also can get rates and information about savings and loans.

Financial Keywords for America Online

America Online is the most popular online service in the world, with more than 12 million members. Because so many people use the AOL online service, I include this section to highlight some of the banking and financial services available through AOL; in particular, I supply the financially oriented keywords that you can use with AOL.

Keywords are the terms that you use to navigate in AOL. After you log on to AOL, you have two ways to find information on the service. The first way is to select a general area, like Personal Finance, from the main menu and then click different selections on subsequent screens. The second way is to press Ctrl+K. When you do that, a window pops up, into which you can enter a keyword. The following AOL keywords are particularly helpful to folks looking for help with banking and personal finance issues.

Banking and Banking Center

Enter the keyword Banking or the keyword Banking Center to go to the AOL Banking Center. From there, you can select any bank online specifically via AOL or link directly to banks on the Internet. You also can view other personal financial data from this screen, including current interest rates.

BankNOW

BankNOW is the software that allows banking from one simple screen. When you enter the keyword BankNOW, you see a list of banks. You can access any of these banks with BankNOW on AOL or link directly to any of these banks' Web sites.

Bank Rate Monitor

Bank Rate Monitor is a Florida-based financial information publishing company. It offers its information on the Web and, when you enter the keyword Bank Rate Monitor, on AOL.

Brokerage

Enter the keyword Brokerage to go to AOL's Brokerage Center. From this site, you can interact with several companies that offer online brokerage services. Some services take place on AOL, others through a link to the vendor's Web site.

Insurance

The Insurance keyword takes you to AOL's Insurance Center. Not only can you look at insurance quotes, you can also read about the insurance business.

Intuit

Enter the keyword Intuit to find information about Intuit, the makers of Quicken, QuickBooks, TurboTax, and BankNOW software, which has its own special area on AOL. This area covers online products, interactive services, and software and support.

Markets

Maybe you need to know the current exchange rate between the yen and the dollar, or perhaps the current Dow Jones Industrial Average. You can find the answers to these questions and more by entering the AOL keyword Markets.

Money University

Let's face it, we can all use a little advice regarding our finances from time to time. Ric Edelman is the "host" of the AOL

Money University. When you enter the keyword Money University, you enter the part of AOL where you can read about Ric and the topics that he discusses, send him an e-mail, or join a chat session with other folks who may have financial questions.

Money Whiz

Another great area that you can use on AOL to figure out your finances is at the keyword Money Whiz. The Money Whiz area boasts a constantly changing series of articles and discussions on all sorts of financial topics.

Motley Fool or Fool

Enter the keyword Fool (or the keyword Motley Fool) to enter the Motley Fool area. The Motley Fool takes a humorous, tongue-in-cheek approach to explaining personal finances. The majority of the material focuses on investing topics, but other issues do come up from time to time.

Mutual Fund

The keyword Mutual Fund delivers you to the AOL Mutual Fund Center. The Mutual Fund area of AOL allows you to research mutual funds, share thoughts with other AOL users, and enter your orders to buy or sell your mutual funds. AOL had only an Investment Center at first, but the Center got so popular and full of information that AOL split the two areas into separate keywords.

Online Investor

Use the keyword Online Investor to enter the Online Investor area, an excellent resource for an AOL customer to read about and participate in the stock market. Which stock should I buy? How does a discount broker work? What's a DRIP? Find the answers to these questions and more in this area.

Personal Finance

The keyword Personal Finance takes you to an AOL location where you can choose many of the other keyword areas covered in this list. If you want to learn more about personal finance in general and aren't sure whether stocks and bonds or online banking is where you want to be, try starting here.

Portfolios

Portfolios are lists of stocks, bonds, and mutual funds that you select and place in a list along with number of shares purchased and amount paid for each. The Portfolios keyword and area enable you to check all the quotes in your portfolio for updated values so that you can see exactly how well (or how poorly) your investments are doing as a group. Hey, I don't know if that's good or bad!

Quotes

If all you want to do is look up a quote for an individual stock or mutual fund, you can find what you're looking for by entering the keyword Quotes. You can check quotes on a large number of exchanges around the world.

Government Sites

Whether you're a banker or a bank customer, government-sponsored Web sites can prove informative — especially regarding issues such as security and government protection. This section describes many of the most useful government sites for bankers and the general public.

The Federal Deposit Insurance Corporation

www.fdic.gov/

The FDIC is the government organization that provides protection to account holders (within certain limits) in case a financial institution goes broke. This is a rich source of information about the FDIC, the laws and regulations governing financial institutions, consumer information, and more.

The National Credit Union Administration

www.ncua.gov/

The National Credit Union Administration is an independent federal agency that's entirely funded by credit unions and receives no tax dollars. It supervises and insures 6,981 federal credit unions and insures 4,257 state-chartered credit unions. The Web site provides information about the agency and about credit unions in general, and includes a search feature that can locate credit unions in your area.

The Office of The Comptroller of the Currency

www.occ.treas.gov/

The Office of the Comptroller of the Currency is the Treasury Department office that charters and regulates national banks. The OCC Web site is loaded with documents and information, most of which are of interest only to banking professionals. However, you can also find useful information on individual banks.

The Office of Thrift Supervision

www.ots.treas.gov/

The Office of Thrift Supervision is the primary regulator of all nationally associated and many state-chartered thrift institutions (often called savings and loans). Like the OCC, the OTS is a part of the Treasury Department. The OTS Web site is primarily designed to provide information to staff of the institutions that it oversees, but the Office of Thrift Supervision has a great reference site that's valuable even if the OTS isn't your primary regulator. For consumers, a feature on the Public Information page enables you to locate and compare statistics on chartered thrift institutions.

The United States Treasury

www.ustreas.gov/

The United States Treasury Web site is the definitive place to find info about money matters. Hey, all the money belongs to this institution anyway! Take a tour of the Treasury Department, read a greeting from the Secretary of the Treasury, and check out all the different departments.

Regulation E: The government's guarantee

frwebgate.access.gpo.gov/cgi-bin/get-cfr.cgi?TITLE=12&PART=205&SECTION=1&TYPE=TEXT

frwebgate.access.gpo.gov/cgi-bin/get-cfr.cgi?TITLE=12&PART=205&SECTION=2&TYPE=TEXT

frwebgate.access.gpo.gov/cgi-bin/get-cfr.cgi?TITLE=12&PART=205&SECTION=3&TYPE=TEXT

frwebgate.access.gpo.gov/cgi-bin/get-cfr.cgi?TITLE=12&PART=205&SECTION=4&TYPE=TEXT

frwebgate.access.gpo.gov/cgi-bin/get-cfr.cgi?TITLE=12&PART=205&SECTION=5&TYPE=TEXT

frwebgate.access.gpo.gov/cgi-bin/get-cfr.cgi?TITLE=12&PART=205&SECTION=6&TYPE=TEXT

frwebgate.access.gpo.gov/cgi-bin/get-cfr.cgi?TITLE=12&PART=205&SECTION=7&TYPE=TEXT

frwebgate.access.gpo.gov/cgi-bin/get-cfr.cgi?TITLE=12&PART=205&SECTION=8&TYPE=TEXT

frwebgate.access.gpo.gov/cgi-bin/get-cfr.cgi?TITLE=12&PART=205&SECTION=9&TYPE=TEXT

frwebgate.access.gpo.gov/cgi-bin/get-cfr.cgi?TITLE=12&PART=205&SECTION=10&TYPE=TEXT

frwebgate.access.gpo.gov/cgi-bin/get-cfr.cgi?TITLE=12&PART=205&SECTION=11&TYPE=TEXT

frwebgate.access.gpo.gov/cgi-bin/get-cfr.cgi?TITLE=12&PART=205&SECTION=12&TYPE=TEXT

frwebgate.access.gpo.gov/cgi-bin/get-cfr.cgi?TITLE=12&PART=205&SECTION=13&TYPE=TEXT

frwebgate.access.gpo.gov/cgi-bin/get-cfr.cgi?TITLE=12&PART=205&SECTION=14&TYPE=TEXT

frwebgate.access.gpo.gov/cgi-bin/get-cfr.cgi?TITLE=12&PART=205&SECTION=15&TYPE=TEXT

You're probably wondering what in the world you're supposed to do with the 15 Web addresses listed above. These Web addresses point you to the 15 sections of the *United States Code* that cover online banking, known as Regulation E ("reg. E"): for the record, Title 12, Chapter II, Part 205 — ELECTRONIC FUNDS TRANSFERS (REGULATION E). The Regulation E Code has a ton of fine print to offer, so it's broken into 15 sections with a separate Web address for each section. Reading the sections one at a time at the separate addresses makes for easy digestion of the Code. (For some explanation and deciphering of Regulation E, check out Chapter 11.)

Software Vendors

Throughout this book, I mention several software vendors that sell banking and financial software and a few vendors that sell important related products. In this section, I list the Web sites for the major vendors, in case you need more product information, software updates, or company contact info.

America Online

www.aol.com

America Online (AOL) is the largest online service in the world, with more than 12 million customers in the United States and abroad. Access all of AOL's content and get a direct link to the Internet for a flat fee of $21.95 a month, or, if you spend only a little time online, sign up for the low-usage hourly fee.

The latest version of AOL (version 4.0) includes the complete Microsoft Internet Explorer, so you shouldn't have any trouble accessing the Internet through AOL. I lay out the online banking options through AOL for your undivided attention in Chapter 6.

Microsoft Money

www.microsoft.com/money

Microsoft Money is a personal financial manager software package (which I cover in-depth in Chapter 8). The Microsoft Money site not only makes the latest trial version of the software available for download, but it also includes oodles of helpful information about the software.

Managing Your Money

www.mymnet.com

Because you can get your software from your bank, the MYM site doesn't offer trial versions of the software online. However, it does discuss several new products under development. Interesting!

Microsoft Internet Explorer

www.microsoft.com/ie

In Chapter 1, I explain both major players in the Web browser market. Microsoft Internet Explorer is one of those two major players. You may already have a copy of Internet Explorer that you got when you purchased a computer, purchased related software, or signed up with your Internet service provider. If so, this site gives you plenty of information on how to use Internet Explorer. And if you *don't* have Internet Explorer, you can download a copy here.

Netscape Communicator with Navigator

www.netscape.com

Netscape Communicator is a major player (along with Microsoft Internet Explorer) in the Web browser market. Communicator is an entire suite of Web browsing tools and Navigator is the browser portion of that suite. If you want to use Netscape Communicator (or do your own side-by-side comparison with Internet Explorer), you can download a copy from this site.

Quicken

www.quicken.com

The Quicken Web site isn't just for software anymore. Quicken.com is a valuable resource for online financial information. You can look for interest rates, insurance, financial market news, stock quotes, and several options for buying financial products. And of course, you can find software support help right online.

QuickBooks

www.quickbooks.com

The QuickBooks site offers a thorough level of software support for QuickBooks customers. Read industry-specific information or use the cool business cash finder, a service that allows you to shop your application for business credit around several financial institutions.

Virtual Internet Banks

Virtual Internet banks are banks that conduct all their business with customers only over the Internet. So, essentially, virtual Internet banks exist only in the virtual world of the Internet (but, of course, even a virtual bank must have at least one branch office from which to operate — that's the law). Virtual banking is in its infancy — as this book goes to press, the list of virtual banks is very short — but you can expect this category to grow rapidly in the next few years.

Net.B@nk

www.netbank.com

WBNK   WBP   WINV

Net.B@nk is the first virtual Internet bank to turn a profit. Net.B@nk offers free bill payment and competitive deposit rates. Federal banking regulations require virtual banks to have at least one office for customers to visit. You can find this bank's mandatory offices in Atlanta.

Security First Network Bank

www.sfnb.com

SFNB is the pioneer in true virtual banks. Like the other Internet banks, its low overhead enables it to offer aggressive loan and deposit rates. In an interesting move, Security First Technologies, the original owner and developer of the SFNB virtual bank, has now sold its Internet banking software to several large and mid-sized banks, including Wachovia and Huntington Banks. Meanwhile, Royal Bank of Canada recently purchased SFNB.

Web Sites for Bankers

In this section, I list several Web sites that include useful information for banking professionals. Some of the Web sites give conventional banking information online; some of the Web sites give advice for banks that want to offer online services. If you're a banker who wants to put the Bailey Building & Loan online, you may find several sites of interest to you and Uncle Billy.

American Bankers Association

www.aba.com

The American Bankers Association is a trade association serving the United States banking community. In addition to the national organization, state chapters are associated with the ABA.

The ABA holds annual national conferences, and helps banks through education, training, information, and lobbying efforts in Washington, D.C.

The ABA Web site includes numerous resources for bankers, including Web links, ABA articles on banking issues, some job search listings, and BankersMart, an industry shopping mall.

American Banker magazine

www.americanbanker.com

American Banker magazine provides a free news summary every day. Full-text articles are reserved for subscribers. If you want to try it out, take advantage of the free offer.

Bank Administration Institute

www.bai.org

Bank Administration Institute (BAI), based in Chicago, is a professional organization that focuses on improving the competitive position of banking companies through research and education events. The mission of BAI is to "establish banking companies as the preeminent providers of financial services by offering high-quality, relevant, objective information and programs."

BAI conducts more than 200 education events, including conferences, seminars, graduate programs, roundtables, and certification programs. BAI also hosts annually the Retail Delivery Conference (usually in late November/early December), an expansive trade show covering online banking, ATM, call centers, and other alternative delivery products and issues.

Credit Union National Association

www.cuna.org

CUNA is a trade association that represents credit unions and credit union members in the United States. Following several challenges to credit unions and how they operate, CUNA has spearheaded an effort to get Congress to pass rules that govern who can belong to a credit union.

Like the banking trade organizations, CUNA offers numerous educational and convention opportunities throughout the year.

The Federal Reserve Board of Governors

www.bog.frb.fed.us/boarddocs/
SRLETTERS/1997/SR9732.HTM

The *Sound Practices Guidance for Information Security for Networks* from the Federal Reserve Board is important reading for any bank with an Internet presence — even if the bank uses only Internet e-mail.

Gomez Advisors Internet Banker Scorecard

www.gomez.com/Banks/Scorecard/

Gomez Advisors surveys online banks and their customers to determine who has the best online banking offering. Gomez also provides this service for online investing sites.

Murphy & Company

www.mcompany.com

What self-respecting author can pass up the opportunity to plug his own company and Web site in his own book? Not me! Seriously, Murphy & Company offers online banking marketing strategy and development services for banks of all sizes. The company offers online banking marketing guides, seminars, and on-site consulting services. Many banks, large and small, have benefited from our assistance in developing online banking marketing plans.

The Online Banking Association

www.obanet.org/

The Online Banking Association is a member-sponsored, nonprofit trade organization based in Corte Madre, California. Although the name says "online banking," the organization also helps members in areas like Electronic Bill Presentment issues.

The Online Banking Newsletter

Phone: 1-800-732-8104

The *Online Banking Newsletter* doesn't have a Web site yet, but it certainly is informative. Make the call and get a trial subscription — and then when it goes online, you'll be among the first to know.

The Online Banking Report

www.onlinebankingreport.com

Jim Bruene publishes the *Online Banking Report* to help bankers keep up-to-date on the latest industry information. Additionally, he periodically publishes a list of online banks.

Part V
The Part of Tens

"Oh yeah, he's got a lot of money. When he tries to check his balance online, he gets a computer message saying there's 'Insufficient Memory' to complete the task."

In this part . . .

The Part of Tens is an oldie but goodie that you find in all *...For Dummies* books. This part includes a chapter filled with invaluable pointers about making online bill payments.

Chapter 13

Ten Tips for Using Online Bill Payment

In This Chapter

▶ Getting the payee and your account number right

▶ Sending yourself a sample payment

▶ Using recurring payments and bill-payment guarantees

▶ Making sure that the payee received payment

▶ Troubleshooting if the payee doesn't receive payment

▶ Timing your payments correctly

*P*aying your bills online is simple, convenient, and a great way to manage your cash flow. Sitting down at the computer and sending off your payments with just a few clicks of the mouse is painless and easy. (Well, maybe it's not quite so painless to watch your money evaporate as the electrons scurry off to the payees, but the actual payment process can't hurt you.)

Let this chapter serve as a checklist of the most crucial things to remember when you make your bill payments. Remembering these tips can improve your bill-paying experience and save you needless trouble.

Make Sure You Get the Payee Name Right

Whether you use Web-based banking or a PFM software package to pay your bills, at some time during the process, you need to establish your list of payees. (I explain what payees are and how to create payee lists in Chapter 4.) Each entry needs to contain the payee's name and mailing address, along with your account number and any other information that the payee needs for processing your payment. When you mail your payment from home in the traditional manner, you normally include a stub or payment coupon along with your check. Information on this stub helps the payee identify your payment and properly credit it to your account. However, online bill payments don't have any such stub; therefore, it's critically important that you enter the correct account information when you set up the payee online. That way, the information is correct on every check that you create online.

Sounds silly for me to say, but you *do* need to get that payee name right, especially when you're dealing with major credit cards. Although you call the company Visa, your payments may actually go to your bank — so the payee name would be First National Bank of My Home Town or something similar.

You need to make sure that you set up the payee name to match the *Make Payment To* name on your bill. A group of different banks or credit unions may all contract with the same company to process payments. By addressing the payment properly, you ensure that the payment-processing company has the information that it needs to apply the payment to your account.

The Account Number Is Critical

Hello again from the strange-but-true files. Some people don't enter their account number when sending an electronic payment — even though the account number is an absolute must.

Most payees request that you put your account number on your check when you pay your bill. The number helps them make sure that your payment is credited to your account. You may get away with omitting the account number when you mail a check from home because you normally enclose a payment stub or coupon with the check, and your account number is on that stub. (That's why the payee includes the stub or tear-off coupon on your bill and instructs you to send it back with your payment.)

As you know, your electronic payments aren't accompanied by the stub that the payee is used to seeing. You're responsible to get the key information from that stub onto your online bill payment by including it in the payee information. Your account number that identifies you to the payee is one of the most critical pieces of information. If you don't include your correct account number, the payee probably can't post the check or electronic payment to your account. Rest assured that the payee can still (and most assuredly will) accept the payment; you just may not get credit for having paid until you squawk.

Test the System by Sending Yourself a Sample Payment

Okay — I confess that I was a little cautious when I made my first online bill payment way back in 1992. (That's 50 years ago in Internet years, dating back to the pre-Webazoic era.) To put my fears to rest and see exactly what the heck happens, I sent my first online banking payment to myself.

I set myself up as a payee, right between the phone company and my Visa card, and I filled some sample information in the account number and memo fields.

When the check arrived, I saw exactly what the check looked like, the positioning of the information on the check, and so on. Plus, I got to see how long the payment took to get from the bank to my mailbox. (Yes, I did deposit the check in my ATM to avoid the puzzled look I was sure to get from a teller — "Let's see, Mr. Murphy, that's a deposit of $1 from . . . Paul Murphy?")

You can use this same technique to test the online bill-payment system for yourself. You may want to redo the test periodically, just to keep an eye on things. (Banks do change their systems and procedures from time to time.)

Recurring Payments Save Time

Using online banking to pay your bills is much easier than writing out a check each month, but you can make your bill payments even easier by setting up recurring payments when possible. Recurring payments enable you to send the same amount of money to the same payee on a regular basis. (See Chapter 5 for more on recurring payments.)

You can't predict the exact balance of certain bills, such as monthly long-distance telephone charges and credit card usage. These bills vary considerably from month to month, and your only option for paying them is to enter a one-time payment each month for the exact amount of the bill. But for payments that are the same every month, recurring payments are real time-savers.

If you have a standard monthly bill, such as a mortgage, you pay the same predetermined amount for each monthly payment. If you have a mortgage that adjusts your interest rate every 12 months, you can set up a recurring payment to pay your mortgage on the first day of every month for the 12 months before the next rate adjustment. Then your job is done — except for keeping enough money in your account — until the mortgage company readjusts your payment and you simply set up a recurring payment for the new 12-month period.

Confirm That Your Payment Arrived

You pressed the button and sent your payment. Good for you! But how do you know that the money arrived at its destination? Try the following methods:

✔ **Call a telephone inquiry system:** These systems — first used by credit card and mortgage companies and now used by a growing number of other types of companies — enable you to use a Touch-Tone telephone to access information about your account 24 hours a day. You can retrieve all types of information, including the balance in your accounts, the dates and amounts of your latest charges, and the date and amount of your last payment. These systems provide a convenient way to find out quickly when the payee received your payment.

✔ **Make an online account inquiry:** A growing number of companies, such as Discover Card, allow customers to access their account information via the Internet. After a brief sign-up process to verify your identity, you can check all the same information usually available on the telephone inquiry systems.

✔ **Read your next statement from the payee:** Your monthly statement following the bill payment is a great source for confirming that your bill payment was processed. It also tells you the date that the vendor posted the money to your account. You can get a good idea of how long a particular payee takes to process the payments by reviewing a couple months' worth of statements. You can then adjust your bill-paying habits accordingly.

Look for a Bill-Payment Guarantee

Many banks offer a *bill-payment guarantee* (which I explain in Chapter 5). Although terms vary between banks, the deal is pretty simple. If you make your online bill-payment request far enough in advance of the actual due date and it isn't posted on time, the bank covers any late fees that you sustain. The bank often can convince the payee to waive the fees, and, if necessary, most banks cover up to $50 in late fees.

The legal type backing up these offers is thicker than mud and most banks refuse to guarantee a few select payments (such as some large mortgage payments, tax payments, and court-ordered payments), but the bill-payment guarantee works for most situations. Even if your bank doesn't offer a formal guarantee, it can often help you resolve disputes over late payments made through its online bill-payment system.

Update Your Payee Information Routinely

Routinely check payee information (available on the bill that you receive in the mail) against your online banking payee list. A wise plan is to check the information every few months — perhaps three or four times a year.

Occasionally, payees such as credit card companies change the address where you send your payment. This kind of change is not unusual at all, and when it happens, you need to update your payee record. Usually, the payee's old address remains functional for a couple of months after any change, so checking your payee addresses once a quarter keeps everything running smoothly.

It's much more rare for your account number to change, but that can happen, too. For example, I ran into this problem once when the local utility company added four digits to everyone's account number in an effort to increase the number of customers that it could manage with its software. Because of the change, the old account number on my online payment didn't match my newly assigned account number, and the payment wasn't credited to my account. I managed to correct the problem when the utility company called to see what was going on. A quick update to the payee record got my payments back on track. If I'd been paying by handwritten checks via regular mail, however, such a change wouldn't matter, because the new account number would have been on the return stub.

Don't Overreact When You Suspect a Problem with a Payment

So you made your payment, you waited a week for the payment to reach the payee, and for one reason or another, the payment wasn't posted when you looked for it. Or, you just received your Visa bill and your payment from last month doesn't appear to be credited to your account. What do you do? Don't overreact and kick your computer for failing to deliver your payment. Just take your time and follow these steps (in order) until you find the problem:

1. **Wait at least five business days before you take any action.**

   That's five *business* days, not five calendar days — basically a full week, assuming no holidays. If on the sixth business day the problem hasn't resolved itself, only then should you go on to Step 2.

2. **Look at your online statement or printed monthly account statement for information that identifies the payment you made.**

   Some systems assign a confirmation number to each payment. Other systems use a check number, and still others just track payments by date and amount. You can write the confirmation number on your bills after making the payment but before filing the bills for your records. If a few weeks to a month have elapsed since your payment, you can also find the confirmation number on your bank statement. As a last alternative, you can call your bank's customer service department.

3. **Review the payment instructions (just to make sure that you paid the correct party on the correct day for the correct amount).**

4. **Call the payee and see whether your payment was simply delayed in the mail when your statement was sent.**

   If you paid the bill close to its final due date, a delay may have caused the payment to arrive too late to be credited on your next account statement. But the payment may have been posted since the statement was mailed.

5. **Contact your bank's online banking customer service department.**

   Give all the information that you've gathered in Steps 1 to 4 (payment identification information, payee information, and dates of your inquiries with the payee) to your bank's customer service representative. Ask for the bank to put a trace on the payment.

6. **Call your payee and explain the situation.**

   Let the payee know that you contacted your bank, which is working to find the payment.

Allow Adequate Time between Pay Date and Due Date

Pay date and *due date* are not synonyms. Pay date is the date when you schedule your bill payment to start moving; due date is the date when the payment needs to arrive at the office of your payee. If you don't allow enough time between these dates, you can incur late fees — and nobody wants that to happen, right? (Refer to Chapter 5 for more on pay dates and due dates.)

Try to leave at least five business days between the pay date and the due date. For best results, schedule payments to arrive a couple of days or so before the due date printed on your bill.

Set Up Online Bill Payment Once, and the Rest Is Easy

When you first decide to try online bill payment, don't be discouraged by the moderate amount of time and effort that you have to invest to set up your payees and establish your online payment routine. The set-up time that you spend up front is brief compared to the time that you save when you begin to use online bill payment regularly. And after you take the time to complete the initial setup, you don't have to mess with setting up those bills ever again. Your process for paying those bills is simple and automatic.

When you receive a bill, you just enter a pay date, enter an amount, and choose the payee. You send the payment electronically and mark the bill as paid before placing it in your file of paid bills. After that, you can be completely carefree. The bank makes the payment on the requested date, regardless of whether you're at home, working late, taking an extended sabbatical in Vienna, or completely forgetting that a bill was due.

Appendix

About the CD

● ●

The *Banking Online For Dummies* CD-ROM includes a variety of tools and software to help you get started with online banking. This Appendix gives you a description of each of the products and tells you how to use them.

System Requirements

Make sure that your computer meets the minimum system requirements in the following list. If your computer doesn't match up to most of these requirements, you may have problems as you try to use the contents of the CD-ROM (and most other current software).

- ✔ A PC with a 486 or faster processor, or a Mac OS computer with a 68030 or faster processor.
- ✔ Microsoft Windows 3.1 or later, or Mac OS system software 7.5 or later.
- ✔ At least 8MB of total RAM installed on your computer. For best performance, Windows 95-equipped PCs and Mac OS computers with PowerPC processors should have at least 16MB of RAM installed.
- ✔ At least 100MB of hard drive space available to install all the software from this CD. (You'll need less space if you don't install every program.)
- ✔ A CD-ROM drive — double-speed (2x) or faster.
- ✔ A sound card for PCs. (Mac OS computers have built-in sound support.)
- ✔ A monitor capable of displaying at least 256 colors or grayscale.
- ✔ A modem with a speed of at least 14,400 bps. However, a 33,600 bps modem or higher is preferable.

If you need more information on the basics, check out *PCs For Dummies,* 6th Edition, by Dan Gookin; *Macs For Dummies,* 6th Edition, by David Pogue; *Windows 98 For Dummies* and *Windows 95 For Dummies,* 2nd Edition, by Andy Rathbone; or *Windows 3.11 For Dummies,* 3rd Edition, by Andy Rathbone (all published by IDG Books Worldwide, Inc.).

Using the CD with Microsoft Windows

If you use Windows 3.1/3.11 or Windows 95/98, follow these instructions to access and install programs from the CD:

1. **Insert the CD into your computer's CD-ROM drive.**

2. *Windows 3.1 or 3.11 users:* **From Program Manager, choose File⇨Run.**

   Windows 95/98 users: **Click Start⇨Run.**

3. **In the dialog box that appears, type** D:\SETUP.EXE.

   Replace *D* with the proper drive letter if your CD-ROM drive uses a different letter. (If you don't know the letter, see how your CD-ROM drive is listed under My Computer in Windows 95/98 or File Manager in Windows 3.1/3.11.)

4. **Click OK.**

   A License Agreement window appears.

5. **Read through the license agreement, nod your head, and then click the Accept button if you want to use the CD. (After you click Accept, you'll never be bothered by the License Agreement window again.)**

   The CD interface Welcome screen appears. The interface is a little program that shows you what's on the CD and coordinates installing the programs and running the demos. The interface basically enables you to click a button or two to make things happen.

6. **Click anywhere on the Welcome screen to enter the interface.**

   Now you are getting to the action. This next screen lists categories for the software on the CD.

7. **To view the items within a category, click the category's name.**

   A list of programs in the category appears.

8. **For more information about a program, click the program's name.**

   Be sure to read the information that appears. Sometimes a program has its own system requirements or requires you to do a few tricks on your computer before you can install or run the program, and this screen tells you what you might need to do, if necessary.

9. **If you don't want to install the program, click the Go Back button to return to the previous screen.**

   You can always return to the previous screen by clicking the Go Back button. This feature allows you to browse the different categories and products and decide what you want to install.

10. **To install a program, click the appropriate Install button.**

    The CD interface drops to the background while the CD installs the program you chose.

11. **To install other items, repeat Steps 7 through 10.**

12. **When you've finished installing programs, click the Quit button to close the interface.**

    You can eject the CD now. Carefully place it back in the plastic jacket of this book for safekeeping.

Using the CD with the Mac OS

If you're using a Macintosh computer, follow these steps to install the items from the CD-ROM to your hard drive:

1. **Insert the CD into your computer's CD-ROM drive.**

    In a moment, an icon representing the CD you just inserted appears on your Mac desktop. The icon probably looks like a CD-ROM.

2. **Double-click the CD-ROM icon to show the CD's contents.**

3. **Double-click the Read Me First icon.**

    This text file contains information about the CD's programs and any last-minute instructions that you may need in order to install them.

4. **To install most programs, drag the program's folder from the CD window and drop it on your hard drive icon.**

5. **Some programs come with installer programs — in which case, you simply open the program's folder on the CD, and double-click the icon with the word "Install" or "Installer."**

    After you've installed the programs that you want, you can eject the CD. Carefully place it back in the plastic jacket of this book for safekeeping.

What You Get on the CD

The *Banking Online For Dummies* CD contains an assortment of useful software, including the two leading Web browser packages and demo versions of some online banking software programs. The following list gives you a summary of the software on the CD:

AmeriBank Demo of the Home ATM: This is a demo of the Home ATM product for online banking and bill payment from Home Financial Network. If your bank is a Home ATM bank, this software shows you the functions and features that you can use to manage your online banking and bill payments. This software was purposefully designed to look and feel like the ATM machines that many of us use every day. For more information, check out www.homeatm.com.

Microsoft Internet Explorer 4.0: This is a recent version of the Microsoft Internet Explorer Web browser and its suite of companion programs. The Internet Explorer 4.0 package includes an e-mail and newsgroup client and other utilities, as well as the Web browser that's the center of attention. You can download this software from the Web for free, but I included it on this CD to spare you hours of download time. For more information on Internet Explorer or to check for new versions, go to www.microsoft.com/ie.

If you're running Windows 98, you don't need to install Microsoft Internet Explorer 4.0. A newer version of the program is included in Windows 98.

Also, if you plan to run Internet Explorer 4.0 under Windows NT 4.0, you need Service Pack 3. If you don't have Service Pack 3, visit the Microsoft Web site at www.microsoft.com. After installing Service Pack 3, continue the installation and follow the prompts on your screen to install the NT version of Internet Explorer.

MindSpring: MindSpring is a leading Internet service provider. If you don't have Internet access yet, the MindSpring software loaded on this CD will do a great job in assisting you during your first trips online. For more information, check out www.mindspring.net.

You need a credit card to sign up for Internet access with MindSpring.

If you already have an Internet service provider, please note that MindSpring Internet access software makes changes to your computer's current Internet configuration and may replace your current settings. These changes may prevent you from accessing the Internet through your current provider.

M.Y.O.B. Plus trial version: The CD includes a fully functional trial version of the M.Y.O.B. Plus small business accounting program by Bestware. This program is an easy-to-use alternative to QuickBooks that is compatible with both Windows and Macintosh systems. Although it has no direct support for online banking, the program can import data that you download and save in a separate file. For more information, check out www.bestware.com.

Netscape Communicator: This is a recent version of the suite of Internet programs from Netscape. It includes the Netscape Navigator Web browser, plus e-mail, news, and more. Communicator is the primary alternative to the Microsoft Internet Explorer Web browser tool. You can download the Netscape Communicator software from the Web for free, but I included it on the CD to spare you hours of download time. For more information or to check for new versions, check out www.netscape.com.

QuickBooks 6.0 trial version: QuickBooks 6.0 is the leading business accounting software package. In addition to managing your business accounts, you can pay bills and submit payroll information electronically. (QuickBooks 6.0 shares the same installer with QuickBooks 6.0 Pro on the CD.) For more information, check out `www.intuit.com`.

QuickBooks 6.0 Pro trial version: QuickBooks 6.0 Pro has all the features found in QuickBooks 6.0, as well as many additional features such as extra reports, time and billing tools, job costing and estimation tools, and multi-user capabilities. For more information, check out `www.intuit.com`.

Using the Directory Links

The *Banking Online For Dummies Internet Directory* in this book describes hundreds of Web sites that you can browse to check out tons of available online banking and financial services. The LINKS.HTM file on the CD-ROM is an HTML page that you can access with your Web browser. On the LINKS.HTM page, you find all the Web addresses from the directory, turned into Web hyperlinks so that you can simply click any Web site from the directory and immediately jump to that site. No need to type in any long, complicated Web addresses!

To access this file from either Microsoft Internet Explorer or Netscape Communicator with Navigator, follow these steps:

1. **Connect to the Internet and open your Web browser.**

2. **Choose File⇨Open in Internet Explorer, or choose File⇨Open Page in Netscape.**

   The File Open dialog box appears.

3. **Enter the filename** D:\LINKS.HTM **and click Open.**

   This filename assumes that your CD-ROM drive is *D.* Substitute the correct letter for *D* if your CD-ROM drive is different. The links page then appears in your WZeb browser window.

4. **Scroll through the list of links and click any link that you want to follow.**

   Your Web browser loads the requested Web page.

If You've Got Problems (Of the CD Kind)

I tried my best to compile programs that work on most computers with the minimum system requirements. Alas, your computer may differ, and some programs may not work properly for some reason.

The two likeliest problems are that you don't have enough memory (RAM) for the programs that you want to use, or you have other programs running that are affecting the installation or running of a program. If you get error messages like `Not enough memory` or `Setup cannot continue`, try one or more of the following methods and then try using the software again:

- **Turn off any antivirus software that you have on your computer.** The automated software installation programs sometimes mimic virus activity and may make your computer's antivirus program incorrectly believe that your system is being infected by a virus.

- **Close all running programs before you install new software.** The more programs you're running, the less memory is available for the installer. Also, installers often need to update system files and won't be able to do so if those files are being used by other programs.

- **Add more RAM to your computer.** If all else fails, you may need to have your local computer store add more RAM to your computer. Admittedly, this is a drastic and somewhat expensive step. However, if you have a Windows 95/98 PC or a Mac OS computer with a PowerPC chip, adding more memory can really help the speed of your computer and allow more programs to run simultaneously.

If you still have trouble with installing the items from the CD, please call the IDG Books Worldwide Customer Service phone number: 800-762-2974 (outside the U.S.: 317-596-5430).

Index

Notes

Notes

Notes

Playing games is really fun...
The Dummies Way™!

Pressman®
©1998 Pressman Toy Corporation, New York, NY 10010

Crosswords For Dummies™ Game
You don't have to know how to spell to have a great time. Place a word strip on the board so that it overlaps another word or creates a new one. Special squares add to the fun. The first player to use up all their word strips wins!
For 2 to 4 players.

Trivia For Dummies™ Game
You're guaranteed to have an answer every time! Each player gets 10 cards that contain the answer to every question. Act quickly and be the first player to throw down the correct answer and move closer to the finish line!
For 3 or 4 players.

Charades For Dummies™ Game
Act out one-word charades: when other players guess them, they move ahead. The special cards keep the game full of surprises. The first player around the board wins.
For 3 or 4 players.

...For Dummies and The Dummies Way are trademarks or registered trademarks of IDG Books Worldwide, Inc.

IDG Books Worldwide, Inc.,
End-User License Agreement

READ THIS. You should carefully read these terms and conditions before opening the software packet(s) included with this book ("Book"). This is a license agreement ("Agreement") between you and IDG Books Worldwide, Inc. ("IDGB"). By opening the accompanying software packet(s), you acknowledge that you have read and accept the following terms and conditions. If you do not agree and do not want to be bound by such terms and conditions, promptly return the Book and the unopened software packet(s) to the place you obtained them for a full refund.

1. **License Grant.** IDGB grants to you (either an individual or entity) a nonexclusive license to use one copy of the enclosed software program(s) (collectively, the "Software") solely for your own personal or business purposes on a single computer (whether a standard computer or a workstation component of a multiuser network). The Software is in use on a computer when it is loaded into temporary memory (RAM) or installed into permanent memory (hard disk, CD-ROM, or other storage device). IDGB reserves all rights not expressly granted herein.

2. **Ownership.** IDGB is the owner of all right, title, and interest, including copyright, in and to the compilation of the Software recorded on the disk(s) or CD-ROM ("Software Media"). Copyright to the individual programs recorded on the Software Media is owned by the author or other authorized copyright owner of each program. Ownership of the Software and all proprietary rights relating thereto remain with IDGB and its licensers.

3. **Restrictions on Use and Transfer.**

   (a) You may only (i) make one copy of the Software for backup or archival purposes, or (ii) transfer the Software to a single hard disk, provided that you keep the original for backup or archival purposes. You may not (i) rent or lease the Software, (ii) copy or reproduce the Software through a LAN or other network system or through any computer subscriber system or bulletin-board system, or (iii) modify, adapt, or create derivative works based on the Software.

   (b) You may not reverse engineer, decompile, or disassemble the Software. You may transfer the Software and user documentation on a permanent basis, provided that the transferee agrees to accept the terms and conditions of this Agreement and you retain no copies. If the Software is an update or has been updated, any transfer must include the most recent update and all prior versions.

4. **Restrictions on Use of Individual Programs.** You must follow the individual requirements and restrictions detailed for each individual program in the Appendix of this Book. These limitations are also contained in the individual license agreements recorded on the Software Media. These limitations may include a requirement that after using the program for a specified period of time, the user must pay a registration fee or discontinue use. By opening the Software packet(s), you will be agreeing to abide by the licenses and restrictions for these individual programs that are detailed in the Appendix and on the Software Media. None of the material on this Software Media or listed in this Book may ever be redistributed, in original or modified form, for commercial purposes.

5. Limited Warranty.

   (a) IDGB warrants that the Software and Software Media are free from defects in materials and workmanship under normal use for a period of sixty (60) days from the date of purchase of this Book. If IDGB receives notification within the warranty period of defects in materials or workmanship, IDGB will replace the defective Software Media.

   (b) IDGB AND THE AUTHOR OF THE BOOK DISCLAIM ALL OTHER WARRANTIES, EXPRESS OR IMPLIED, INCLUDING WITHOUT LIMITA-TION IMPLIED WARRANTIES OF MERCHANTABILITY AND FITNESS FOR A PARTICULAR PURPOSE, WITH RESPECT TO THE SOFTWARE, THE PROGRAMS, THE SOURCE CODE CONTAINED THEREIN, AND/OR THE TECHNIQUES DESCRIBED IN THIS BOOK. IDGB DOES NOT WARRANT THAT THE FUNCTIONS CONTAINED IN THE SOFTWARE WILL MEET YOUR REQUIREMENTS OR THAT THE OPERATION OF THE SOFTWARE WILL BE ERROR FREE.

   (c) This limited warranty gives you specific legal rights, and you may have other rights that vary from jurisdiction to jurisdiction.

6. Remedies.

   (a) IDGB's entire liability and your exclusive remedy for defects in materials and workmanship shall be limited to replacement of the Software Media, which may be returned to IDGB with a copy of your receipt at the following address: Software Media Fulfillment Department, Attn.: *Banking Online For Dummies,* IDG Books Worldwide, Inc., 7260 Shadeland Station, Ste. 100, Indianapolis, IN 46256, or call 800-762-2974. Please allow three to four weeks for delivery. This Limited Warranty is void if failure of the Software Media has resulted from accident, abuse, or misapplication. Any replacement Software Media will be warranted for the remainder of the original warranty period or thirty (30) days, whichever is longer.

   (b) In no event shall IDGB or the author be liable for any damages whatso-ever (including without limitation damages for loss of business profits, business interruption, loss of business information, or any other pecuni-ary loss) arising from the use of or inability to use the Book or the Software, even if IDGB has been advised of the possibility of such damages.

   (c) Because some jurisdictions do not allow the exclusion or limitation of liability for consequential or incidental damages, the above limitation or exclusion may not apply to you.

7. U.S. Government Restricted Rights. Use, duplication, or disclosure of the Software by the U.S. Government is subject to restrictions stated in paragraph (c)(1)(ii) of the Rights in Technical Data and Computer Software clause of DFARS 252.227-7013, and in subparagraphs (a) through (d) of the Commercial Computer–Restricted Rights clause at FAR 52.227-19, and in similar clauses in the NASA FAR supplement, when applicable.

8. General. This Agreement constitutes the entire understanding of the parties and revokes and supersedes all prior agreements, oral or written, between them and may not be modified or amended except in a writing signed by both parties hereto that specifically refers to this Agreement. This Agreement shall take precedence over any other documents that may be in conflict herewith. If any one or more provisions contained in this Agreement are held by any court or tribunal to be invalid, illegal, or otherwise unenforceable, each and every other provision shall remain in full force and effect.

Installation Instructions

To install the valuable programs on the *Banking Online For Dummies* CD, read the following instructions.

If you use Windows 3.1/3.11 or Windows 95/98, follow these instructions to access and install programs from the CD:

1. **Insert the CD into your computer's CD-ROM drive.**

2. *Windows 3.1 or 3.11 users:* **From Program Manager, choose File⇨Run.** *Windows 95/98 users:* **Click Start⇨Run.**

3. **In the dialog box that appears, type** D:\SETUP.EXE.

4. **Click OK to see the License Agreement window.**

5. **Read the License Agreement and click Accept to use the CD.**

   The CD interface Welcome screen appears.

6. **Click anywhere on the Welcome screen to enter the interface.**

   The next screen lists categories for the software on the CD.

7. **To view the items within a category, just click the category's name.**

8. **If you don't want to install the program, click the Go Back button to return to the previous screen.**

9. **To install a program, click the appropriate Install button.**

If you're using a Macintosh computer, follow these steps to install the items from the CD-ROM to your hard drive:

1. **Insert the CD into your computer's CD-ROM drive.**

   You see the CD-ROM icon on your Mac desktop.

2. **Double-click the CD-ROM icon to show the CD's contents.**

3. **Double-click the Read Me First icon.**

4. **To install most programs, drag the program's folder from the CD window and drop it on your hard drive icon.**

5. **For programs that come with installer programs, simply open the program's folder on the CD and double-click the icon with the words "Install" or "Installer."**

For all the details about the CD, see the Appendix.

YOUR ONLINE RESOURCE

WWW.DUMMIES.COM

Discover Dummies™ Online!

The *Dummies* Web Site is your fun and friendly online resource for the latest information about *...For Dummies*® books on all your favorite topics. From cars to computers, wine to Windows, and investing to the Internet, we've got a shelf full of *...For Dummies* books waiting for you!

Ten Fun and Useful Things You Can Do at www.dummies.com

1. Register this book and win!
2. Find and buy the *...For Dummies* books you want online.
3. Get ten great *Dummies Tips*™ every week.
4. Chat with your favorite *...For Dummies* authors.
5. Subscribe free to *The Dummies Dispatch*™ newsletter.
6. Enter our sweepstakes and win cool stuff.
7. Send a free cartoon postcard to a friend.
8. Download free software.
9. Sample a book before you buy.
10. Talk to us. Make comments, ask questions, and get answers!

Jump online to these ten fun and useful things at **http://www.dummies.com/10useful**

SURF THE NET

WWW.DUMMIES.COM

For other technology titles from IDG Books Worldwide, go to **www.idgbooks.com**

Not online yet? It's easy to get started with *The Internet For Dummies*®, 5th Edition, or *Dummies 101*®: *The Internet For Windows*® *98*, available at local retailers everywhere.

IDG BOOKS WORLDWIDE

Find other *...For Dummies* books on these topics:

Business • Careers • Databases • Food & Beverages • Games • Gardening • Graphics • Hardware
Health & Fitness • Internet and the World Wide Web • Networking • Office Suites
Operating Systems • Personal Finance • Pets • Programming • Recreation • Sports
Spreadsheets • Teacher Resources • Test Prep • Word Processing

IDG BOOKS WORLDWIDE
BOOK REGISTRATION

Register This Book and Win!

We want to hear from you!

Visit **http://my2cents.dummies.com** to register this book and tell us how you liked it!

- ✔ Get entered in our monthly prize giveaway.

- ✔ Give us feedback about this book — tell us what you like best, what you like least, or maybe what you'd like to ask the author and us to change!

- ✔ Let us know any other *...For Dummies*® topics that interest you.

Your feedback helps us determine what books to publish, tells us what coverage to add as we revise our books, and lets us know whether we're meeting your needs as a *...For Dummies* reader. You're our most valuable resource, and what you have to say is important to us!

Not on the Web yet? It's easy to get started with *Dummies 101*®: *The Internet For Windows*® 98 or *The Internet For Dummies*,® 5th Edition, at local retailers everywhere.

Or let us know what you think by sending us a letter at the following address:

...For Dummies Book Registration
Dummies Press
7260 Shadeland Station, Suite 100
Indianapolis, IN 46256-3945
Fax 317-596-5498

BESTSELLING BOOK SERIES